LOST
A
N
D
FOUND

An Autobiography About
Discovering Family

By Micky Neilson

Micky Neilson

For more information contact:
Riverdale Avenue Books
5676 Riverdale Avenue
Riverdale, NY 10471.

www.riverdaleavebooks.com

Design by www.formatting4U.com
Cover by Scott Carpenter
Digital ISBN 978-1-62601-284-4
Print ISBN 978-1-62601-285-1

First Edition June 2016

DEDICATION

This book is dedicated to my immediate family, to my newly (re)discovered family, to "the Brothers," to Lori Perkins and Max Ximenez for believing in this story when others turned their backs on it, and to Jaime Cerota Costas for her steadfast support. There are countless others who have touched my life, who are mentioned throughout this book. You all have my heartfelt, undying gratitude.

TABLE OF CONTENTS

PROLOGUE

As the plane began its descent I was an emotional disaster.

I sat, wringing my hands, nearly overwhelmed by the enormity of it all. Here I was, traveling to connect with the person I had dreamed of meeting since I was old enough to speak: the person who I had been told throughout my life was dead. I had almost given up; almost accepted that I would never, ever see my Mother. But after 38 years, I was finally going to meet her for the first time.

Flying makes me nervous anyway, but as the wheels touched ground I could barely stay in my seat. My wife, Tiffany, kept a concerned eye on me but she had learned long ago that when I was in the midst of in-flight anxiety to just let me work through it. She knew when I needed my space.

My half brother, Marshall, had contacted the local news media (something we had all agreed to), so I had the added jitters associated with knowing the event would most likely be filmed and broadcast. My eight-year-old daughter, Tatiana, scampered down the gangway. I followed, holding hands with Tiff, still shaking. As we left the gate, I received a phone call from Marshall saying that Fox 11 News was waiting, along with Mom, and that they were at Baggage Claim. This was it: the moment I had waited for my entire life.

The baggage area was accessed via revolving doors. These doors were automatic, with sensors so you didn't have to push on them. I had only been exposed to a door like this once before, in Vegas. I looked through and could see a reporter, cameraman, Marshall, my half Sister Gynene, Mom's husband Gary, and of course… Mom, waiting expectantly. She looked beautiful. I wanted to hold her more than anything.

But I had to get through those stupid doors first.

Someone went ahead of me, and I followed. The person exited the other side and the doors stopped. I knew they were automatic so I just waited for them to start moving again. Unfortunately I wasn't far enough forward to trigger the sensor, so there I was, being filmed standing like a doofus, outwitted by a revolving door while my long-suffering mother and captivated family waited anxiously. Everything in that instant seemed to halt. I stood taking in the sight of Mom, with her effortless smile and her gorgeous white hair, hands clasped near her heart in anticipation, and I thought about the strange, impossible journey that had brought me to this moment in time.

CHAPTER ONE:
THE BEGINNING

My Dad was an intense man, downright scary at times, and deeply religious.

There came a point in our lives where every other phrase out of his mouth was "praise God." He stood about 5'5" and had a stout build. His face was lined, and his hair was thin and mostly gray, styled in a kind of mushroom/bowl cut. He didn't smile or laugh terribly often, and when he did, a set of half-broken teeth were exposed. Over the course of his life he swore that if he had absolute faith and concentrated hard enough, he'd be able to grow a whole new set.

The older he got, the more his teeth decayed.

Dad had given me the name Yakimoki—later he told me it meant "impetuous"—but mostly he just called me Moki. Dad was Shihan Calvin Neilson. I later found out that "Shihan" is a rank in martial arts, but Dad used it as a first name, not a title.

In my very early years, I had blond, curly hair—we're talking almost Shirley Temple-caliber curly. And I can say without too much hubris that I was a cute kid. Dad would later tell me that when he took me to the local Chinese restaurants, the waitresses would fawn over me, scoop me up and take me into the kitchen. Dad also told me that I wouldn't be cute forever. That always ticked me off.

Apparently I was a pretty lively little tyke. Dad claimed that when he took me to see a Bruce Lee movie I stood up in the seat and yelled at the screen: "Kick him in the crotch!"

I don't remember that. In fact, I have only a handful of memories clustered around the age of five, living with Dad in Oklahoma:

First, a birthday at Dad's dojo (for the uninitiated, a martial arts training facility. Like the Cobra Kai dojo in the original *Karate Kid*, just without the sleeveless uniforms and emphasis on leg-sweeping). I received a toy—a front-end loader with an electric motor, and I thought it was absolutely amazing.

Second, sitting on the mats in the middle of the dojo, crying as if it were the end of the world. One of Dad's students came in with a big paper grocery bag, and he pulled out the most gigantic teddy bear I'd ever seen. It was bigger than I was. It was white, with big, round, perfect eyes and an everlasting smile. That teddy bear would be my steady companion for many years. Over time the cottony faux fur turned a dingy gray, the smile's stitching came undone and one eye worked loose and became lost, but I loved it just the same. I loved it as I loved Dad: unconditionally.

Third, I woke up in a room where I slept with Dad, in the dojo, inconsolable due to a nightmare—of a horrific Frankenstein-like creature that had risen to peer up and over the edge of the bed. I yelled to Dad, who slept next to me, that there was a monster under the bed. He said that was impossible; there was no bed. We were sleeping on the floor.

4

Finally, I remember flying in a plane. I think Dad was with me. What I remember most is puking. A lot. The plane was a little twin-engine job, and for a while Dad had a picture of me and the pilot—a guy with dark hair and a thick mustache—standing in front of it. To this day I have no idea who that guy was.

And to this day I still hate flying.

That picture, along with one of me sitting on the mats in the dojo with my curly hair, and another of the outside of the dojo—where the words "we are opposed to communism in every way" were painted—were the only photos we possessed. Dad, I would later learn, almost never allowed his picture to be taken.

* * *

We left Oklahoma in what I thought for the longest time was a military truck. (I found out later that it was a covered pickup with long, fold-down seats on either side of the bed, similar to what Army trucks have in back.) This was around 1977/78. We had left behind everything; just picked up and, as my Dad would have said, "skedaddled."

We ended up in Albuquerque, New Mexico, where we stopped for a very practical reason: the truck broke down right in the middle of the street.

Dad sold the truck, but Albuquerque wasn't where he wanted to be. We got another crappy vehicle with expired tags. Now, one thing that Dad really excelled at was art. He used some of his art materials to craft a tag for the vehicle (it looked pretty authentic until you got up close) and we headed toward his intended destination: Tombstone, Arizona.

If you've never been to Tombstone, I recommend you go; it really is a fascinating little place. Anyone who's up on their history (or has seen the absolutely awesome Kurt Russell/Val Kilmer movie *Tombstone*) knows that this is where the infamous gunfight at the OK Corral took place. To this day, "The Town Too Tough to Die" presents itself as a wild west boomtown, complete with wooden boardwalks, hitching posts, Wells Fargo wagons and building facades. I don't know if they still do it, but back then they used to dress up in period costumes on Sundays (or maybe it was once a month) and stage gunfights in the street.

It wasn't long until we got rid of the clunker, and we soon found ourselves in an apartment complex. There, Dad basically served as the maintenance guy/all-around handyman in exchange for a break on the rent. I must have been six or seven by this time.

Dad would walk around to all kinds of businesses and offer to paint signs, murals, create logos, you name it. Wherever he went, he never let me out of his sight. He got a job for a while where he transformed what seemed to be an old theater into a kind of attraction, creating a hallway/tunnel entrance that resembled the rocky adit of an underground mine. Me and some older kids got to help out, creating the whole thing out of chicken wire and paper mache.

Somewhere in the midst of all this, I had started asking about my mom. Did I have one? If so, where was she? Where was the rest of the family?

Dad sat me down for one of his serious talks. We had a lot of serious talks. Usually after I got spanked with Dad's belt or, if I had really screwed up, a ping pong paddle he kept around for just such a purpose.

We had other serious talks too, but those came later, becoming more and more outlandish and fantastic the older we both became. The first "Mom conversation" went something like this:

Mom and Dad were on a plane from Mexico, flying into the states. They worked for the government, doing search and rescue. Mom had a cyst on her ovary, and it exploded, killing her.

I wanted to know what she was like. Dad said she had long black hair, down to the heels of her feet. He said she was the only person he knew who could whoop him in martial arts. She was Spanish, he said.

I asked what her name was.

April, he told me. Pronounced "Ah-breel." April Salvez.

I was deeply saddened that I would never get to know Mom; never see her or hear her voice or feel her embrace. I often imagined what she must have looked like, how she must have acted. What a completely badass martial artist she must have been. Dad told me that one day, we would travel to South America, and venture into the Amazon Rain Forest, and there, deep inside the misty jungles we would find a forgotten land—a land of square trees and golden frogs. And there also we would find the Cave of the Seven Winds. And inside the cave, I would be reunited with the spirit of my Mother.

I thought of that cave often. I imagined myself entering and seeing a beautiful woman in a long white dress, with black hair down to the ground. I imagined that in this magical place, even if Mom was a ghost, I could run to her, wrap my arms around her and hold on tight, while repeating over and over again how much I loved her.

* * *

One day, while I was "helping" the workers on the theater entryway, I looked around to find that Dad wasn't there. I asked some of the guys where he had gone off to, and they didn't know. Moments passed, and I started to panic. What if something happened to him? What if the people he was afraid of came and took him away? Or worse?

Part of me was horrified at the thought of Dad not being around anymore... but a small part of me was curious, too: what would it be like to just go off on my own, to run and never look back? To have adventures like Tom Sawyer... it sounded tempting, to be sure. But how could I ever find the Cave of the Seven Winds by myself?

It wasn't long before the part of me that was scared of a life without Dad overpowered the curious side, and I cried and cried. I loved Dad so much; to my young mind and heart his word was gospel. His presence was all-encompassing. His knowledge was infinite. He was my world.

Ten minutes or so later Dad was back. He had run out to grab some supplies, and whoever was supposed to watch me and tell me where Dad was had gone off to do something else (that guy probably got a serious ass-chewing). I was greatly relieved. But the seed of curiosity had been planted, and throughout the rest of my time with Dad, there would come moments where I would imagine life without him.

He continued to go from job to job. Sometimes it seemed like we were okay on money, and sometimes it seemed like we were completely broke. We stayed in a trailer park for a while. Dad drank coffee like it was, as he would say, "going out of style," and one of his favorite things to eat was burnt toast. I mean *burnt.* If it didn't come out looking like a flattened briquette, he'd send it back.

In the food joints we frequented, Dad would draw caricatures of the other regulars. The manager actually started posting these drawings on the walls. Dad would give each person a nickname. I found out later that he had done the same thing with his students in Oklahoma.

For whatever reason, Dad had stopped teaching martial arts. I think he just wanted to continue laying low, and starting up another dojo would have drawn too much attention. He had taught me some basics, though, starting with, you guessed it, "Kick 'em in the crotch!"

He offered to teach me everything he knew, but at that age, I really wasn't interested.

* * *

At some point around this time Dad planned an "operation" with what I later realized were either military or ex-military folks. Dad once said that if he had 40 well-trained men he could take over the United States. The mission they were mapping out was aimed at stealing a WWII-era plane, which they wanted to fly to Mexico. Don't ask me why anyone would want to steal an old junker of a plane and fly it to Mexico, but that was the plan. I was even going to serve as a decoy. I'm sure Dad had an exit strategy for me, but I don't remember what it was.

For whatever reason, the operation never materialized. But just the idea that he was planning it made me feel uneasy. I was seeing a side of Dad that was disturbing, a side that I would be seeing more of: the anarchist, non-conformist, militant side. I didn't know exactly why it troubled me, but it did. I think on some level I might have known even then that I disagreed fundamentally with his point of view.

* * *

A year or so passed, and Dad became increasingly eager to spend time away from people, away from civilization. He wore his belt buckle to one side (I think it was the left) and had me do the same. I didn't notice at the time that everyone else wore theirs in the middle. I would ask about that later.

At one point we stayed at a place out in the desert called the Double U Ranch. This may have been where I rode a horse for the first and only time. By "rode," I mean I hugged it tightly, got bucked off immediately and busted up my arm, thankfully without breaking it.

We had a kind of rustic little two or three room cabin that we stayed in, and one night, Dad came in from standing outside, looking up at the stars, very excited. I had taken out all of my toys from a big footlocker that we traveled with, and was playing happily with all my favorites (including my Six Million Dollar Man action figure, the one with the "bionic eye," where you could look through the back of his head, and my Evel Knieval—with motorcycle!) and had them spread all over the place. Dad told me that I had to come outside at once.

I went out. He pointed up to a cloud formation and asked if I saw it. I didn't know what "it" was, but he said the clouds formed a Christian Fish. It was a sign. Now you might think that a manifestation of the Christian Fish would presage some religious event, but according to Dad it meant that an alien spaceship was on its way to pick us up, and to take us to a place far, far away.

At roughly seven years old, who was I to argue? Like I said, Dad's word was gospel. Aliens? Awesome! I get to see them? And ride in their spaceship? SO cool! I ran in and started packing up all my toys. I had that footlocker full again in no time. I was so excited to see the aliens. I asked Dad what they would be like, if they were nice or mean, what their ship looked like, if they had beds we could sleep on, etc. He mainly told me I'd have to wait and see. So I went out and I waited.

And waited. And waited.

Hours later Dad would tell me to go to bed, that the time hadn't come; not yet, but it would.

The aliens never came, but something else had manifested that night: the first hairline crack in the dam of my Dad's seeming infallibility. My unshakeable faith in him was upset, even if only slightly.

An idea began taking shape after that; the notion that maybe, just maybe, not everything Dad said was gospel. Maybe he could actually be wrong.

And if he was wrong about that, the obvious extension of my line of reasoning would become:

What else might he be wrong about?

CHAPTER TWO:
EXILE

I'm not sure what sparked it, but sometime in late '80, early '81, Dad decided to check out from society altogether. Kind of like Superman retreating to his Fortress of Solitude, except we ended up in a desert and not the Great White North.

The nearest town was roughly five miles away. Gleeson. The swath of land that Dad staked a claim to was in the middle of nowhere, off of a small dirt road, near a few cattle farms. We had a single pop-up trailer to start off with. With that and a healthy supply of beans and rice, we started two years of seclusion.

Mostly the days were scorching-hot and the nights would chill to the bone. For a while we had cats and dogs. I vividly remember picking quills from the mouth of one of the dogs after it had apparently tried to eat a porcupine.

Dad would beat the dogs sometimes, and eventually they ran away. I always blamed him for their departure, feeling that they left to escape his abuse. Maybe they made it to one of the nearby farmhouses.

Something else Dad had during that time was

guns. Three of them, if I remember correctly. Rifles. At least one was a bolt-action he called "Big Bertha." "No Trespassing" and "Private Property" signs were posted everywhere—Dad and I spent a great deal of time building a fence, with wooden posts gathered from nearby abandoned mines. He fenced off a large section of land, posted the signs, and we strung rusty barbed wire. Dad called the land his compound.

We bathed once every few days, undergoing something Dad described as a "cat bath"—you filled a small plastic tub with soapy water, stripped down, and washed with a washcloth. No such thing as shampoo or toothbrushes.

When food became scarce, we'd ride our bicycles into town. Sometimes Gleeson, sometimes farther into Tombstone. For a short period of time we had a two-seater bike that we could both pedal (Dad usually ended up doing most of the pedaling) and then later we had two separate bikes. Those bike rides were something I dreaded. There was one hill that was a lot of fun to come down on the way out, but a real pain in the ass to work your way up on the way back. Often, while pedaling for what seemed like an eternity, I'd fantasize about cars giving us a lift back home. Once I even daydreamed that Jimmy Carter gave us a lift in his limo.

Flat tires were fairly common. So were flash floods. The floods would leave patches of soft dirt in the low spots on the road, easy areas to wipe out in.

Sometimes we'd end up being out late, and we'd have to walk several miles, due to either a flat tire or road conditions. Quite often we'd just look at the stars.

There was one night in particular, where the full

13

moon was out, and we were walking our bikes home. We stopped, and Dad pointed out a snake track that crossed the road in the soft dirt ahead of us. The track was nearly a foot wide, and it slalomed from one side of the road to the other, disappearing into the desert. We wondered at the size of snake that must have made that track. I imagined a leviathan, a rattlesnake with a head the size of my old footlocker and fangs as long as sabers.

* * *

There was a printer in Tombstone, and for several months Dad put together a small newspaper. We built a newsstand out by the dirt road, and I'd sit there for hours, waiting for cars to pass by so I could sell them a "souvenir paper." Sometimes Dad and I would draw caricatures as well.

There were two police officers who would sometimes visit. Dad seemed to get along with them, but he also told them that if anybody came after him, he wouldn't hesitate to shoot first and ask questions later. He said he just wanted to be left alone.

At night Dad would tell me stories. Some of them he made up, and some were memories (though with Dad it could be really difficult to tell the difference). I, of course, wanted to know more about Mom, and one of the stories Dad told was that he and Mom were doing Search and Rescue somewhere (he might have said it was Mexico, I don't remember). He said they were driving at night along steep mountain roads to go and rescue someone, and he lost control of the car. The vehicle veered off of the road and they headed straight for a drop-off and sudden death. As the car's front tires cleared the edge, they came to a sudden stop. He said Mom was resting her legs on the dash and her legs went through the windshield, slicing the skin to ribbons, but they had both lived because a length of barbed wire strung between two wooden posts had gotten wound up in the car's front axle and arrested their momentum.

Another story Dad told was that one night he woke up while I was sleeping, as he heard the struggling of a car's motor. He said he went out to the dirt road, where he greeted an old man wearing pristine white gloves (the old man would not shake his hand). The geriatric motorist was driving an antiquated "wind-up" car that had broken down. Dad said he pushed the car as the old man got in and it started up… and as Dad watched the man drive away, both he and the car disappeared into thin air.

He said that on some nights you could still hear that sputtering motor on the road outside.

Dad also spun the ongoing adventures of Jack, John and Buckwheat… three kids who snuck into a haunted house. In each telling they would face some new, scary, fascinating challenge. They fought animated suits of armor and escaped rooms where floor tiles would fall away one at a time into a bottomless abyss.

My favorite story, and the one that scared me the most by far, was a variation of what I later learned to be a fairly popular spooky story: Bloody Mary. In Dad's version, there was an old fishing village with an abandoned lighthouse on a nearby promontory. At night kids would sneak in (always in a pack of at least three—it was important never to attempt it alone), and proceed to the lighthouse keeper's quarters, where there was a small bathroom. There they would stand before a mirror with a candle next to their face and say "Bloody Mary" 13 times and if they made it to 13, legend was that Bloody Mary would appear. Out of all the times the kids went to the lighthouse though, none of them said the words 13 times; they always got too scared and ran away.

Until one night, when some drunk teen decided to go and perform the ritual alone. Moments later, the entire town heard his scream. The town's one police officer showed up and ran into the room, where the teen lay on the floor, except he was no longer a teenager: he was a white-haired old man, and he was close to death. He motioned for the policeman to lean closer, and when the officer did, the aged teen whispered something into his ear, and then breathed his final breath.

Throughout the rest of his life, the police officer would not tell anyone what those final words were, and in time the secret died with him.

This story fascinated me, scared the bejeebers out of me, and frustrated the Hell out of me. What were those final words? Like so many other secrets Dad kept, he would never tell.

He did encourage me to come up with my own stories, though. Which I did. Mostly I would jump on the Jack, John and Buckwheat bandwagon, offering up my own versions of their adventures. I was a ghostwriter in the universe Dad had created, but it exercised my creative muscles. I look back on those times now as the early fostering of my imagination, and I have to say, those recollections in particular are pleasant.

My "schooling" also took place during this time. While on our bike rides, Dad would make me go over my addition, subtraction and multiplication tables. I absolutely stunk at math. At night I would read books—kid's stories. Even at that age I knew I wanted to write. I pointed out a name on one of my books— "Whitman"—and asked what it meant. Dad said that was the publisher. I asked what a publisher did and Dad said, "they're the ones who make the book." From then on I told Dad I wanted to be a publisher when I grew up.

There were a series of adventures that first year— close calls with spiders, scorpions, at least one centipede (or was it a millipede? I still don't know the difference) and snakes. There was one in particular— not a monster snake like the Kraken-esque serpent from our night under the full moon, but a big one nonetheless, a rattlesnake that took up residence under our trailer. Dad drug it out with a rake, which he had me press down on its neck while he took off to grab something. I didn't hold down hard enough and it wriggled out from under the rake and was slithering into striking distance when Dad arrived and chopped off its head with a machete.

Later that night, Dad cut it up for food, and we found that there were baby snakes inside. It was a mother (obviously) and had apparently thought the space under our trailer would be an ideal spot to give birth. I actually felt sorry for it.

There were old mines to explore as well. And explore them we did. The tricky thing about the mines was, you could be walking and not realize that there was a vertical shaft until it was nearly too late. Some of those shafts were deep enough that if you dropped a rock you could almost count to ten before you heard it hit bottom.

As I've hinted at, the years we spent out in the desert weren't all bad. Even though, for the longest time, they ranked up there with "periods of my life I really could have done without." As I've gotten older however, I've truly learned to believe that things happen for a reason. All of the hardship I've described thus far, and everything I'm about to describe, as bad as it got, even when I thought it couldn't get any worse: I still believe it all happened for a reason.

* * *

Time passed, and Dad's demeanor seemed to change. He grew angry with increasing ease and frequency. He felt certain that the planes which flew overhead were taking pictures of us. He felt like the government was closing in once again.

Sometime after our first year out there a group of military or ex-military men came and trained with Dad. They stayed there for a few days. Dad spoke again of how he could take over the United States with 40 well-trained men. The group that had come out to train numbered less than ten, but it was still enough to make me worry about the path Dad had seemingly chosen for us.

He spoke more and more about how corrupt and communistic the government was, and about how it was a sign of the end of days. Armageddon. Dad read

18

me passages from the Bible daily, and Revelations was his favorite section. He equated world events and politics with the opening of the Seven Seals. To him, it all made perfect sense. I didn't know what to believe... but I did know that I didn't want the world to come to an end, whether we'd be saved or not.

Our food supplies dwindled. Dad got creative, and particularly excited when we found a beehive at the entrance to a nearby mine. He fashioned "beekeeper suits" for us, taped his machete to the end of a martial arts "bo" staff, and cut down the hive to get at the honey. My beekeeper suit wasn't exactly bee-proof, but I only got stung once during the whole ordeal. And the honey was actually pretty good.

Not everything we scrounged from the desert was so agreeable, however.

For a long time we ate what he called "mesquite beans" (I don't know what the proper name for them is... they looked like pea pods that grew on the thick bushes—I can actually taste them as I write this. If I never eat another one for as long as I live, I'm really okay with that). And we cut the buds off cacti, removed the needles, peeled them, and ate those. A word of advice, if you ever eat the bud of a cactus, no matter how diligent you are about removing the needles, there will always be some left. Trust me on this.

Our water reserves must have run out around that time as well, because Dad and I took empty milk cartons one night and rode out to one of the nearby cattle ranches. We filled the cartons from the water tanks used for the cattle's watering troughs. Dad said it was mineral water, and that it was fine for us to drink.

I thought it was just about the nastiest water I'd ever tasted.

We drank it for several weeks. I was not having much fun at this point. We were in the middle of a sun-scorched desert, going hungry, drinking water meant for cows, and Dad was determined to take down the government, and take me along for the ride. I really didn't think things could get much worse.

I was wrong.

Remember that dirt road, where Dad built the newsstand for us to draw pictures for passersby? Well one day, a car pulled up to that stand. Dad went to the hill overlooking the road, and for some reason, at the sight of this person, Dad freaked. He became hostile. He got one of the rifles. I was freaking out at this point too, but that was just the beginning.

Dad handed me a gun as well.

He said that he was going to talk to the man out by the road. He told me that I was to go the top of the hill, lie down in the dirt, and point my gun at that man, and watch the two of them through my scope. He looked at me with that intensity I had come to know and respect and fear, and he said that if he gave me the signal—arms up, palms facing outward—I was to shoot that man in the head.

I said I didn't want to, but Dad said it was "kill or be killed." All I knew was that I didn't want Dad to die, and so I went to the top of the hill as Dad went out to the road… and I lay down on my belly and put the man in my sights.

Dad approached the stranger, rifle in hand, barrel pointing skyward, shouting. He ordered the man to walk to a wooden post not far away, what he called a checkpoint. The man complied. Dad and the man exchanged words that I either didn't hear or can't remember. I watched carefully, agonizingly, waiting for Dad to give the signal.

He never did.

The man returned to his car and drove off. I took my eye from the scope and sat, numb and overwhelmed by the entire experience.

To this day, I still don't know whether or not I would have pulled that trigger if Dad had given the signal.

I can't even express how grateful I am that I didn't have to find out.

One thing was for certain though: that event changed everything. I didn't know it then, but a sequence of dominoes had started to fall, and my life would never be the same.

CHAPTER THREE:
LEFT TURN AT ALBUQUERQUE

Sometime after the incident with the motorist, Dad and I were in Gleeson, at a friend's house. It must have been around Christmas, because I remember going out with the man and his kids, weeks before, to chop down a Christmas tree.

We were standing in the front yard. I think we were getting ready to leave, when several police cars pulled up, accompanied by a military Jeep and some men in camouflage BDUs.

Two policemen approached and immediately grabbed me, holding me by the arms. Dad raised his hands as the policemen said they were placing him under arrest. Dad looked at me, saw that there was no way out, and put his hands behind his back to be cuffed.

I was yelling and screaming and crying, and the policemen tried to lead me to one of the cruisers, but I kicked and dragged my feet, and one of the officers said that if I didn't cooperate, they would have to put me in handcuffs. I resisted less, and they finally got me into a police car.

From there on out it was a bit of a whirlwind:

Dad was taken to jail, and I eventually went back to stay with the friend whose house we were at when Dad was arrested. I'm sure they kept me at the police station for quite a while and asked me all kinds of questions, but I don't remember the specifics.

At one point the people I was staying with drove me out to our desert dwelling so I could pick up our possessions. The place had been picked clean. On top of that, it had been shot by what seemed like a small army. Our trailer looked like the Bonnie and Clyde car. The whole place was wrecked, and the few photos that I cherished—me sitting on the mats at Dad's dojo, me standing in front of the small airplane—were gone. In a very short amount of time, my life had been turned upside down, and the one constant, my Dad, had been taken from me.

I found out much later that the year Dad was arrested in Arizona was 1982. The arrest was for assault with a deadly weapon. For the longest time, my belief and my recollection was that the motorist was identified as an off-duty police officer, but having gone through the legal records, that doesn't seem to be true.

I do know that it wasn't long before Dad was out of jail, awaiting trial. I was happy and relieved to have him back, but I was also scared that he would be sent back to jail for a very long time.

During that period we stayed with a person who I can only assume was a court-appointed custodian. Maybe he was a parole officer, I'm not sure. Either way, it wasn't long (probably less than a week) before Dad made his move. He told me one night that we were leaving, and that we wouldn't be coming back.

We took what few possessions we had and fled to Albuquerque, New Mexico.

* * *

Shihan Calvin Neilson and Yakimoki Neilson disappeared. Dad, at some point, procured someone else's driver's license. Someone by the name of Fred Bissonnette. Dad told me that we'd be using different names for a while, because if the police found us, he would be taken away and locked up forever. The government, he swore, was behind it all.

Dad got his picture taken at one of those passport photo places. He put his photo over Fred's on the driver's license and re-laminated the card. Poof! Shihan Calvin Neilson was now Fred Bissonnette.

Shortly after, Dad said: "Okay, you need to go by a different name. You can pick any name you want." Well now, that was kinda fun! I could pick *any* name I wanted... "Sparky," or "Slaphappy" or "Captain Destructo!" Or maybe something more subtle, like "Baron Bonecrusher!" No, that wouldn't work. I needed a normal name. After all, we were trying to blend in.

Well, my absolute favorite cartoon character at that time was Mickey Mouse. I told Dad that the name I wanted was "Mickey." Dad agreed. I was on cloud nine.

I had to write the name several times to get used to it. Only problem was, I wasn't the world's greatest speller back then. I spelled it M-I-C-K-Y. No 'E.' How convenient it would have been if we'd watched the Mickey Mouse Club, where they spell it for you right there at the beginning of the show. But no, I got it wrong and it stuck, and I use that name, with that spelling, to this very day.

I still have a suitcase with "Micky Bissonnette" written on it.

* * *

Things were rough for a while. I remember Dad stealing candy bars, and instructing me to shoplift as well. The difference was, I actually got caught. Dad chastised me in front of the store clerk for being dishonest and promised a harsh punishment. Once we left the supermarket of course it was a different story: he admonished me for getting caught.

Despite the early struggle, it wasn't too long before Fred and Micky Bissonnette started scratching out a pretty decent living. Dad drummed up work painting signs, murals, banners; anything art-related. Odd jobs here and there at first, but as time went on, more and more projects came our way. We became active in a local Mormon church, and for the first time I made some friends my age. I was actually having some fun.

But the lying part didn't come easy to me. I hated it, and I told Dad over and over again that I that I was tired of pretending to be someone else.

Maybe that act of taking on another persona, and my ability to do it convincingly was what gave Dad the idea to take me into a local TV production company for an open audition.

I read for the guy who ran the place, and apparently I nailed it. He said his company did local commercial work, and that we should call and check in from time to time.

Dad called routinely, and before long it actually paid off! I read for a few different things, and even landed a non-speaking role in a commercial for the local power company. My part was a kid in a school play, putting on an Abe Lincoln beard in a mirror backstage. It was one of the most exciting moments of my young life. I was going to be on TV! It seemed that things were really looking up.

Not long after that I auditioned for a McDonald's commercial. They liked another kid better, but they liked my voice, so we did dialogue replacement. It was an interesting experience seeing the final product—my voice issuing from the mouth of a young black actor.

Even Dad caught the acting bug. He and I answered a casting call for the movie *Red Dawn* (awesome movie by the way. If you haven't seen it, you're missing out on some classic 80s cinema— "Wolverines!"). Dad read the part of the grocery store clerk in the scene where the teens are loading up on supplies before going into hiding. As you may have guessed though, we didn't get the parts.

Evidently the money that came in from the commercials and the money Dad had saved from doing his art projects was enough to start up a little business. We opened an office in a strip mall, where Dad advertised that we could make everything from logos and business cards to signs, brochures and camera-ready art. We even had copy machines! The shop was called "Destiny Art Creations"—we could meet all your art and advertising needs! Dad even took on a few employees. He didn't pay them, of course—

they got a commission off of work that they brought in, but the business was actually doing okay. Not well enough for us to have our own place though—we slept in a back room.

I made friends with the employees and I was thrilled to be interacting with people on a daily basis. Even better, I got to join the Boy Scout Troop that was sponsored by the church. I started working on merit badges. I even went on a few camp-outs. But more importantly, I was associating with kids my age. Social interaction was something that I desperately needed to work on. The mockery and lampooning that kids frequently engage in, good-natured or otherwise, was completely lost on me (and to be completely honest, that's something that hasn't changed all that much—I enjoy good-natured "smack talk" with friends, but for the most part people who interact with others almost solely through ball-busting and disparagement bug the crap out of me). Despite my unfamiliarity with adolescent rapport, I met a few kids who I started to consider real friends. We even made up our own clubs: the Star Wars Fan Club and the Indiana Jones Fan Club. We had secret codes and everything.

Anyway, the highlight (and as it turned out, the lowlight), of my Boy Scout experience was the Jamboree—a kind of uber-camp-out with numerous troops coming together for several days. We got to work on merit badges, dress up like Indians, tell ghost stories... all kinds of fun. I especially enjoyed the "Indian leg wrestling," where one kid would lie down in the center of a ring, and the other kid would lie next to him, head facing the opposite direction. Both kids

27

would lock their arms, raise their legs nearest to each other two times, and on the third, slam their legs together and, just like arm wrestling, try to pin the other guy's limb. For a kid my size (I've always been smaller than average in both height and weight), I did really well.

The "lowlight" I spoke of happened during the part where I was supposed to learn to swim. Dad took me to a pool a few times when I was really little, and to say I disliked it would be a huge understatement. I just remember screaming a lot. Anyway, Dad thought it would be okay if I joined the other kids who had lined up to jump off the deep end.

I jumped, and immediately started flailing like a cat in a bathtub. This of course had the effect of causing me to sink. I fought my way back up just as one of the Scout Leaders tried to assist by extending the pool skimmer, which he hit me in the head with. I went back under, and I remember thinking to myself *this is a really stupid way to die* as I started taking in water. It was then that one of the braver kids caught me under the arms and hauled me up. They laid me on my back and I spat water out, but I was okay.

Dad had watched the whole thing and hadn't moved a muscle. He later told me that God was watching over me, and that he knew I'd be fine. I remember thinking to myself that God hadn't shared that info with me, and that I could have used some help.

At any rate, for the first time I was living something that had started to resemble a normal life. But the more I spoke to the other kids and learned what a "normal life" really was, the more I realized that I was kidding myself. Dad and I weren't normal.

Our lives weren't normal. We were impostors; liars and pretenders and somehow that made it even worse. I wanted to go to school. I wanted a normal family. I wanted to tell people the truth.

But that was not meant to be.

I bugged Dad repeatedly to tell me again what had happened to Mom. There was a part of me even then that wondered if he wasn't telling me everything about the circumstances of her death, especially when he found it so easy to lie about so many other things. After all, both of our lives at that time were based on fabrication.

The shadow that seemed to pass over Dad so frequently settled on him once again and he sat me down for another of his "serious talks."

He said, with complete conviction, as he always did, that he and Mom were flying from Mexico to the United States. This was the same as what he had told me before: that she had died during the flight when a cyst on her ovary ruptured. But this time the rest of the story was different. They landed and Mom was alive, but as they deplaned, when Mom stepped onto the tarmac... Dad got teary as he said "the government assassinated your mother."

This was a lot to take in. I was old enough now that I started to question things, and I wondered (to myself) whether this could possibly be true. Did the government really just go around shooting people? I didn't know what to think. The more I thought about it though, the more I wasn't entirely convinced.

Dad's revised account of Mom's death was unusual, but as far as "unusual" goes, something he told me later really takes the cake.

For many years both Dad and I wore our belt buckles to the left side. As a kid growing up, I thought it was normal. As I interacted with other kids more often, I realized that everyone else wore their buckle in the middle. For a while Dad told me (and others who would ask) that it represented our religious and political beliefs. One night, Dad told me the "real" reason...

There was a black planet, he said, located behind the sun. There were aliens from this planet, and they walked among us, posing as humans. They were evil, and they had worked their way into our government infrastructure, into powerful and influential positions throughout the world. The belt buckle we wore on the left side was a sign to others who knew of the aliens that we were believers as well.

I asked if there was any way to tell when someone was from the black planet.

"Only one way," he said. "When you look in their eyes, you can't see your own reflection."

Naturally, this scared the crap out of me. For the next several days I stared into the eyeballs of everyone I knew just to make sure I could see myself in there, and I did the same thing to people we'd meet for the first time. I'm sure I must have freaked more than a few people out—"Hello sir, nice to meet you. Why is your kid standing two inches from my face scrutinizing my eyeballs?"

* * *

Have I mentioned how much Dad loved his coffee? Every morning, he and I would hit up McDonalds. I'd get their breakfast and Dad would have his coffee. He made friends there; one of our friends was an old guy who'd had a stroke. He had trouble remembering words sometimes. He'd get frustrated and slam his fist on the table, but Dad was always patient, and would calm him down. And eventually they'd figure out together what he was trying to say.

I remember Dad telling our friend one morning that we'd be going to California. Dad talked about going to all kinds of places, so I didn't think much of it at first. But then he told the church we were leaving, and told me to share the info with my Boy Scout friends. I protested, of course, but Dad said I could join the Scouts in California; that our lives would be even better.

One morning the old guy at McDonalds was trying to tell me something about California, something I'd see there. He couldn't think of the word. He cursed and smacked his fist against his head and Dad handed him a napkin and a pen, and asked if he could draw what he was thinking of.

A few seconds later he slid the napkin to me, smiling proudly.

He'd drawn a palm tree.

CHAPTER FOUR:
THE LONG ARM OF THE LAW

What, exactly, caused Dad to decide that the time had come for us to move on, I don't know. He had a habit of just pulling up stakes whenever he felt like it.

Regardless, "move on" is exactly what we did. We ended up in Anaheim, California, where we rented a room in a condo. This must have been late '84, early '85. We were still going by Micky and Fred Bissonnette, and Dad cooked up this cover story he wanted me to tell people to explain why I wasn't in school. Ready? I was a child genius.

Yep. A prodigy. That was the cover story. I was to say that I graduated The Albuquerque Technical Vocational Institute at the age of nine. I was 12 at this point, and even then I knew this cover story wouldn't hold water. But hey, that's what Dad told me to tell people, and that's what I told 'em. I even had a résumé (which I didn't remember until going through records later) that made all sorts of outlandish claims, but we'll get to that in a while.

Dad went back to the usual—hustling door to door asking who needed signs painted, logos drawn up, etc. We attended a local church, we went to

McDonalds every morning, and Dad put me back in Boy Scouts.

It was as close to "routine" as my life had ever been. I wrote my friends back in Albuquerque, and even though I was in the Scouts in California, it wasn't the same. I missed my friends, and I wasn't making new ones.

The Scouts didn't last. I found out later from a letter I found that Dad, who had volunteered as a kind of consultant, was basically asked to leave and not bother coming back.

All of it just seemed wrong. I didn't know why, but things were off... the cover story, the Scouts, the entire change of location... it just felt out of whack. Sure, California had palm trees. Yeah the weather was nice. But that didn't change the fact that my Spider Sense was tingling like nobody's business.

Remember how I mentioned that my life changed irrevocably when Dad was arrested in Arizona? Well, it was about to change again.

On May 16th, 1985, shortly after my 13th birthday (May 3rd), Dad and I were sitting at McDonalds, as usual. Dad was having his coffee and I was reading the funny papers.

Two police officers entered, made a beeline for where we were sitting, and identified themselves. One of them started asking Dad questions—"Who are you?" "What do you do?" that type of thing—while the other pulled me aside and made similar enquiries. The officer talking to me asked if the man I was with was my Dad. I said he was. He asked my name. I told him "Yakimoki Bissonnette." Whoops. "Uh, I mean, Micky." Then the officer asked why I wasn't in school.

I recited the information that Dad had taught

me—that I graduated from the Technical Vocational Institute in Albuquerque, New Mexico.

The officer then told me that they had actually checked into that… and that there was no record of me graduating from there.

Well as you can imagine, it all went downhill from there. I said I didn't understand why the records didn't show me graduating from TVI. They asked Dad where I went to elementary school, which he had no answer for. They asked if they could contact my grandparents on either side and Dad said no. They asked for a birth certificate and Dad told them there wasn't one.

Not surprisingly, they decided to take us to the police station for further questioning.

At the station they put is in separate rooms and continued with the questions: how long was I with Dad, did I ever know of any other family, did I ever go to school, where did we live and for how long… a parade of inquiries that I knew would only lead to one thing: Dad being taken away again.

It had started off as a normal day, but now there I was, in a police station, separated from my father, being asked for information that I really didn't have, or was afraid to give because I wanted to protect Dad as much as possible.

It took a few hours, but eventually of course they found out that Dad had been arrested in Arizona. The charges at that time were Assault with a Deadly Weapon and Violation of a Release Order.

They confronted him with that information, and then the questions started all over again. At that point the jig was up. I told them that I never went to school, that I never graduated from TVI, that I spent my whole life with Dad and never knew any other family.

Dad was arrested, and this time there was no bail.

I, of course was crying my eyes out. What would happen to me? I thought they might throw me in jail too... or worse. I thought of Dad's horror stories of government assassinations. It seemed so far-fetched... but what if I was wrong?

By the end of the day I ended up in "protective custody," and was taken to the Albert Sitton Home, a children's home for abused, abandoned and neglected kids.

Paperwork was filled out; I was issued a towel, a toothbrush, etc. and shown to my room, a small space with a single bed and a door with a tiny window.

That night, after "lights out," was the worst. At least in Arizona when Dad was arrested I was able to stay with our family friend and his kids. But this time was much different. I was in a completely foreign, sterile, uncomfortable environment with a bunch of strangers and troubled kids. And to my mind it seemed very likely that the government really had been looking for us; that they had made a mistake last time by letting Dad out of their sight, a mistake I felt sure they wouldn't make again. Now that they had us... I was more and more convinced that they would keep us separated forever.

It was the most alone I've ever felt. The kind of alone that caused endless tears, reminiscence and longing; a soulful yearning to once again be in the presence of the one person who had been a binding thread in my life, for better or for worse.

* * *

Over the next several days I mostly kept to myself, lost in a kind of fog. One saving grace in the midst of all this, believe it or not, was school. I was excited to be taking classes. Art, history, English, math (not fun, considering I sucked at it), and more were all taught right there at the home. I was also excited to maybe make some friends; interact with kids my own age like I had in Boy Scouts.

As you might imagine, there were all different kinds of youths at the Albert Sitton Home—with every kind of behavior problem you can think of. Some were prone to violent outbursts, some were suicidal; some had suffered from neglect, and some had suffered from the opposite: they had gotten attention, but attention of the worst kind.

Kids who were a few years older attended many of the same classes, and a couple of the bullies set their sights on me. They had a good deal of fun at my expense, and when I stood against them, I was often outnumbered and overpowered. Of course, at that time it really didn't take much to overpower me... I must have weighed less than 80 pounds.

I did manage to make a couple friends—one of whom didn't speak any English. He was a little Vietnamese kid who would practice punching drills with me.

I did well in my classes, especially art, which I attacked with a passion. It felt comfortable and rewarding; something familiar that I actually had a talent for. I adjusted to the daily schedule: wake up, shower, brush your teeth, go to classes, eat, go to more classes, watch a movie, maybe get some tokens for the arcade (where I became obsessed with *Dragon's Lair*), brush your teeth, go to bed, repeat. The strangest part of this routine was actually the showering. I had only taken a few showers in my entire life, when Dad and I were living in the apartment in Tombstone. It felt odd and somewhat pointless to me to take a shower, but I suffered through, and now of course I feel disgusting if I go a day without one.

One highlight in addition to some of the school classes: getting to watch movies. Don't ask me how it was okayed (or actually, it probably wasn't), but one of the workers actually brought in *Terminator* for the "older" kids to watch. I was blown away by the action and the effects, but aside from all that, it was the first time I saw boobies on a TV screen (I had seen a *Playboy* magazine once before that, and determined even at that early age that I thought naked women were *really* cool).

I'm still a big *Terminator* fan, too.

Some kids were allowed time on an Atari later at night, and that became a highlight for me. Aside from that, bedtime continued to be the most difficult. I didn't hear from Dad, so at night I would lie awake for hours. There was a song that was popular at the time, "Cherish the Love" by Kool and the Gang. I had a little radio in my room, and it seemed that the station I set it to would play that song over and over. The power a song can have, especially when it's closely associated to a deeply emotional chapter of your life, is pretty amazing. I absolutely did cherish the love of Dad, and I missed it more than words can express. Many nights I cried myself to sleep with the lyrics of that song repeating in my head.

* * *

A few weeks went by, and a worker was assigned to review the petition in my Dad's case. She interviewed me and Dad separately.

Many years later, when I retrieved my juvenile records, I was able to secure the court report. The report contained the caseworker's notes, Dad's arrest report, and my "résumé." The résumé wasn't included in the copy I received, but it was described, and is worth mentioning here...

In addition to the TVI graduation, it stated that I was a brown belt in martial arts (Dad had shown me a few moves, but that was about it), a publisher at the age of three (I claimed that I drew a snowman for Dad; apparently that qualified me), had graduated high school (in the interview I admitted that I hadn't), had attended a bible school (I told the caseworker that I wrote a letter and was accepted... I don't remember any of that today), and had a few years of survival training (now that one wasn't a lie—if living in the Arizona desert for two years on nothing but beans and rice didn't qualify me, what would?).

In the caseworker's notes for Dad's interview, she detailed the following: Dad said that the charges against him were all garbage. He repeated the story of my mom dying from a cyst on her ovary that burst, then later in the interview he told the worker that mom died by being injected with a slow-acting poison, administered by a communist agent outside Tijuana (this is one version he never told me). He claimed that while in the desert, he taught mercenaries who were going to Andorra, wherever in the world that might be. But that wasn't the best part. Get this: Dad said that our desert compound had "beautiful accommodations." That's bad enough, but with Dad, when he was telling his tall tales, he always had to take it one step too far. He actually told the caseworker that we had a helicopter pad. A freakin' helicopter pad! To be fair, in a way he was right; there was a helicopter pad. A *really* big one. It's called "the desert."

He said that the property was government property that he had claimed, but the file for the claim was removed by the State of Arizona. He, of course, said that the government was after him, because he was anti-communist, that we would be shot and killed, etc... But then apparently he went off on a whole different tangent.

Dad raved about something called "the Faction." The Faction was who was after us. Arizona was involved in the Faction, and California was cooperating. The Faction, he said, had removed anyone we had ever associated with, including their families. The Faction wiped out all files pertaining to myself or my Dad. According to him, the Faction even influenced the court case years before in Arizona, as the State told him the charges would be dropped. Again, Dad said he believed that as soon as he was released, he would be assassinated. And apparently the Faction wanted to kidnap me... because of my photographic memory (my memory sucks).

He then proceeded to threaten the commission of another crime in order to avoid extradition. Inexplicably, he then claimed that he would "drop a bomb on Thursday." Why Thursday? Who knows. Drop a bomb on what? Got me.

Regarding family, Dad said that he had wealthy parents in Canada, and that he and Mom met while teaching guerilla warfare in Vietnam. He claimed that they were married in Mexico... and he said that I had an older brother (something Dad never told me) living in Barcelona with our grandparents.

Near the end of the interview Dad said I was an exceptionally good son. And that he was very proud of me. He said he respected me, and talked to me four times a day; that he trusted me implicitly and loved me immensely.

And out of all the things he said in that interview, that last bit was the only real truth. But of course, it was what mattered most. Even after I read that document years later, shaking my head at all the craziness, it still hit me: Dad loved me, I loved him. A beautiful and simple fact amid a sea of falsehoods.

* * *

As far as my interview went, I basically told the worker everything I could remember from Oklahoma on, and not much more, except that I sent "mental messages" to Dad every night, telling him everything would work out, it would be okay. I prayed and prayed and prayed that God would reconnect us, that it was all just a temporary nightmare, another hurdle to overcome. I believed that we would be reunited.

The recommendation of the caseworker following her review was that I be declared a dependent of the Orange County Juvenile Court.

More time passed, until the day of Dad's hearing came. I was allowed to attend. I saw Dad come out in his jumpsuit, sit, and answer questions. He looked older, his hair grayer, his face more lined.

The only words I remember from the whole event were in a statement by the prosecuting attorney saying that the court-appointed defense was "fly fishing for carp." The judge snickered.

There must have been a recess, because I remember getting to sit with Dad and his attorney. I spoke with Dad briefly, and I recall his lawyer telling him to plead guilty. I also remember Dad steadfastly refusing. They were all a bunch of communists in his eyes, intent on "railroading him out of town," and he wouldn't give them the satisfaction of a guilty plea.

The lawyer made it clear that he didn't feel that things would go our way. I remarked that what had sealed it was obviously the prosecutor's "fly fishing for carp" line.

It wasn't long before we got the verdict, and sure enough, Dad's lawyer was right; it didn't go as we hoped. Dad was to be extradited to Arizona, where he would stand trial.

As for me, I would stay in California. The chasm between Dad and me widened, and the realization that I was well and truly on my own became even clearer.

CHAPTER FIVE:
THE REAL ALIENS

The search for my missing family began in earnest. My dad's fingerprints, his stories about military service and parents in Canada all led to dead ends. This of course resulted in me speculating that Neilson wasn't even our real last name. Was Dad using an alias even as far back as Oklahoma? If so, why? I didn't want to think about that. I just wanted all the craziness to end.

The police and Social Services all did their parts, but after a few more weeks it was determined that while the investigations into my past would continue, I would be placed in a foster home.

Dad and I had lived with a Mormon family briefly in Albuquerque, but the idea of becoming *part* of some existing family of strangers, of being expected to treat them as a mom and dad was varying amounts bizarre, intimidating, and exciting all at once. Perhaps the most exciting prospect was the idea of having a mom for the first time.

What would she be like? What would a typical household be like? And what about going to a real school? Living a life for the first time that could actually be called... normal.

Days seemed to stretch into infinity, but finally the time came to meet my prospective foster parents—Ernest and Janet Parker. They seemed nice enough. Hell, they seemed normal, and that was a great start. The children's home had become stifling. In some ways, it felt like I was in jail too, and I wanted freedom. I wanted to get out.

My social worker put the wheels in motion. Papers were signed, hoops were jumped through, red tape was sifted and cut, and then one day I found myself sitting in my social worker's car, on my way to a new home and a new family in Yorba Linda. It was like something from an old Disney cartoon, the one where a drunk stork delivers a baby giant meant for the beanstalk to Mickey and Minnie... except in my case the Social worker stork was dropping off a 13-year-old kid. BAM! Here you go, kid, say hello to your new mom and dad.

Whatever happens, it's okay, I told myself. *This is only temporary. Dad'll be out of jail soon and then everything will be back to the way it was.*

I toured the house. It was pretty big. Bigger than I was used to, that was for sure. I met Brian and Rich, two other foster kids who were close to my age, though a little younger, as well as a handicapped girl that Ernest and Janet cared for. I explored further, put my stuff in the room I would be sharing with the two younger boys, and for a while I just tried to take it all in.

We played, ate peanut butter and jelly sandwiches, drank Kool Aid, and later that evening I met Kyle, Janet and Ernest's natural son. He was a big kid in his mid teens who wore make-up and sported coal-black hair styled after the Cure's Robert Smith.

He had his own room, the walls plastered with posters of 80s Goth bands.

That night I went to bed feeling mostly relieved and more hopeful for the future than I had since Dad's second arrest.

* * *

When the time came for my first day at school, I felt the same as I had going into the new foster home: nervous, anxious, excited… I had no idea what to expect.

The way I felt stepping foot into junior high school is the way I imagine Neil Armstrong must have felt stepping foot on the moon.

It was a completely foreign world. Unlike the moon, however, this foreign body was populated by alien life forms. and not even aliens from the same planet. It was like an intergalactic alien convention. I was intrigued, but mostly kept to myself as I navigated this strange new territory.

I got my class assignments: amazingly, I was on track with all the other eighth graders, except for math and English. I was ahead one grade in English, behind one grade in math.

But the most exciting thing? I was assigned a locker! My own locker! It was *mine*, and I could put *my* stuff in it. How cool was that? Of course, I didn't have much stuff yet, but that would change... as soon as I figured out where my classrooms were.

I don't have a good sense of direction to begin with, but I did manage to find my first class, where the teacher made it a point to introduce me to everyone: "This is our new student, Yak… Yoka… Yoki…

maki..." and of course the other kids thought this was the funniest (and weirdest) name they'd ever heard. I hoped that I wouldn't have to go through that embarrassment for every classroom.

I was wrong.

Lunch was an adventure. I didn't know anyone, so I had no idea what to do, other than stand at a low wall overlooking the football field. It was there that I had my first real interaction with one of the aliens. Two girls approached, looking at me and giggling. I, of course, thought that they wanted to start a conversation, be friends, even. As they passed, one of the girls reached out, put her hand between my legs and squeezed... not gently. It wasn't enough to cause much pain though, so I looked at them wide-eyed and smiled like "hey, thanks." They pointed and laughed and went along their way.

I went back to my locker at the end of lunch and there I had my first real verbal interactions with the aliens. One girl asked me if I had any friends, in a mock-pity kind of voice (which was completely lost on me). I said I didn't, really. She was soon joined by a few other girlfriends, and one of them decided to remark on how skinny I was. "Look at him, I mean he's like, a stick." The other girls thought this was hilarious. It was one of those situations where someone says something and you think of several very clever comebacks five minutes later. At least, I thought the comebacks were very clever; something along the lines of: "Yeah, I'm like a stick, like the stick you've got lodged up your ass." The French have a phrase for when you think of a good comeback a while after the insult has passed.

I don't remember the phrase.

I really didn't understand where the hostility was coming from, and by the time I left school, I was starting to get the sense that the whole experience was going to suck. Hard.

At least I had a pretty decent time at the foster home playing with Brian and Rich. Brian had started collecting GI Joe action figures, which I thought were the coolest things on Earth. He let me borrow some of his Joes, but we didn't have any bad guys to fight against, so we had Joes fighting Joes, which really just ain't right. But hey, we made do.

Kyle came home late, and spent the rest of the time in his room.

The second day came and I thought for sure things at school would get better. They didn't. One kid said "hey," and offered his hand, which I moved to shake, and he pulled it back and said "thought you had a friend!" and walked away.

Things progressed without much change. Life with Dad had been challenging to say the least, but in many ways it had been simple compared to what I was going through in junior high.

Oh, and one other thing *really* didn't help: my wardrobe. Janet had taken me to a second-hand store and basically let me pick out whatever I thought looked cool. Good idea, right? Well it's not like my idea of "cool" coincided with any kind of fashion trends. And I have learned in the years since that I certainly don't have an innate sense of fashion.

One of the winners I picked out was a silk shirt that had a giant orchid and leaves spread across the front, a visual assault and battery that was fully executed when

46

the shirt was buttoned. I had slacks, too, and dress socks, but most damaging of all was a cream-colored 70s double-knit polyester leisure suit. Yeah, you read that right. I thought it was awesome. It had big green buttons and green stitching. Green! Looking back now I fully realize that I looked like a leprechaun pimp.

The combo of the orchid shirt and the leisure suit was a devastating ensemble. At the time, I had no clue that much of the ridicule I endured was caused by my clothing choices.

* * *

At the end of the first week Brian, Rich, and I went to play in a golf course that lay beyond the cul de sac at the end of our street. As we crawled through the bushes and climbed trees to stage GI Joe battles, we noticed old, lost golf balls… a LOT of them, scattered all around the periphery of the course. I had a thought, which I voiced to the others, and this thought soon took the shape of a plan: we would collect these balls, clean them up, and sell them to golfers. We spent the rest of the day collecting. A lot of the balls were Titleist, which I was convinced was pronounced "tit-lee-ist." That in itself was a source of much amusement.

Something else I observed that weekend, and beyond, that disturbed me a bit was how Janet treated the kids. Yelling, mostly, but she had a habit of putting her hands on the kids, pushing, pulling, etc. Nothing too dire but it was enough to set me on edge.

I had quickly come to dread school. I told myself that things couldn't get any worse.

Sound familiar?

47

Then, one of the most embarrassing moments of my school career happened, and it centered around one thing: a Scantron test.

Now, I had never seen a Scantron sheet in my life. As I'm sure everyone who's reading this knows, Scantron sheets were narrow pieces of paper with *A, B, C, D, E* bubbles in rows. You would read questions from a booklet, and select the correct answer from multiple choices in the booklet by penciling in the appropriate bubble.

The teacher didn't explain any of this because everyone in class had been taking Scantron tests for years. Everyone except me. I asked someone what to do, and was told to put the correct answer on the form. So I selected the correct answer, and wrote, in *really really* small words, the entire answer on the margin of the Scantron sheet. For every question. That's not an easy feat to accomplish. The teacher walked by, saw what I was doing, and proceeded to ask in front of the whole class, why on earth I was writing my answers on the sheet. The class thought this was the funniest thing they'd ever heard. Most of them. The rest just thought I was *really* weird. I'm sure a few thought I was just plain stupid.

I said that I'd never taken a Scantron test before, which led to a brief explanation of my predicament— that I grew up with just my Dad, that he never put me in school, that he was arrested and now I was in foster care... Most of the kids still looked at me like I was a total freak. But a few expressions changed to genuine interest.

After that, though, some of the kids actually started talking to me.

It began with brief acknowledgments from some

of them, a "hey" here and a "what's up" there. At one point I even went to the kid who'd offered his hand and pulled it away… I told him he'd gotten ink on his palm. When he opened the palm to look, I pressed my hand into it and said, "now I know I gotta friend." He smiled and nodded.

Soon me and Brian and Rich had our freshly washed golf balls ready. We stuck them in egg cartons, and we sat at the edge of the fairway and sold the balls for 25 and 50 cents, depending on the condition. We made something like 12 bucks, and the first thing I did with my cut of the money was buy a Cobra action figure… "Saboteur." For the first time, I had an opposing member to go up against Brian's Joes. I wasn't ready for all-out war yet, but it was a great first step. Things were looking up, I thought.

After a little while I befriended two other kids… both social outcasts. Both younger than me, and one of them Indian with a thick accent. They were ignored or mistreated by many of the other students, just like me. This commonality was enough to bind us, in addition to one other: they "still played with toys." They collected action figures and vehicles, which I thought was pretty damn cool.

Something else was happening at school, too: kids were asking me about where I came from, what my situation was before I got there. I told my entire PE class my life story while we sat cross-legged on the basketball court.

With the passage of my first month at the Parker household, things were going okay, except for the fact that I hadn't heard from Dad. My social worker checked in to tell me that I was officially, legally a dependent of the court. I wasn't sure how to feel about that. I asked him to find out why I wasn't getting Dad's letters.

Over the following weeks I continued to survive at school. I never really felt like I fit in or was accepted in general, but I wasn't being ridiculed daily, which was fine with me. Meanwhile, my golf ball side business enjoyed enough success to provide me with a small squad of Cobra action figures, which I led to several glorious backyard and golf course victories against Brian's vaunted Joes (that's my side of the story, anyway).

Not long after, I was contacted by my social worker and informed that I would be talking with a psychiatrist. He informed me that this was standard procedure for all foster kids. I later found out this wasn't true, but I understand the reasoning: after all I had been through, and given my dad's behavior, they wanted to make sure I didn't have a screw loose... one that might fall out later in life and lead to a loss of my marbles.

I saw the psychiatrist once every couple weeks. After I saw him a few times, he remarked about the kids I was hanging out with, and what I thought about the fact that they were younger than me, that they still played with toys, etc. I understood what he was getting at, but I really didn't care. I enjoyed hanging out with them, and I enjoyed "playing with toys."

Later on in life, when I worked at Blizzard Entertainment, guess what I had sitting constantly on my desk? Yep, toys.

* * *

Before I knew it, Christmastime was coming around. My first Christmas with a whole new family, and it felt... weird. Still no letters from Dad. At this point I had written him five or six times. The approaching holiday made me miss him even more, but I tried my best to put it out of my head.

There was, however, one shadow that was again cast over the whole affair: Janet's treatment of the kids. Most disturbing of all was an incident where she grabbed Rich and pulled him by his ear. I felt strongly that this was not okay. The incident stuck with me, and I worried that if she was willing to do that, what else would she try to get away with? Also, Janet was pushing for me to call her Mom, something I wasn't comfortable doing. I could tell that she felt snubbed by this, but calling some relative stranger Mom simply didn't feel right.

Christmas went pretty well. Then it was back to school, and even school was tolerable.

In late January, my social worker came to visit. He had news about Dad and how long Dad's sentence was going to be: 18 years, with possible time off for good behavior after nine years. I'd be 22 years old when he was released.

This hit me like a freight train. I had been fooling myself into believing that Dad would be out soon. A couple years at most... but 18 years? Nine if he was good? I was devastated, and for a while, inconsolable. In later years, whenever I would tell someone about Dad's sentencing, people have always been surprised, and felt like he got put away for much longer than he deserved. In later years I too felt that there must have been more to the whole thing. But at the time of hearing the news, all I felt was shock and anguish. I wanted to know why I wasn't getting letters. The worker said that they were looking into it, that they had tried to get me visitation but it hadn't worked out. There was still no progress on finding any other family members, or my real name, either.

The social worker asked if there was anything he could do.

I told him about the incident with Janet pulling Rich's ear.

Now it turns out that the state frowns on foster parents getting physical at all with their wards. Things happened pretty fast after that. There was an inquiry into the matter, and Janet and Ernest were cleared, but they wanted me out of the house.

The social worker had visited on January 21st, 1986. I was back in the Albert Sitton Home by January 24th.

CHAPTER SIX:
STARTING OVER

I didn't know how long I'd have to stay at the children's home the second time around; I only knew that I didn't want it to drag on. I'd had a taste of "the outside," and I liked it.

It turned out I didn't have to wait very long. Within a couple weeks, I was heading to my next foster home.

It was huge. Located at the top of a winding loop in Anaheim Hills, it even had its own little driveway, which I thought was really cool. It also had a half-acre backyard that I would come to know intimately.

My new foster parents were the Coolidges: Renee, a nurse, and Shawn, a cantankerous old cowboy construction worker.

I had two older foster brothers, Roy and Alex. Roy was getting close to graduation. A drumming enthusiast, he was tall, a good student and an all around mild-mannered dude. Alex was a younger, acne-scarred teen who radiated a sense of really not giving a crap about much of anything.

Right around this time I got a new social worker, an African-American lady named Joyce Collins. She was soft-spoken and very kind.

At the house, I warmed up to Roy pretty quickly. I was a little apprehensive about a new school, and upon viewing my wardrobe, Roy thought it prudent (once he and Alex stopped laughing) to give me some pointers on what to wear.

Renee and Shawn took me to get clothes, and they actually took me to real stores! With brand names! By the time I was done I was rocking some Polo shirts, cargo pants and Reeboks. Thus empowered, I felt ready to take on school again. I would be going to El Rancho Junior High.

And you know what? I got off to a decent start. The change in clothing made a huge difference, along with the fact that I was picking up on social behaviors and learning not to be so awkward. At the outset I wasn't a complete pariah. I was making progress!

I learned pretty quickly that weekends would be spent working, mostly on the backyard. The yard was a beast—we weeded, raked, mowed, and de-snailed every inch of that half acre. Alex and Roy hated every minute of it.

I did manage to get in some TV time—Saturday morning cartoons. GI Joe, Transformers, Voltron, Thundercats. The mid to late 80s were a treasure trove of pure pop culture gold, and I loved every minute of it. The work was a pain in the ass, but overall I had it better at this new foster home than I'd ever had it before.

I decided that at school I needed to do something that would gain me some visibility... maybe increase my chances at, oh I don't know, actually making friends. I found out pretty quickly that the kids in my drama class could be a little "out there" themselves, and they pretty much didn't care if you were "cool" or not. Drama was its own microcosm within the school, where it was okay to just be you.

The first performance I put on in front of the class was a lip-synch to "I Want to Be a Cowboy" by Boys Don't Cry. The skit was a huge success. People laughed at me, for the first time, in a good way.

At the house, Shawn offered for me to join him at his construction site. I decided to try it out. He wasn't really much fun to work for. All he did was grumble and bark orders, and the work held no real interest for me. By the end of the day I got a little bit of money, and an open offer to continue working on weekends if I wanted to. I declined.

All in all though, life was feeling refreshingly normal.

Then I got my first letter from Dad... as well as the five others he had written that had been held back. All at once. One of them was a photocopy of Dad's letter rather than the letter itself.

The content of some of the letters was hopeful ("My love for you, YAKIMOKI—my GOD given Son; is greater and more PLENTIFUL, than all the stars in ALMIGHTY GOD'S HEAVENS," he wrote). He said that he had filed several lawsuits and that we would be together again soon. He said he met some friends in prison who were from Vietnam, that he told them all about me and that he wanted me to write to them. He listed their names. The names were Vietnamese. I still don't know what that was all about. I didn't really want to write letters to strangers.

I was genuinely happy to hear from Dad finally, but the thing that worried me most was that he told me to run away. Just get on a bus. He gave me addresses of folks who would take me in, and said he'd send me a money order.

Then I read another of the letters. Where the one was hopeful, this one was frustrated. Apparently Dad's lawsuits were leading nowhere. Dad was pursuing action through the ACLU to learn details about my placement, but they told him that they could do no more than inform him that I was in a foster home. In the letter, written when I was still living with Janet, Dad accused Janet of trying to steal me from him. He wanted a pastor that he had contacted to take custody of me.

Dad said that all incoming mail to him was being screened.

It was a lot to take in. I had no idea what to do. I certainly didn't think it would do anyone any good for me to just run away. I wanted to write Dad back immediately, but I wasn't sure how to tell him that I didn't plan on jumping on a bus. I really didn't know what to tell him.

I wrote a few drafts of letters, but none of it sounded right. I decided I would draw him a picture; maybe that would console him somewhat. At least I had finally heard from him. His letters brought back memories of our time together and reminded me of my love for him, but his insistence on me running away brought other memories as well: the hard times, the strange behavior, the anti-government rants, the guns in the desert, the day I laid on a hill and put a stranger in the sights of my rifle—the parts of my old life that felt not only distant, but... undesirable, to say the least.

I finished the picture for Dad and wrote, telling

him about the other letters I had sent previously. I told him that I loved him. I didn't say anything about running away. I worried about his response; that he would be ashamed of me. I waited anxiously for his next letter.

Meanwhile, once a week I started seeing a new psychiatrist—Allison. She was a poised older lady with glasses. The first few sessions were mostly getting-to-know-you stuff. I didn't feel like talking in the beginning; I mostly just answered questions.

At school, the more I observed social behaviors, the more I noticed that the "cool kids" got the most attention by doing things they weren't supposed to do. Bad behavior was rewarded with higher status. Of course, I wasn't really analyzing the situation in those terms at the time, I just began aping behaviors that seemed to make others the center of conversations.

And thus began the "mischievous" period of my life. It started fairly small—rolling up strips of paper, bending them, and using rubber bands to shoot the projectiles at other kids. Not the kind of thing that would land me in jail, but not the kind of thing I was opening up to my therapist about either.

Dad wrote back. He wasn't angry with me, which was a huge relief. He said he was studying law, and that he would take care of everything; that we would be together soon. I thought that sounded... unlikely. I wrote back, telling him about the new foster home and the new school.

I started warming up to my therapist a bit more. She had all kinds of questions about how it was for me growing up, and she was deeply interested in helping me figure out where I was born. She asked me something no one else at that point had asked me: was I circumcised? I didn't know what this meant, so once she explained (going so far as to draw me a picture of a circumcised and an uncircumcised penis). I replied that I was, in fact, circumcised. This led her to believe that I was most likely not born in Panama or South America. It was her opinion that I was born in the United States. But, of course, I had no proof of that… I was told that, in the eyes of the state, I was an "undocumented alien." Unless some proof of my place of birth was discovered, this would mean that I would go through the immigration process. I didn't know much about this either, but it didn't sound like fun.

Dad sent me a letter wishing me a happy birthday and telling me that he was still working on his legal education, and that it wouldn't be long before the two of us would be reunited.

And then, I had my birthday! It was the first time I had a birthday with presents that someone spent a fair amount of money on. I got a bike! I got clothes! I got toys! And, at this point I had started really getting into Garfield, so I got a Garfield stuffed animal! Yes, it was the prevailing opinion of most people that stuffed animals were for girls. I didn't care; it was an amazing feeling to get all of those gifts. I couldn't wait until Christmas!

Renee and Shawn suggested that I should start calling them Mom and Dad. I thought about my real dad and my real mom. I wondered again what Mom looked like, what her personality had been like. Was she like me? I might never know.

I told Renee and Shawn that I wasn't comfortable calling them Mom and Dad. They said they were okay with it, but I could tell that Renee especially was put off.

Roy and Alex weren't doing so well. Alex especially. The housework was driving both of them nuts. Then, at dinner one night Alex made a crack about Shawn being corny, and the old guy went off on him, telling him he'd take him out to the garage and have him put on the boxing gloves; see what kind of a man he was.

Two weeks later Alex ran away from the house.

* * *

The school year ended with me feeling pretty okay about it, and then summer was in full swing. I was encouraged to go to summer school, to catch up (especially in math).

Letters from Dad, who was still working on legal recourse, came in frequently and I wrote back consistently, keeping him updated on my life.

We didn't talk much about Alex at the foster home, but I could tell Roy was not happy. He complained often about the chores affecting his schoolwork. He also worked with Shawn at the construction site, an arrangement that he was not at all happy with.

Me, I got along okay with Shawn, despite his habit of walking around the house in old tighty-whitey underwear that was no longer tight or white.

On the nights when Renee was working, Shawn would shout out from his room "Miiiick!!" I'd go running into where he was lying in bed in his skivvies, and he'd ask me to go to the garage and pick out a

John Wayne movie for him. "Pick out a good one!" he'd say.

In the garage was a tall bureau chock full of VHS tapes consisting of exactly two genres: War and Western. I'd grab him a tape and later that night we'd hear this sound: "booooooooopppppp"—that was the noise the TV made when the tape in the VCR ran out. I'd go in and find Shawn conked out, snoring away, and I'd shut off the television.

Something else Shawn kept in the garage, which I heard about from either Roy or Alex: *Hustler* magazines.

I, of course, took it upon myself to investigate, and sure enough, there were boxes full! Yet another milestone in a teenage boy's life.

* * *

The visits with my psychiatrist were going well. She asked me if I had nightmares. I told her about the recurring nightmares that I had been having since early childhood: spiders. I've been arachnophobic my entire life and my spider nightmares are the worst: I'm usually in some dark wooded area, surrounded by webs no matter which way I turn. And then the spiders come—squat, fat, eight-legged creepy crawlers, some of them with vibrant markings. I would run, and in the dream they would get bigger and bigger. In one dream I backed up against a tree. Then the tree started to *move*, and as I turned around I saw that what I had leaned against was a giant spider that bore the same markings as the tree and had wrapped itself around it. I'd wake up yelling my head off.

Allison wondered if I had experienced some kind of trauma earlier in life involving spiders. I hadn't, that I could remember. Perhaps subconsciously at this stage in my life I felt like a fly caught in a spider's web. Like so many things it was just one more question about my past with no definitive answers.

That particular session ended early. I had seen a comic book shop just down the street, and I had some lunch money, but Shawn hated comics. He said they "rotted your brain." I decided to go to the comic book shop anyway.

There I perused through the titles and found one that jumped out at me: *Conan the Barbarian.* He looked like a complete badass—bare-chested, a massive broadsword in his hand and a voluptuous woman curled around his leg. I bought a couple issues and went back to the therapist's office. I read a bit and was hooked immediately by the high fantasy of Conan's world.

When Renee came to pick me up, I stuffed the comics under my shirt and tucked the bottoms into my pants.

That night I read the rest. Conan was so many things: strong, fearless, and desired by beautiful women; a peerless warrior. Yes, I wanted to be Conan, and I couldn't get enough of those comics. And so a tradition began: I would go to my therapist appointments, and if I had time, I would run to the comic shop, grab a few issues of Conan, and smuggle them into the house.

* * *

I started summer school, and found that it was a bit more laid back, and therefore I could be more relaxed as well. There was an older teacher who absolutely had to come speak to the student next to you while sticking his butt right in your face. I called it the "prune moon." The name stuck, and I started a rapport with another kid in the class, Chuck Richards. Chuck had an oddball sense of humor much like mine, and was a prankster. We hit it off pretty quickly.

Chuck was a good-looking guy, and he struck up easy conversations with the girls in the class. I felt more at ease, and the two of us became a team when it came to chatting up the females. We even managed to get one of the girls to hang out with us at a local park. We ended up playing "spin the bottle," and we all finished the game in various stages of undress, but that was as far as it went.

The summer flew by. Chuck and I hung out together more often. He taught me to fly fish. We fashioned slings and from the backyard of his house we would fire rocks over his back wall, across the street and onto the roofs of other houses. Chuck and I seemed to feed off of each other.

While Dad wrote non-stop at this time, the consistency of my return letters to him had slowly ebbed. He asked me to write often, but I got more and more caught up in the life that was evolving in California, and I began to distance myself from the life I had led before. And in distancing that life I was distancing Dad.

* * *

Summer school ended, and before long it was time for my next year of junior high—ninth grade! Chuck went to another school, but we had forged a tight friendship and would continue causing trouble for some time.

Something important to mention here—as I'm sure pretty much everyone reading this knows (although this was all new information to me), junior high school normally consists of seventh and eighth grades, and high school is grades nine through 12. Well for several years, El Rancho Junior High taught grades seven, eight and nine... but that was coming to an end. We were to be the final ninth grade class!

This was exciting for a number of reasons, the foremost being that the following year, when we went to Villa Park High School, it would be the first year they would have ninth graders, but we'd be in 10th grade and so we wouldn't be the lowest *schmoes* on the totem pole!

The future was looking pretty bright!

Dad's letters, in the meantime, took a slightly different tone. He was still warm overall, but he warned me not to become a "robot."

There was still a small part of me that wondered: was I being brainwashed by "the system?" Was I doing exactly what the government wanted me, and everyone else to do? I felt pretty normal, and that felt great, but was "normal" just "compliant"? I didn't know, but I knew that although I missed my Dad and loved him, my quality of life with Renee and Shawn was better than it had been with Dad.

The clothes, the school scene, the fun I was having… this was what life was really all about, right?

* * *

At school I wondered what else I could do to ascend to a higher place in the junior high-erarchy... then it struck me: sports! I tried out for soccer, and completely sucked at it. Track and field? Nope. Then I decided to try wrestling.

The tryouts I walked in on had a loud-mouthed kid who had obviously been wrestling for a while. He decided I would be an easy target to make fun of, so he made a few remarks about how I would need to get used to being on my back. We started practice, and after a bit of awkward grappling with one of the kids, I looked over and noticed Loudmouth was being pinned. Seizing the opportunity, I walked over and said something along the lines of, "who's on his back now?"

This enraged Loudmouth, and he challenged me to wrestle. I thought to myself: what would Conan do? He wouldn't take any crap from some snot-nosed pup!

So I assumed a stance that was more akin to the fighting stances my dad used in martial arts, and the rest of the kids looked at me like I was nuts. I had never grappled before in my life. Loudmouth closed the distance, drew me close, twisted and threw me flat onto my back.

Just as the first word of smack talk exited his mouth, I sprang back up and went at him. He threw me again. I got up again. And got thrown. This was repeated at least five times before the coach decided he'd seen enough. I had gotten worked over pretty good, but I never showed a sign of quitting. Loudmouth was exhausted, and the smack talk had ceased.

I knew my attempt at wrestling was another bust, but despite being tossed around like a sack of potatoes, I could tell that I had gained a modicum of respect from many of the other wrestlers. I didn't have to wait long to get the news:

I had made the team.

Renee and Shawn agreed to let me stay late on weekdays for practice. The workouts were hell, especially for the first few weeks, but between the new clothes and my antics in drama class and my endeavors in wrestling, I could tell that people were starting to view me differently.

It was around that time that I really started to come out of my shell.

* * *

October came and I learned that we would be moving. Not far, from Anaheim to Orange County. Renee and Shawn told me I could continue going to the same school, which made me happy. And Allison was in Orange anyway, so I could keep seeing her (and I could keep smuggling my Conan comics). And, although the new place would have a backyard, it wouldn't be nearly as big! No more three-hour weeding sessions!! I figured Roy would be ecstatic.

But I could tell his relationship with Renee and Shawn had deteriorated. I hoped that he would stay. He was a good role model, a good big brother. At times I wondered how different my life would have been growing up with a real big brother. Was there one out there somewhere? A whole family, maybe? At that point I figured I would never know.

CHAPTER SEVEN:
SHENANIGANS

We moved, and there was a ton of work to do, getting the house in order, unpacking, etc. After the first few weeks, Roy had reached his limit. He said that he wasn't getting time to do his schoolwork, and rather than let his grades slip, he was going to leave. And soon, he made good on his word.

He told me he would visit when he could, which made me feel better. Still, that positive influence was gone.

Not long after Roy's departure, Renee and Shawn got a new foster kid, an eight-year-old girl named Melissa. It was clear from the start that Melissa would get most of Renee and Shawn's attention. That was fine with me. I was more than happy to hang out with Chuck and some of the other neighborhood kids.

Which brings us back to the mischief. Some of the things I did during this period of my life were funny, and I still laugh when I look back on them, but most of what I did was harmful and stupid. I've often said that if "modern day me" met "back then me" I'd kick my own ass for being an idiot.

On weekday evenings I would join the neighborhood kids in adventures through the drainage tunnels that ran underneath the nearby railroad tracks. We'd hide out in the concrete bunker (catch basin? I don't know what those things are called, exactly) where water drains off of the street. Sometimes we threw rocks at cars as they drove by.

Meanwhile, the wrestling team started having matches. If there was more than one kid in a single weight class, those kids would have to wrestle to see who would compete. There was one other kid in my weight class, and we squared off. I took him down and kept him down with a "head and arm," and earned the spot to compete.

My first wrestling meet was a "buy"—meaning there was no one from the opposing team in my weight class. I was wrestling somewhere in the 80 to 90 pound range. Yes, I was still rail thin.

* * *

Christmas drew near. The frequency of Dad's letters had actually increased. His latest told me that he was now officially an "attorney of records." He said that he was bringing litigation against California and "the entire system." He also said that he was arranging for us to meet for Christmas. I wrote back, saying that would be awesome.

I got another letter from Dad a week later, still anxiously awaiting a letter from me, saying that he would physically fight to see us reunited.

Just before Christmas, another letter. He still hadn't received my response to the first. This time he told me to run away again, to a monastery. Saying, "We must both fight and battle, Yakimoki, for our freedom."

My social worker, Joyce, told me that Dad was trying to arrange a visit. I would need to meet with Dad's attorney first. They wanted to know if this was okay with me. I said sure, but I was honestly a little nervous about the whole thing. My old life was becoming a speck in my rear-view mirror, and I realized, with a bit of shame, that I wanted it that way. Why would I run away to a monastery? I felt like Dad must not understand what I was going through, that I really didn't need even more upheaval in my world... and I had no idea how to say these things to him. The last thing I wanted to do was crush his spirit.

Christmas was almost on top of us, and I still had anxiety about the meeting with Dad's attorney... then I found out that it was postponed until after Christmas break. As terrible as it sounds, I was relieved.

I found out years later, going through juvenile records, that the visitation didn't happen for a few reasons: key people going on vacation, wires getting crossed in communication, and my foster parents' desire for the timing not to interfere with my first "real Christmas."

The Real Christmas came, and I was overjoyed. I received a ton of presents, including a Garfield telephone! My own telephone! A telephone is a big deal (or at least it was back then) for any teenager. But for me, it was beyond my wildest imaginings. It was like some kind of dream—the best Christmas yet.

Melissa received a crapload of presents, including a Teddy Ruxpin. Teddy wasn't still the rage at that time that he had been before, but he remained pretty popular. He had audiocassettes you'd stick into his back. His eyes would move around and his mouth would open and close, and he was just about the creepiest thing I'd ever seen. He reminded me of the animatronic characters at Chuck E Cheese. Sometimes he would come on for no reason at all, just activate and start talking and singing. I was convinced he was possessed.

A few days after Christmas I got another letter from Dad. At this point he'd received mine. He said again that we'd be together soon, and that "The Crusades and Armageddon, inevitably are in progress."

I decided that I'd write back soon, but not tell him how awesome my Christmas was.

* * *

In the meantime, Chuck and I hung out more and more.

On Friday and Saturday nights, Chuck would come over, we'd walk a couple blocks to the corner store, buy a six-pack of Jolt Cola ("all the sugar, and twice the caffeine!") and stay up late watching *Star Trek* reruns.

We started acting out our own movie/TV parodies, recording them on audiotapes. As the year 1987 rolled around, I was having the time of my life.

* * *

Joyce was still working on arranging the meeting with my Dad's attorney. They scheduled it for late January. I had no idea what to expect. Would I be whisked away yet again? Did Dad arrange to have me taken to some monastery? Or transferred back to Arizona? I

69

was tired of having everything turned upside-down. I wanted to stay put.

I asked if Allison, my therapist, would go with me. She agreed.

At school, I grappled for the chance to compete and won again! But when we went to the meet, I was told that as usual there was no one on the opposing team in my weight class. BUT... the coach made a deal to have me do an exhibition match, with a kid who was in the next highest weight class. At least I wouldn't have gotten all dressed up in my singlet for nothin'!

The kid was much taller than me, but slightly skinnier, which is saying something 'cause I was thin as a reed. Still, his height was intimidating, and he looked at me like I'd be a pushover.

When the whistle blew, I shot in on him and executed a double-leg takedown. He spent the rest of the match on his back. I didn't get the pin, but I won the exhibition on points nonetheless, and got my hand raised.

More important, I won some more respect from the rest of the team.

* * *

The day of the meeting came. My attorney, my therapist, and I met Dad's attorney. He told me that Dad was doing okay, and he wanted to know if I was receiving Dad's letters. I told him I was. He wanted to know if I was doing okay. I told him I was.

And that was pretty much it. No relocating. No major upset. And for the time being, no visit with Dad.

When we left the meeting, it felt like an enormous weight had been lifted. My life at home, at school, my friendships... were not in immediate danger.

It was time to relax. And to cut loose.

* * *

Chuck and I started loitering at the Orange Mall. We bought "cap traps," basically a gag gizmo that would fire off a cap when pressure was released from it. We put these under the receivers of the public telephones so when people lifted the receiver it would go off with a bang and scare the crap out of them. We sat nearby and giggled our asses off.

Our favorite prank though was to steal condoms, then take one and stuff it with toilet paper... there was a male mannequin at the entrance to JC Penney. While Chuck stood in front of me, I'd stick the base of the condom in the mannequin's fly and zip up so it would stay. When we stepped away it looked the guy was standing there with his johnson hanging out.

Some nights I would sneak out of the house and meet Chuck, and we'd go around the neighborhood. We started with TP-ing and quickly moved on from there. Some of the pranks were of a nature that we wouldn't even see the payoff for, but the *thought* of the result was more than enough. There was a median that ran down the middle of the main street outside my development. Located on that median was a manhole for drain or sewer access. We removed the manhole cover, camouflaged the hole with bushes, and made a shallow, circular hole in the dirt that we placed the manhole cover in. We thought it was the funniest thing in the world, imagining the city worker coming out to inspect it, lifting the cover and finding no hole there!

Another popular late-night gag was to take some of the centerfolds from Shawn's *Hustler* collection, walk around until we found vans with the rears facing out (so when the target walked out in the morning they wouldn't see the rear of the vehicle) and tape the centerfold to the spare tire. We laughed like hyenas just thinking about those vans driving around the next day with some naked gal spread-eagled on the back.

We made it out to Disneyland a few times. There was a tram back then that ran high over the park and through the Matterhorn Mountain where there was an animatronic Yeti. We would each buy a bag of Jelly Bellys and pelt people walking around in the park below with the beans.

* * *

In the early part of the year there were a couple more additions to the Coolidge household: Shawn's niece Lucy, who I think was in her late teens/early twenties, and Renee's daughter from another marriage, Liz, who was 16. Liz was pretty, and someone I had a crush on for her entire stay. Lucy and Liz treated me well when they were around, but most of the time they were off having adventures of their own.

* * *

Wrestling meets continued. I won some, I lost some. But the team did well enough to earn a spot in the City Tournament... and I would have a chance to wrestle there.

Dad kept writing letters, sometimes on a jail laundry slip, saying that we were foreigners in this country; that he was working on having me transferred to Arizona.

I asked my social worker and foster parents about the possibilities of such things, and they let me know that Dad was not in a position to make things like that happen, which was a relief. I still felt that nagging fear every once in a while that the life I was building could be ripped out from under me at any instant.

* * *

To say that I was a crappy older brother to Melissa during this time would be an understatement. It didn't help that Renee and Shawn focused most of their attention on her, but I certainly made no effort to be a positive influence in her life, and she and I did not get along.

So of course, I messed with her as much as I could.

One time Chuck and I drew a top-down diagram of Melissa's room, with a figure in the wall behind her headboard. We took the drawing to Melissa and told her that when the house was being built, a construction worker died and his body was still trapped in the wall. Much crying ensued.

One weekend day, Renee, Shawn, and Melissa were gone while Chuck and I stayed at the house watching TV. There was a giant (almost life-sized) crayon drawing that Melissa did, a basic depiction of her in a dress. Renee and Shawn displayed it proudly in the dining room, and when Chuck and I went to get a snack, Chuck thought it would be funny to poke a hole in the crotch of the drawing.

I thought it was funny too, but I knew there'd be hell to pay. I thought: *we have to make it look like an accident...* so I tore the paper. I tore it way too much, nearly ripping the entire thing in half. Melissa was going to be devastated. It was her favorite drawing. I'd be grounded for a week at least.

Then I remembered that the roll of paper Melissa used was still in the house. I found it, along with her crayons. We took the drawing down, put it next to a sheet of paper from the roll, and I went to work. I knew that Renee and Shawn were on their way home soon, and I had to be quick.

I'm a pretty good artist, but one thing I'm really good at is reproducing art. I created an exact replica of Melissa's drawing... except for the hair. I couldn't find the right color crayon in Melissa's bin. I picked the closest color there was and literally as Renee and Shawn pulled into the driveway I finished the hair, we taped the picture to the wall and threw the old one in the trash.

Renee, Shawn, and Melissa all came in. Melissa went about playing while Chuck and I tried to act inconspicuous, all the while terrified that someone was going to notice.

Shawn walked into the dining room, passed the drawing... and stopped. My heart stopped along with him. He stood there for a second, then shook his head as if to say "nah" and continued walking.

No one ever knew the difference.

* * *

Meanwhile, the day of the City Tournament arrived. I'd never been so nervous in my life. I was set to wrestle the top guy in our weight class.

The time came, the ref blew the whistle, and it was on! We grappled, and I ended the first period ahead on points, which meant I got to start the second period in the offensive position (the other wrestler on his hands and knees with me at his back and to the side, trying to control him, get him on his back, and pin him). I couldn't believe it… the best wrestler in the weight class, and I was ahead on points. The whistle blew, we fought for position, and he reversed me. I ended up losing my lead, and he won the match. I came in fifth overall.

In some ways, of course, I was extremely disappointed. But, I was also very proud of scoring those early points. The other guy was only human after all, despite the fact that I had psyched myself into nearly losing the match before it even started. The experience taught me that my own mind could be my worst enemy.

Soon after, another school year ended. I couldn't believe I would finally be attending High School next. I ended up with two *A*s, two *B*s, two *C*s and one *D*. Not bad for someone who went to public school for the first time in eighth grade.

* * *

Over the summer Liz and Lucy continued with their social lives, and Chuck and I kept messing around—this time with a Ouija board. For those who've never used one, a Ouija board is a board with all the letters of the alphabet on it, as well as numbers 0–9, the words "yes" and "no" and "goodbye." It comes with an oracle, a plastic triangle on short legs with a viewing hole in the apex. The board is described as a way to "explore the supernatural." You sit down with one or more friends, place your fingers lightly on the oracle, or planchette, and ask questions. The oracle moves, and you can see the answers to your questions through the viewhole.

Back then I wasn't really sure what I believed in just yet, and I was very, very curious. Well, Chuck and I started using the Ouija, and more often than not, we got it to move and succeeded in getting our questions answered. I was pretty impressed by the results. There were times, however, when we couldn't get the oracle to move, or it would just stop moving for seemingly no reason. We'd get frustrated and try different techniques to "reestablish contact," including reading passages from the Bible, which worked most of the time.

We decided to try out other techniques as well. I had read about a method where you put paper over the board, and replace the oracle with a triangular piece of cardboard with two legs glued to the base and a pencil stuck through the apex. The idea is that you get the spirit to write something on the paper.

We tried and tried, and couldn't get the planchette to budge. We read Bible passages, and then moved on to insults and provocation, and the oracle finally started to move. We watched wide-eyed as a single word was spelled out in cursive on the paper:

BEWARE.

I thought Chuck was screwing with me, but there was one hitch: the word was written oriented to me, upside-down to Chuck. It seemed highly unlikely that Chuck could perfectly spell out a word upside down by pushing around a piece of cardboard.

We kept messing with the board, but we never tried the pencil and paper again.

On a different night, Chuck and I were hanging out with another friend. We'd been fooling around with the Ouija board, then decided to try something different. There was a thing back then called "Leon Neon"—plastic glow-in-the-dark tubes that could connect end-to-end. We made a big loop, squeezed three of us into the bathroom, which had a wall-sized mirror over the sinks, and shut off the lights. We made the shape of a ghost with the Leon Neon... Chuck was the left hand, and he was near the wall by the door. Our buddy had formed the head, and I was the right hand. As we were making the ghost dance in the mirror, I felt something close tightly around my right ankle. It held firm for a split second, then let go. I looked in the mirror, where I could see that both the left hand and the head were still moving, so if Chuck or my other friend had snuck down to grab my ankle, either of them would have needed to hand off their "ghost body part" to the other. Certainly possible. But what really made me think was this: the hand had shot out from my right side.

To my right was a *solid wall*.

I had started out not knowing what to believe in, but I ended up with a much more defined attitude toward ghosts, spirits and other things beyond our understanding. I believed very much in energy; positive and negative. These concepts would form the foundation of what I would believe in years to come.

* * *

Toward the end of the summer, my status as an illegal alien came up once again. If I expected to start working when I turned 16, I would need a Social Security Number, and in order to get that, since I didn't have a birth certificate, I would have to establish citizenship. My social worker Joyce wasn't sure exactly how this would work—there was no precedent for my situation that anyone knew of. They couldn't verify me as a citizen, but they couldn't verify any other country of residence either. Joyce said she would start looking into it and get back to me.

* * *

September came… and it was time for high school at last!

Tenth grade at Villa Park High. I was beyond excited.

And my classes included Driver Safety!! Was it really even possible, would I actually drive a vehicle in the near future? Insane!

Most of the class from El Rancho didn't end up going to Villa Park. When the family moved, we had moved into another school district. I finished the year at El Rancho, but I wouldn't know most of the other tenth graders in this new district.

Still, I didn't feel the same trepidation on the first day of high school that I did in junior high. Wrestling and drama had been rites of passage. I didn't feel like the weirdo outsider anymore.

I felt like I belonged there.

Before long I started hanging out with a girl who

I shared some classes with, who also happened to live just a few blocks from me. Her name was Samantha, and though I liked her as more than just a friend, she made it clear to me that our relationship was to be strictly of the non-sexual variety (at this point, sex with an actual female was just some highly desirable, yet seemingly unattainable goal. It was a pipe dream, pun fully intended). Despite this, we hung out quite often. I spent hours in her bedroom, mostly listening to music and talking. Samantha introduced me to Guns N' Roses, Black Sabbath, Motley Crüe... and soon some of her friends became my friends. They were the "hessians," considered by most of the faculty and a fair amount of the students to be the rebels. They all hung out together at lunch, in their jeans and jean jackets with back patches, sneaking smokes.

I got along well with them. They didn't judge me or look down on me. And despite the fact that I didn't smoke, and I was just becoming familiar with the music they all listened to, they made me feel welcome.

Chuck and I hung out less and less.

Wrestling season came around again, but I passed, for a number of reasons. I wanted to focus on other things... drama class, art, hanging out with my new friends, hanging out with Samantha. But there was one other thing I had set really set my sights on:

Getting a job.

My social worker Joyce told me that she was still working on the whole Social Security Number issue but it would take time. There was another worker who was handling my "change of undocumented alien status" but I didn't want to wait. I wanted to start making money.

There was one kid from junior high who ended up in Villa Park with me, a redheaded kid named Tom Schultz. I hatched a plan: I would use Tom's Social Security Number. I guess you could call it identity theft, but is it really theft if the other person agrees to let you use his identity? I'm no lawyer, but however you cut it, I'm relatively sure it was illegal.

I did it anyway.

Come November, there was a job opening at the Orange Mall, at a tiny little place called Hot Dogs and More. The "more" was nothing to get excited about, but hey, it was a job. Somehow I sold the whole idea to Renee and Shawn. I applied, but the manager wanted to see a birth certificate.

I borrowed Tom's, and they went for it.

That night, I was actually working! My first real job!! Of course, there were some problems.

Mainly, my nametag read "Tom." Many times I would be busy cleaning a counter or switching out wieners or whatever, and the other guy I worked with would be saying "Tom!" "Tom!" "Hey, Tom!!!" I was oblivious.

And there were times when Samantha or some of the other kids would drop by, and they would call me Micky. When the other worker asked why, I told him it was just a nickname. Somehow I don't think he bought it.

As the end of the year rolled around, I would receive paychecks; Tom would cash them and give me the money (I'm pretty sure I gave him a cut, for using his name and all). Things were going okay except for one major issue: money kept coming up missing from my register. Not much, a little bit here and there. The other guy I worked with had access to my register, but he had been working there for a while, and his register was never short. I thought maybe I was just screwing up, miscounting the money customers were giving me. I decided to pay more attention. I had just gotten the job; I didn't want to lose it!

* * *

Dad and I were still corresponding. He was frustrated that legal recourse had not resulted in his freedom. He said the lawyers could not "understand the intrinsic energy of our Ki and Ch'i." He wanted me to memorize the Constitution, saying that our rights were being violated. He called the system Anti-Christs and the Sick Satans of Doom.

I had spent long enough among "normal people" that I knew Dad was unusual, to say the least. But was he crazy? He said when we lived together that throughout his life people had called him crazy. These were things I hadn't thought about in quite a while... I had gotten to the point where I tried to think of my old life as little as possible, but one place where I still couldn't escape it, was in therapy. So I decided to take Dad's letter to Allison. I wanted her to read his words.

She said that based on her assessment from the language in the letter, Dad sounded exactly like a paranoid schizophrenic, and she explained to me what that meant. I had to admit, it did seem like her description fit Dad's behavior pretty well.

Dad had always told me that God spoke to him. Was he just hearing voices in his head that he ascribed to the Lord?

81

The situation seemed hopeless: Either Dad was right about the things he said, and I was falling into the system's trap, or he was crazy, and would continue to act crazy unless he got help (and Dad would never in a million years take anything a doctor prescribed for him).

There was something else that disturbed me: if Dad was crazy, did that mean I had the potential to be crazy as well?

Allison said that schizophrenia was hereditary, and in most cases it would start to manifest in the early teenage years. She said she was relatively sure that if I was schizophrenic, I would have shown signs by then.

Still, I wondered: would I someday start hearing voices?

* * *

As the year 1988 jumped off, things at work weren't going so well. My register kept coming up short, by larger amounts. At this point I knew it had to be the other guy I was working with, though, of course, he denied it. It happened a few more times, and I was let go.

Regardless, the bug had been planted: I really enjoyed working and making money, and I pushed harder for getting my Social Security Number.

CHAPTER EIGHT:
NATURALIZATION

In Drama Class I went full-bore and got a lead role in the play *Barefoot in the Park*! I played the part of Victor Velasco, quite the ladies' man, which everyone thought was actually very funny. For me it was bittersweet. I got a lead role in a school play, but I got it because I was physically and romantically almost the opposite of what the role signified (even though I spent time with Samantha, I certainly wasn't seen as someone who had "a way with the ladies").

What the hell, I thought, and embraced it. The play got quite a reception, and I loved every minute of it (well, almost... I hated the butterflies in my stomach just before the curtain went up. I got nervous before my wrestling matches too. And when I get nervous, I get gassy. Enough to clear out the bleachers).

* * *

As the year progressed, both my social worker and I were getting frustrated with the "legal status" situation.

The biggest problem was they didn't have any

documentation to get the wheels turning at Immigration and Naturalization Services. Nobody could provide any paperwork to show where I was born. Dad had told me I was born in Mexico.

They tried several different routes until one day my social worker sat down and told me this, off the record:

They would use documentation for an unnamed baby that had been brought across the border in 1972. There was paperwork attached to this incident, and they would use that paperwork as a starting point, claiming that I was that baby.

That's right: Yakimoki Neilson. Born in Zacatecas, Mexico.

If they didn't do it this way, there would be no Social Security Number in my near future.

I told them to do whatever they had to do to enable me to work legally. And so, they got the ball rolling, but the "naturalization" process would take time.

My whole life during this period was one giant naturalization process: introducing a foreign element (me) into a setting and hoping like hell it could flourish as if native. Everything I did (even—or maybe especially—the stupid stunts I pulled) was an effort to adapt. But my past just wouldn't go away. No matter how much I tried to outrun it, that speck in my rearview mirror refused to disappear.

I found myself thinking once again about what really happened to Mom. Assassination by the government just didn't ring true. But why would Dad lie about that? Unless he really was crazy, and maybe he actually believed it, even if it didn't happen. But… there was another possibility as well.

It had been suggested a few times that maybe Dad took me from my mom. I didn't want to accept that, because I loved Dad and I didn't want to think of him as someone who would do such a thing, but the more I considered it, the more real that notion became in my mind.

This line of thinking brought me back to the idea that Neilson wasn't my real last name, which in turn led to the question: what if the birthday I was celebrating wasn't even my real birthday?

I determined that dwelling on such things would do nothing but depress me or drive me nuts (which, given my genes, might not be such a long drive).

And so I pressed on.

Things were going well at school, although my teeth were a mess. I had an impacted tooth that was stuck up in the roof of my mouth, leaving a gap in my teeth on the left side, which made me highly self-conscious when I smiled. Beyond that my teeth were kind of all over the place, some of them pushing against each other. I dreaded the thought of needing braces. After a few orthodontist appointments though, the diagnosis was much worse: they wanted me to wear headgear!

For any kid that's like a death sentence, much less a kid in my situation. This came along at a time in my life where I was finally starting to feel accepted. No way was I going to walk around school with a satellite array on my head. I would never get laid, for God's sake! (Not that women were lining up, but still…)

The plan was to wear braces, and have a wire attached to the impacted tooth. Tension would pull or guide the tooth into the open space over time.

I agreed to wear the headgear at night.

* * *

One weekend a few months into the year, two Mormon missionaries came to the door. We started talking, and I told them that Dad and I had attended the Mormon Church. They asked if I planned on going back, and I told them that I hadn't really thought about it, but they could check back with me if they wanted.

Like I said before, this was a time in my life when I was trying to figure out what I believed in. Dad had his own ideas on religion, but it was basically a spin on traditional Christianity. I always wondered why he went to the Mormon Church, when it seemed so different from his own faith.

I decided that learning more wouldn't be such a bad thing.

The missionaries returned a few weeks later and I agreed to do bible studies with them once a week. I enjoyed the time discussing their religion. More weeks passed and bible study led to me attending church.

I didn't understand why I was responding to Mormonism the way I was.

Asking myself the questions I had about my mom and my past, questions that I hadn't asked in so long, bringing my old life back to the surface... I think maybe it brought other things with it as well.

Mormonism was familiar. In a way it was like reconnecting with Dad and an aspect of my life with him that didn't feel negative, or smothered in doubt and deception. I had some great times when Dad and I stayed with the Mormon family while I was in Boy Scouts.

I wanted to believe in Mormonism, I wanted to

give it a chance. I studied and I prayed and at a time in my life when so many things were uncertain and I felt as if I had little to no control, this was something I had complete control over. I could believe whatever I wanted to believe. It was entirely up to me, and that felt good.

I wrote a letter to Dad, telling him that I was attending the Mormon Church, certain that this would make him proud.

Meanwhile, Lucy left, and Liz followed soon after. Melissa and I continued either not getting along or ignoring each other as much as possible. My birthday once again drew near.

The braces were an interesting thing to adjust to. I had small rubber bands inside my mouth, and sometimes when I would yawn one of them would snap and fly across the room. And of course there was the constant fear that I had a chunk of food stuck in my braces when I smiled. Again, self-conscious. I wore the headgear at night… most of the time.

At school I was doing well, especially in art. We made our own T-shirts for one particular project. My shirt had Freddy Krueger on the front and a quote from Edgar Allen Poe (which was also shown before *Nightmare on Elm Street 3, Dream Warriors,* which I managed to see and thought was the coolest thing ever): "Sleep, those little slices of death, how I loathe them."

I actually wore the shirt around school and didn't get beat up.

* * *

My birthday came. More Garfield! More clothes! More toys! I got my first cassette tape, "Dead Man's Party" by Oingo Boingo. It had the song "Weird Science" from the movie of the same name, which I had watched a hundred times. I could quote the bar scene word-for-word.

I was 16 years old and I'd be able to drive soon. Of course, I didn't have a car, but just the idea of driving was amazing to me. It was a time of wide-eyed optimism.

Not long after my birthday, I got a reply from Dad. It wasn't what I was expecting. He wasn't at all excited about my association with the Mormons. In fact, he called them communists!

I was utterly confused. Hadn't we attended the Mormon Church together years ago? One thing from my past that felt solid and real and now Dad was ranting about it.

I thought once again of my therapist's assessment of Dad—paranoid schizophrenia. Well this was it; this was pretty clear evidence in my mind.

Dad really was crazy.

I wrote a curt letter, assuring Dad that I wouldn't let the Mormons convince me to do anything I didn't want to do, but that it was my decision to assess whether Mormonism was right for me.

I had defied Dad's wishes subtly in the past, by not running away when he told me to, for instance… but this was different. This defiance held conviction behind it. I was making a stand. A line had been crossed, another thread that connected Dad and I had been cut.

I was becoming my own man.

* * *

Over the summer, I kept hanging out with Samantha and some of her friends. I started growing my hair out. I was in summer school again, taking drivers' ed. My social worker Joyce told me that they were getting closer to getting me an alien ID card, but it didn't look like it was going to happen for summer, which was extremely frustrating.

I continued doing bible studies and going to church. The missionaries were adamant about the fact that I needed to be baptized. They told me wonderful stories of how they connected to the spirit of Christ once they accepted him into their hearts, about how they could feel his divine essence flowing through them.

As the summer wore on, I didn't receive a reply letter from Dad. I talked to Samantha about my considering being baptized, and she encouraged me to do what I felt was right. After thinking about it for quite a while, I decided to take the literal plunge.

Once I had made my decision, the missionaries moved quickly to make it happen. I asked one of them to do the actual baptism, and I invited Samantha and another friend.

There was a brief ceremony. I was dressed in white, as was the missionary doing the baptism. We stood in a pool of water, and when the time came, the missionary dipped me like we were doing a tango. Into the water I went…

With a completely open mind, and an open heart, excited to feel the divine essence that the missionaries had described.

I hate having my head submerged in water. The only other time my head had gone under water was the time I almost drowned in Boy Scouts. But this was different. Instead of tiptoeing to the brink of death I was opening my soul to rebirth. And when I emerged from the water...

I didn't feel any different.

It was declared that my covenant with God was complete. I was officially a member of the Mormon Church. There was much excitement in the room. But there was disappointment in me.

I literally felt zero difference from when I went under the water, except that I was wet, and I don't like being wet.

Did I do something wrong? Did I somehow trick myself into thinking I had opened my heart fully when I hadn't? These were the questions that plagued me in the days following the baptism. My friends asked me if I felt any different, and I told them the truth: no, I didn't.

As the summer wound down, I found myself being less convinced that I had done the right thing. It was a decision made in haste, and one I had begun to immediately regret.

There was still no letter from Dad.

Had part of my decision to get the baptism been made just to spite Dad? If I had determined to no longer believe what Dad said, to no longer just accept his word as the truth, then why should I just blindly follow some religion? I began attending church less and less.

By this time I had built up quite a collection of Conan comics. The god of Conan's barbarian race is

Crom, and if you pray to Crom, you might as well be praying to a loaf of bread because Crom just sits on his mountain and laughs at you. That made the barbarians self-reliant; hard; tough as nails.

I didn't think Crom was laughing at me, but I did think of something Dad had always said: "God helps those who help themselves."

CHAPTER NINE:
BROTHERHOOD

I finished driver's training and it would soon be time to start 11th grade... and that's when I got the good news: my paperwork at Immigration had gone through! I would be getting a Temporary Resident card. Social Services was working on getting me a Social Security Number still, but my "alien ID number" would allow me to get a job. I was overjoyed!

With renewed determination I filled out job applications at different places, including a little six-screen movie theater at the Orange Mall called the AMC Six Theaters.

Not long after, I got a call back and went in for an interview. They were willing to work around my school schedule, giving me a few nights a week and weekends.

Before I knew it I had gotten the job! I couldn't believe it! I would actually get to watch movies for free on my breaks! I could get discounts to see movies at other theaters! Free popcorn and soda! It was better than Christmas!!

I would be starting off where all new hires

started: the concession stand. A supervisor showed me when and how to dump the popcorn out of the popper, how to operate the registers, etc.

Pretty soon I was off and running. Oh, and I got "the outfit"—white button-up shirt, black polyester pants with a silk stripe up the side, black vest, and a black bowtie. Pure swank, baby. I also had to wear black socks, which I was responsible for.

AMC had six theater houses in that location, all small. Three on either side of the one large concession stand. The theater had been considered large at one time and would show all the latest blockbusters. By the time I was hired, however, the 20-theater mega-plexes had really just started to draw in the crowds and the little AMC theater had been relegated to showing movies that had transitioned out of the big theaters and would soon be on their way to video or HBO.

One thing AMC had that the big mega-plexes didn't was cupholders that could accommodate large-sized cups!

Working the concession stand was fun at first, and the time went by quick especially when we had rushes, which we did whenever Disney movies were starting… mobs of kids who would sweep through like a tornado.

But I knew early on that what I really wanted was to be an usher. Those guys walked around like they owned the place. They weren't stuck behind the stand slingin' popcorn. No sir, they could sit in on movies, just before the end so they could open doors and tell people to "exit to your left, please." Then they got to clean the theater, douse the house lights, and set off to the next one. And, of course, they made more money.

Yep, that was what where I wanted to be, but it would take a while. For the time being, I was stuck behind the stand. So I decided to make the most of it. I did things to amuse myself, like making a sign for one of the soda pumps that said "Kern's Kiwi Nectar." Whenever someone would ask for it I'd tell them it was all out. I'd yell out that I could "help the next homo sapiens in line." I would also take crushed ice and throw it onto the ceiling over someone else's station so the water would drip on them when they stood at the register. I was having fun, but I was missing a partner in crime.

One night before closing I looked in the schedule book, flipped the page, and couldn't believe what I saw: there he was, standing proudly, broadsword held ready, a generously endowed female clinging to his tree-trunk leg. It was Conan! Someone had drawn Conan in the schedule book. And it was good. Damn good. The drawing was signed "Samwise."

Samwise was a character from Lord of the Rings. Who was this guy? I would have to find out.

I turned the page and drew a Conan of my own, in a different pose. I looked at the drawing done by Samwise, and was struck by how much better his drawing was. Jerk! I signed mine anyway.

* * *

The next time I worked, I saw that one of the ushers had a nametag that said "Sam." He was a husky fellow, with dark brown hair that was long in the back and short in the front—not quite a mullet, but close. He had a baby face and an easy way about him. His name was Sam

Didier, and yes he used the name Samwise on his art because he was a big Lord of the Rings fan. I introduced myself, and told him that he was a killer artist. I told him I drew the other Conan, and he was kind enough to say that mine was good too. We talked about Conan and art for a while until it was time for him to clean a theater. While he was gone I sketched a new Conan in the schedule book. Later that night, after Sam had gone home and I returned from a break, I found another Conan, signed "Samwise."

His was still better.

That night I also took a look at the titles of the movies we would be getting soon. One of them was called *Predator*. I hadn't seen any of the previews for the film, but the name sounded interesting, and I saw that it would star Arnold Schwarzenegger, so I definitely wanted to check it out.

The next time I worked, I snuck into *Predator* on my break. I was hooked immediately—enthralled with this group of elite soldiers being hunted by some invisible enemy. I stayed late that night and watched the whole thing, and similar to *Terminator*, it impressed me as a film that showed just how good movies could be.

* * *

I hadn't been working at the theater for very long before a new school year began—11th grade was upon me! I saw a couple kids at school who worked at the theater, Matt and Rich Miller—two blond-haired surfers, twin brothers. They were definitely part of the "cool crowd," so I kept to myself at first.

All in all, I wondered what the new school year would hold for me... and then, another pleasant surprise: I got my Social Security Number and card. I've discovered since then just how important that Social Security Number is—one more thing that makes you a slave to the system, I'm sure Dad would have said, but let me tell you: I was happy to have one!

I got to know the Miller Twins. They were goofy and hyperkinetic and loved to party. The more I got to know them, the more I liked them. I made other friends there as well, and there were even some good-looking girls at the theater with whom I was striking a rapport. But my closest friend at the theater was quickly becoming Sammy.

We swapped more drawings and tales of high adventure. We also shared a quirky sense of humor that embraced the random and the nonsensical. After a fairly short amount of time, the movie theater had become my favorite place to be.

There was one other place that I discovered however, right across the street—a Brunswick Bowling Alley with a little room that had a few pool tables. Sometimes I would go from work and shoot pool.

Whenever I left the house to walk the several blocks to work, I would just wear my white shirt and black pants and go straight to the theater. Renee and Shawn never stopped by, so at one point I got the genius idea that every once in a while, I could *say* that I was going to work, but actually go to the bowling alley and play pool for six hours. The only problem was they would think something was up if I left the house not wearing my theater uniform as I always did, so there were several nights I ended up at the bowling alley, playing pool in my white shirt and polyester pants.

* * *

At school I had started weightlifting and it was actually producing some results.

I also found that because I knew the Miller Twins, I could hang out with them and their friends and be accepted, or I could hang out with the hessians. So... I did both!

It was an amazing time in my life. Social status is so important in school, and I had come so far: from the weird skinny kid who literally no one wanted to talk to, to a guy who could associate comfortably with two of the biggest cliques in school, as well as the drama crowd. People knew my name and frequently said "hey" to me in passing. People listened when I talked. So many aspects of my life were coalescing...

And the Mormon Church didn't seem to align with where I was, what my priorities were. The bible studies and constant reminders to attend church had become a distraction. I wanted to really start enjoying life. I wanted to be with a girl, maybe try alcohol at some point. I was at a crossroads, and the road I felt drawn to was not the path of Mormonism.

I had a heart-to-heart with the missionaries, basically telling them that I needed time away from the church. They agreed and promised to check in on me every once in a while.

When I wasn't working on weekends, I goofed off with Sammy. Someone else Sammy was good friends with at the theater was a towering, stone-faced teen named Eric. Sammy called him "Ogre." He was a fellow usher, but Sammy knew him from high school. Ogre was part of a circle of friends they referred to simply as "the brothers." They were a tight-knit group, all into the same kinds of things—weapons, Tolkien, D&D, Conan, martial arts, partying (even though I didn't drink and they did)... they even had their own handshake! The more I got to know Ogre, the more I liked him. He was quiet at first, but once you got that guy talking about something that interested him, you couldn't shut him up!

I soon met the next brother, Brian. The rest called him "Rider." He was a mechanic, gruff and surly, cock-sure and downright rude at first. He had the brass to call people "hero" condescendingly. At first I thought I wouldn't get along with him, but Sammy assured me that Rider would grow on me.

The last brother was Tony, an Italian who bore a small resemblance to Al Pacino. Tony was in the Navy and was out on leave. His real name was Cosmo... calling him "Tony" (or Tone Dog) was a privilege reserved for the brothers. He was an infectiously boisterous intellectual with a pragmatic view of the world. He drove a Dodge Daytona that everyone called the "DayTony." Sammy drove an old Mustang with a long-haired skull hanging from the rear-view mirror. Ogre had a POS Opal. Rider had the coolest vehicle of all: a giant yellow Bronco with massive tires and the loudest horn you've ever heard in your life. And he wasn't afraid to use it. Of course all of this just made me want my own car even more.

I got to hang out with all of the brothers, and

before too long I had to admit that Sammy was right. Rider grew on me. He had the quickest wit of anyone I knew other than Sammy himself, and he was just as genuine as the rest of the group. They all shared a deep connection—they felt more like blood brothers than friends.

The five of us then spent one epic weekend in the desert, shooting guns, cracking jokes, videotaping all of the insanity. At night we sat around the fire, they drank, we cracked more jokes and we shared stories. I shared mine.

And by the end of that weekend they had embraced me as one of their own.

I even learned the secret handshake. But—Rider, Ogre, Tone Dog, and Samwise... they all had cool nicknames except for me. It was determined that moving forward I would be known as "Michelob." And so it was written! I didn't have a family of my own, but the four of them vowed to be my brothers. I hadn't chosen to be with Dad, I was born into that situation. Foster parents had chosen me, not the other way around... but this brotherhood, this was a family I chose.

CHAPTER TEN:
USHERS

As 1989 got off and running, things at the theater were going well. There was a blonde girl who worked concession, with puffy cheeks and a pointed nose. I called her the penguin and whenever she came near I laughed like the character of the same name from the old Batman TV show—"wa wa wa waaaa." Despite that, I found her very attractive. I told her on multiple occasions that I wanted to bear her children.

One night after we both got off work, we sat in her car. My hair had gotten pretty long at this point, down to my shoulders, and she started brushing it. Before I knew it, we were kissing. Kissing led to more fooling around. We didn't go all the way, but it was my first real experience that even came close to sex, and I was ecstatic.

I was also unsure how to follow up the next time I saw her. Things at work between us became awkward, and we never hooked up again after that. It was, nonetheless, a window for me into a whole new world.

* * *

Tony had gone back to his duty station in Hawaii at this point, but I still palled around with Sammy and Ogre and Rider. I hung out with Samantha and the Hessians as well, but I spent most of my time with the party crowd that the Miller twins circulated in. Of course, they and everyone else drank... they were always able to get alcohol despite being under age, and I had ample opportunities to partake if I wanted to, but I was having enough fun. I didn't really feel a desire to get drunk, though I was curious as to what the sensation was like.

I had not heard from Dad in several months. I was worried, and asked my social worker Joyce to look into the situation.

At AMC, the theater managers began transitioning me to more and more usher duties. I was out of "the box" for the first time. I was moving up in the world! I got a 25 cent raise and soon I was being scheduled for concession sometimes, but also as an usher.

I loved being an usher. You greeted people at the door, tore their ticket, kept any eye on the schedule in order to "break" movies (which just meant waiting at the back of the theater for the movie to end, then opening the doors and telling people which way to exit), and you cleaned the theaters.

It was an opportunity to shoot the shizzle with Sam more often, and of course it afforded ample opportunities for shenanigans.

At one point Sammy and I were standing at the back of the theater, during a show. The movie was *Beaches*, which was a somber flick, a real tearjerker (we used to hand out tissues when the movie was

101

over). I thought we needed to liven things up a bit. Sam and I had watched *Naked Gun* about a hundred times. In the movie was a guy with a mustache, a newsboy hat and a striped shirt. He did a little dance that we thought was hilarious, so we made up a name for him (he doesn't have a name in the movie): Pierre LeCroix.

Anyway, I thought it would be funny to replicate his dance, down the aisle (like I said, the theaters were small and only had one aisle, in the middle).

So I busted out in a dance, complete with kicks and points and jerky, spasmodic motions. I worked my way halfway down, then danced my way back up, and just like that, "aisle dancing" was born!

Aisle dancing was a big hit. Everyone loved to watch it, and some of the other ushers would do it as well. The challenge was to dance all the way to the screen and then back up.

During one aisle dancing performance, I decided to do a little something extra. Sammy was in the audience, on his break, so I took off my vest, whipped it around above my head, and threw it to him.

When the movie was over, one of the customers was irate. He told the manager that an employee was in the theater "strip-teasing in front of my wife!!" I was across the main floor, standing with another usher named Rick. The customer pointed in our direction and said "it was him!" The customer left; the manager strode over and told Rick "clock out, you're done for the day!" I was tempted not to say anything, but I spoke up and told the manager that I had done it. He looked at me and said: "Oh… all right, well don't do it again."

I got away with all kinds of tomfoolery, including "door posing." There were two theaters close to the concession stand with their doors facing outward, one on each side. Sometimes when there was a huge crowd, we would throw open the double doors, strike a pose, and hold that pose while the doors slowly swung shut. We did everything from "The Sands of Iwo Jima" (posed like the soldiers raising the flag, using a broom as a stand-in), to Chippendales (removing our shirts, leaving on the bow ties, and flexing). Later we would get descriptions from the concession workers of the customers' befuddled looks and hushed exchanges of "did you just see that?"

One of our favorite gags though was called "customer disorientation." Sammy and I practiced until we got the process down to a science: one of us would stand just outside the doors, and as a customer would approach with a newly purchased ticket in hand, if it was me outside, I would tear the ticket, and tell the person that the theater was to their left, and point to their right. Sammy, standing just inside the doors, would then ask to see their ticket, he would verify it, hand it back and tell them the theater was on their right, and point to their left. Then the two of us would hide and snicker as we watched the baffled customer wander back and forth squinting up at the marquee signs.

During my time at the theater I had the opportunity to see a lot of movies... some good, some bad, but either way I couldn't get enough. I loved movies then, and still do now. What an amazing art form: combining visuals and sound to tell a story in a way no other medium except live theater can come close to.

Before long I was trained on how to close the theater. Closing kept me out late, especially on Friday nights, when the theater hosted *Rocky Horror Picture Show* at midnight. Which meant we didn't close until somewhere around 2:00 a.m..

The Rocky Horror crowd was entertainment in itself. If you've never attended an audience-participation movie like *Rocky Horror*, you're missing out on quite the experience: people would dress up as characters from the movie (which included Rocky himself, who wore nothing but a gold Speedo), then sit in the theater and recite a litany of amusing phrases in response to the dialogue. They would get up and dance along with the song and dance numbers from the movie, and at certain times they would throw rice, toast, squirt water pistols—it was a complete madhouse. But of course most of the employees (including myself) got to the point where we could shout the phrases right along with the crowd.

We'd keep one theater open to accommodate *Rocky Horror*, and while that movie was showing whoever was closing concession would go through a precise routine: clean the popper, the nacho cheese dispenser, the hot dog warmer, the soda stations, lock up the displays, and mop. The closing usher would clean the popcorn, toast, rice and various other dregs (yes, that included the occasional condom) that remained after *Rocky Horror* broke.

One night while closing, I had taken the trash to the Dumpster behind the theater and was walking back to the front to be let in. I passed a group of three teens (not, to the *Rocky Horror* crowd's credit, among the regulars), one boy and two girls, sitting against the sidewall. One of the girls said, "hey, nice polyester." I said thanks and the other two started laying into my outfit as well. We exchanged a few more choice words, and I was fuming by the time I got back into the theater. I took a jumbo-sized soda cup, filled it, went up onto the roof, and stood there looking down. A second later I dumped the entire contents of the soda cup on top of them, and listened contentedly to their shrieks.

One of the girls ran away so fast she left her purse. I put it in the lost and found in the box office, and to this day I don't know if she ever came back to reclaim it. Either way, I never saw the hecklers again.

* * *

My penchant for getting into mischief continued in school. In my English class, I thought it would be funny to pin a centerfold on the wall next to the pencil sharpener. The teacher speculated that something was amiss when every male student in the class suddenly needed to sharpen his pencil. Unfortunately I got caught. My therapist was notified, and we had a nice long talk about that particular stunt.

As my birthday approached, I finally got a letter from Dad. He said that he had been working hard, writing letters to secure his release and ensure our reunion, so that we could both leave the country. At this point I had pretty much become jaded to that kind of talk, so it didn't bother me. I was confident that I wouldn't really be going anywhere any time soon.

More importantly though, Dad said that he wasn't mad at me about the whole Mormon thing—that I was old enough to make my own decisions, that he loved me and would support me, which made me feel relieved. It felt even better to write back to him and let him know that I was no longer attending the church.

Meanwhile, Sammy and I had joined a local gym. We took a martial arts class from a sensei who was tough as nails. We spoke Korean in the class, which I always got mixed up (I would say "good evening" in Korean as we were leaving), but I found that with martial arts, similar to weightlifting, it came to me with a bit of ease. Both Sammy and I quickly excelled.

By my 17th birthday, I was riding high on life! Things at work were going well, I had an amazing circle of friends, I was saving up for a car, I was healthy and strong... the future had never looked quite so bright.

And then something happened, something that threatened to bring it all crashing down around me. It came out of nowhere, not from my Dad, but from a source I could not have guessed, and was not prepared for.

CHAPTER ELEVEN:
EBB AND FLOW

Shortly after my birthday, Renee and Shawn announced that they were moving to Burbank.

Burbank.

The school year was ending, and after the summer I'd be going into 12th grade. After all the time I had spent making friends and finally feeling like I belonged at school, my foster parents were talking about thrusting me into an entirely new environment, forcing me to graduate with a class that shared no history with me. I would be taken from the job I had grown to love, and I would be separated from my brothers, the family I chose.

It was unacceptable.

I pled my case to my social worker, Joyce. She understood, but was unsure if there was anything she could do. I told Sammy and a few close friends what was going on, but kept mum to coworkers and friends at school.

I poured my heart out to my therapist Allison, who swore to appeal to Social Services to do everything within their power to place me in another foster home in the same area.

The prospect of getting used to yet another new home and family was unsettling, but nothing compared to the devastation I was sure to feel upon being fully uprooted.

As the school year ended and I handed my yearbook over to person after person for signing, I wondered if this would be the last I would see of them.

Renee and Shawn wouldn't budge. They were determined to relocate, and nothing I said or did was going to change that. I understand now that they had to do what was best for them. At the time though, I didn't understand at all. I was just frustrated. Social Services was looking into available foster homes and was running into a dead end, and I was running out of time.

I attended summer school again (my grades at the end of the year were poor—I got my first 'F.' With my job and increased social stature had come a drop in my grade point average) but it was a haze. Tony took leave from the Navy and the brothers shared another legendary desert trip, but I worried that this newfound bond, which had only gotten stronger, would dissolve.

I spent the next several weeks in a state of dread as the time of the move drew near. Social Services told me that finding a foster home for a teenage boy was difficult, but they were doing their best.

The day of the move came in August. Social Services said they were still trying, but for the time being I had to go with Renee and Shawn. AMC agreed to give me a few weeks off, but after that, of course, I wouldn't have the job anymore. I promised the brothers that this wasn't the last they'd see of me.

We relocated to the new house. The neighborhood felt foreign and unwelcome, worlds

108

away from the environment I had come to love. I strolled around, looking for something to do. I went and saw a movie, by myself. It was *Lethal Weapon 2,* one of the coolest action movies I'd seen in a long time, but even that didn't lift my spirits for very long. I was alone. And it really became clear that for me, "home" wasn't wherever Renee and Shawn were. It was where my friends and my job and my school and the rest of the life I had built was. And no one was going to take that away from me.

I called Joyce, and asked her to expand her search. I would take a public bus if need be, I didn't care. She said there was nothing necessarily in the rules against that, and she would see what she could do.

I spent several hellish days waiting until I finally got the phone call: it was kind of a long shot, but Joyce thought she had found me a home. She soon informed me that I would spend a week with the new foster parent. If, at the end of that week either party decided it wasn't going to work, I would return to Renee and Shawn. That was fine with me. Long shot or not, I didn't care. All I wanted was a chance to reclaim the life that had taken so many years to build.

CHAPTER TWELVE:
SLAYING DEMONS

Makala Holcroft was a single foster mother in her early forties. She lived in Garden Grove, several miles from the Orange Mall and Villa Park High School. She worked carpentry for convention centers, getting things set up before big shows and tearing everything down afterward. She was also raising a troubled young boy named Fred.

Joyce took me to the house and introduced me to Makala and Fred, and said she would check in with me in a week to see if things were going to work out.

I asked Makala about her name. It was Hawaiian. I thought it was cool that she had an odd-sounding name like mine. The house was nice—a couple thousand square feet in a neighborhood that was predominantly Vietnamese. In fact, I would find out later the area was called "Little Saigon."

We spent the week in a "feeling out" period. Makala offered that if I stayed, she would drive me to work, but I would have to take the public bus to school. In the meantime, we could use her vehicle for driver training. It sounded like a really good deal to me.

Makala was a no-nonsense type who had an ethereal air about her. She had adopted Fred, a ten year-old bundle of raw energy. He had been through a rough past and was struggling with some behavior disorders. I was amazed at how patient Makala was with him.

But, she could also be tough to read. As the week passed, I still wasn't a hundred percent sure where I stood. My future was in her hands. I was just a leaf blowing in the wind. The not knowing was killing me. After the week was up, Joyce arrived and asked both Makala and myself what the decision was. I knew what my answer was but I wanted Makala to say it first. Everything hinged on her.

She took a moment to appraise me, then told Joyce that she would be okay with me staying. A huge weight was lifted from my shoulders. This was it; the chance I had so desperately hoped for. Joyce wanted to know my answer. Happily I said that yes, I wanted to stay.

The next day Joyce took me to Burbank to pick up my stuff. It hit all of us at the same time, that after three and a half years, it was time to say goodbye.

Renee and Shawn told me that they would welcome me back once I graduated, that they would pay for college, I could work with Shawn if I wanted to.

As Renee said goodbye, she said tearfully: "I don't know if I was a good mom." I had never seen her so emotional; never seen her feelings laid bare in such a way.

I told her that she had done just fine. Looking back now, do I think she could have done things differently? Better? Sure. But as I write this, I can also think of a hundreds of things I should have done differently, that I should have done better.

Melissa and I hadn't always gotten along, but she was sad to see me leave as well. We all dried our eyes, and then it was time to go.

* * *

It didn't take me long to settle in at Makala's house. I got back to work, relieved to tell Sammy that Brother Michelob wasn't leaving. I had kept my membership at the gym, so Sammy and I got back to martial arts classes as well.

Senior year would be starting soon. I had my permit, and Makala allowed me to drive her vehicle (a pickup with a camper) while she rode passenger. The more I did it, the more I got used to it. I couldn't wait to get a vehicle of my own! For the time being though, Makala got me a city bus pass.

The school year soon started. I would get up early, take the city bus for about half an hour, then walk three blocks to school. Not so bad really, and besides, I was attending senior year with the rest of my class. I could hardly believe it. Sometimes I would walk from school to work, and sometimes on weekends Makala would drive me to work and pick me up. Life was settling back into balance again.

At home I was somewhat conscious of the fact that I was acting as a role model for Fred. Makala started teaching me how to cook and do laundry. She tried to tell me that when I turned 18, I wouldn't be a part of the system anymore. Things would be different.

I would need to be self-sufficient. I heard what she was saying, but I didn't fully grasp it. I was just enjoying the ride.

And speaking of "enjoying the ride," I was having a blast in driver's training. I'll never forget the first time I got onto the freeway, with two other students in the back and the instructor in the passenger seat. It seemed like the vehicles on either side were just inches away. I couldn't believe people drove like that all the time. Doing 50 miles an hour on the freeway even for just a few miles felt like I was driving the Indy 500.

Amid all the craziness, I hadn't written to Dad. He, of course, didn't know yet that I had a new foster mom, so he continued writing to my old foster parents, who forwarded the letters to me.

In those letters, he had started referring to me as Yakimoki Zeilzonahua Quipu, telling me that I was an Incan prince and that when he was released, we would return to our homeland of Peru. He decorated the letters with cryptic symbols amid Christian fishes.

Meanwhile, my therapist Allison asked how often I thought about my mom. Whether she was alive or not, and if she was, where she might be? If I might have other family and where they might be? I told her the truth—that for the most part I tried not to obsess over it, because if I kept asking myself questions that didn't have any answers, maybe I would go crazy like Dad. Allison assured me this would not be the case; that despite all I had gone through, I was, in fact, remarkably normal.

November rolled around. I took my driving test, and passed it! Makala let me drive her truck to work a few times. I couldn't believe that I was actually behind the wheel... by myself! It was an incredible feeling... kind of what I imagine a bird must feel when it flies. I could just hit the gas and go... and forget about everything.

I wondered how I would ever be able to afford a vehicle of my own, however. I had started looking at the prices on clunker windshields at used car lots, and even they were way beyond anything I might save up for in the near future.

And so a few weeks later I got one of the biggest surprises of my life when I came home and Makala informed me that I was the owner of a car!

As Makala led me outside, my head was still spinning.

It was an old Dodge Demon—yellow with a green top. Dodge, I found out later, didn't make a ton of Demons. They basically looked like a Dart or a Duster. Makala had bought it for something like 1800 bucks, which I swore I would pay back to her. I thought it was the coolest car in the world, and I couldn't believe it was mine. Actually having a vehicle of my own had seemed like a nearly impossible dream, and now that dream was a reality.

I sat on the driver's side, admiring the interior.

Then I drove it.

It was a beast to my young mind, a rumbling behemoth. MY behemoth. I couldn't wait to show it off to Sammy and the others at the theater, to the kids at school—Hell, to everyone!

The Demon had character, but I needed to add a few touches before it would feel like something that was truly mine. There was a little figure I had bought

114

at a gaming convention, a grim reaper (I drew the grim reaper every chance I got, almost as much as I drew Conan). The first thing I did was glue that reaper to the dash. Then, I took a blurb that was on the first page of every Conan comic, cut it out, and taped it to the left of the instrument panel.

With those additions, the Demon was ready for action.

My star at school had been somewhat on the rise. I wouldn't be voted Homecoming King or anything—true popularity still eluded me—but I was becoming more well-known. Once I got a car though it seemed like I suddenly became everybody's best friend.

Of course I wouldn't be shallow enough to use my vehicle as a means to attract women or anything like—well, no that's exactly what I did. Unfortunately within a few days I was stupid enough to let a particularly attractive female freshman drive my car. Without a license, of course. When the police pulled up behind us, she pulled over and frantically switched places with me. Somehow the officer wasn't fooled, and I got a point against my license.

My car was a big hit with the brothers. The seat belts in the back could be let out to a ridiculous length, something like eight feet. The bros would toss the belts out the window so the metal tongue would drag on the asphalt and kick up sparks.

I learned early on that the Demon had its flaws. The one that we all thought was the most hilarious was a tendency for the motor to kick back on—just for a second before dying out again—after the key had been removed.

At the movie theater, I quickly discovered that the

Demon could take a beating. There was a grocery store nearby, and shopping carts always seemed to get left behind in our parking lot. So... we came up with a novel way of getting rid of the carts: slamming our cars into them at 30 miles an hour. We'd hang out, smash the carts, and award points for how far they flew. On its first run, the Demon demolished its way to first place. The only real damage the car took from all the cart crunching was a jarred headlight. From then on, whenever I drove by a house at nighttime that one headlight would shine up into second-story windows.

Now you might think that an activity like shopping cart derby is a touch irresponsible. And you would be right. The longer I owned the Demon, the more I wanted to test its limits, and responsibility flew out the window along with the extended seat belts.

On late nights after closing at the theater, I'd hit the vacant 22 Freeway and peg the Demon's speed at 120 MPH. Other times I thought it was super cool to skid into corners.

In the right hands the Demon would have been a fierce and dependable machine. In my hands it was becoming a loaded weapon, a loose cannon. And I was becoming a reckless twit who didn't appreciate what he had.

And then came Midnight Madness.

Midnight Madness was basically this: Seniors with vehicles would pay to play the game, which was kind of a scavenger hunt. Everyone would meet at the school parking lot at midnight, and there they would receive a clue. That clue would lead them to a location, where they would find a second clue to another location, and so on until the final location,

116

where the winner would collect the pot of all the money everyone had paid and all the drivers would party their asses off. I can't even tell you how excited I was to be a part of the whole thing. It was the height of coolness.

And so I went to pick up my friend Jake, who lived up in the hills, not far from where I had lived with my previous foster parents. I was driving with Jake to get to the school parking lot at 11:45 at night, through the winding S curves of Anaheim Hills, racing against a car driven by another Villa Park student.

I had just passed the car I was racing, going insanely fast. Jake was holding on for dear life. I came up to a 90 degree curve, braked as I yanked the steering wheel, and—

Nothing happened. The car kept going straight, right off the road, slamming into a side hill covered with ice plant. We hit hard. It took both Jake and I a minute to gather our wits. I asked him if he was okay and he said he was. I wanted to find out how badly the Demon was damaged, so I opened the door, stepped out, and immediately fell into a ditch.

Jake would later recount that all he saw when he looked over was my long hair, sticking straight up as I dropped. The only thing that was missing was a puff of smoke like in the old Roadrunner cartoons.

I crawled to a spot where I could see exactly what had happened and beheld the Demon, front end buried in the ice plant, rear end barely perched on to the edge of the road, and the body suspended over the ditch that I had fallen into.

The vehicle I had been racing pulled to a stop. Once it was determined that we were definitely not injured, the driver volunteered to give me a lift to the movie theater where I could call a tow truck.

Minutes later I was dropped off at the theater, and Jake and the others were on their way to Midnight Madness.

I tried to sort through the mess I'd gotten myself into. How would I tell Makala? There was nothing to do but tell her the truth. I called her from the theater, explained what had happened. I could tell that she was beyond disappointed, which made me feel even crappier. She told me she had AAA, and to get a tow truck.

I caught a ride back to the crash site and sat, waiting to be towed. Several minutes later it arrived. The driver got out, surveyed the scene, and quickly determined that a regular tow truck wouldn't cut it— they were going to need a flatbed.

And so I waited some more. Now it just so happened that one of the clues for Midnight Madness was up in the hills, and so, as I sat there feeling like a pathetic waste, half the senior class drove by, honking, hooting, hollering and heckling. I had felt bad before; now I felt like the biggest ass on the planet.

The flatbed finally arrived, and I rode with the driver home. Makala didn't really want to talk or even look at the vehicle when I came through the door.

At this point I seriously wondered if she regretted allowing me to stay.

The next morning she and I both got a look at the extent of the damage. It was bad. Really bad. The front end was trashed. The engine wasn't damaged, but the front axle, wheels, suspension, etc. were unsalvageable. I waited, sure that Makala was going to call up Joyce and have me shipped back to Burbank. Finally she turned to me and announced that she would not pay for repairs. If I ever wanted to drive again, I would have to fix the car myself.

On Monday I was back to taking the bus to school. Just one week prior I was a senior with a bitchin' ride; then all of a sudden I was back down to the bottom of the food chain. I wasn't a nobody, though—on the contrary, it seemed like literally everyone had heard the story of the dumbass who crashed his car into the ice plant. At last I was finally, truly popular... for being an idiot. I wanted to crawl into a hole somewhere and disappear for the next few years of my life.

Another week or so and mercifully winter break came. I started learning everything I could about how to fix my car. I was never a gearhead, so this was completely foreign territory for me. I still can't lift the hood of a vehicle and identify most of what's under there, but during that winter break I was focused; determined to be driving again when I returned to school.

Makala helped out. She drove me to junkyards, where I sought out replacement parts. Sometimes the parts fit, sometimes they didn't. But I was making progress. Before too long I had replaced the shocks, the front rims and the radiator. The brakes were still giving me a lot of trouble, though.

Then Christmas came. Makala wasn't as well off as Renee and Shawn, so it wasn't quite the same, but what she did get me was pretty amazing: a class ring. It was gold with an emerald setting. I was ecstatic. I wanted to keep the ring in pristine condition, so I made sure to take it off when I was working on the Demon.

New Year's passed, and 1990 was upon me. I had almost gotten my car to a point where it was actually drivable. I had been working on the brakes, and finally got the last parts I needed. I went to make some final adjustments before a test drive, and I realized I was still wearing my ring. I took it off, put it on the roof of the car, and tinkered until the front brakes were intact. I put the rims and tires back on, and I was behind the wheel in short order.

The car didn't handle right, and the frame was bent, so the right front corner drooped like the face of a stroke victim, but it was functional; it would get me from point A to point B. I could drive to school once again! I was still as excited as could be when I pulled back into the driveway, and realized I had never put my ring back on. With a dawning horror I remembered that I had put it on the roof of the car. I prayed that it fell when I pulled out of the driveway.

I scoured the driveway, and every inch of my street and as much of the road beyond as I could, but I never recovered my ring. When I told Makala, she was devastated. It was just one other thing that I would have to pay her back for, and only with the passage of time do I realize that some things can never truly be repaid.

After the loss of the ring, I started to think that maybe the Demon was cursed; perhaps the grim reaper wasn't such a great choice for a dash decoration after all. Regardless, I left it on, and come January I was back in school.

* * *

There was a lot of talk about what everyone would do after graduation. Some people had plans and lofty goals, and some didn't have any kind of plan at all. And what about me? I was becoming acutely aware that this was it: six months and it would all be over. Then what? I knew I wanted to pursue art, maybe acting as well. Community college seemed like a good option. There was educational assistance I could get through the state. A scholarship... Makala had also offered to let me work with her after graduation, but our relationship had deteriorated. I think the class ring was a kind of final straw. She enforced more rules, more discipline, and the idea of her telling me what to do at work *and* at home didn't appeal to me. I still hadn't written to Dad yet, I was too caught up in my own life; my own problems, but I told my social worker that I wanted to visit him in Arizona after I graduated.

I remember military recruiters walking the campus, shaking hands, offering incentives for anyone who wanted to join the service. They spoke to me. I listened to what they had to say, said thanks but no thanks, and didn't think much more about it.

At work I was back to my old tricks, ramming shopping carts, aisle dancing. The wreck at Midnight Madness would have been a hard lesson, if I had bothered to learn it at the time. I still drove like crap in general, although I wasn't in a hurry to race anyone. Besides, the Demon still wasn't the same as it had been before. And, like my relationship with Makala, it never would be.

After all I had been through I felt closer to the AMC theater crew than ever, and I had really taken a liking to a girl named Carly. She was tough and pretty. Our personalities clicked, and our friendship began developing into something more.

School passed in a blur of short days and schoolwork that no longer felt like work. The teachers were more relaxed, and overall cast an air of "congratulations, you guys made it, enjoy these last few months." It was a strange but exciting vibe, the opposite of the rule enforcement taking place at home.

Soon it was April. I found out that my therapist Allison was preparing to move to Arizona. I would have only one more session with her, although she gave me her home number if I needed to talk.

My birthday was a stone's throw away. My attitude, my whole outlook had steadily transformed over the first quarter of 1990: I became more and more confident that I was going to make something of my life. Turning 18, graduating… it was still somewhat scary, but more than ever it was full of promise; freedom. I could do whatever I wanted, whenever I wanted. As my confidence mounted, my relationship with Makala decayed even further. I wanted to be in a position where no one could tell me what to do, and it seemed like the more I realized my independence, the more Makala wanted to clamp down on me and enforce rules. She wanted to know where I was at all times and when I was going to be back; I was determined to come and go whenever I pleased.

Then, Makala informed me that new foster kids would be arriving, and that they would need my room. I would have to sleep on the couch. The chasm between us widened.

When the day of my 18th birthday finally arrived,

Makala and I hadn't spoken much. She got me a card, and had offered to throw a party but I told her I had plans of my own.

There was something that had been brewing in my mind for a while: the question as to whether or not I should drink alcohol, and if so, when. With everything that had happened, with all the pressure and the sense that one act of my life was coming to a close and another was set to begin, I decided that the time had come for me to imbibe.

Sammy hooked me up right. I went to his house, where he presented me with part one of my present: a bottle of Jack Daniels whiskey. I had my first shot. It felt like liquid fire in my throat. Part two was a mint-condition Savage Sword of Conan number one. The handwritten note on the back of the protective sleeve announced: "Must be read or at least flipped through to be in the right drinking, brawling, wenching state o mind. Love, Sammy."

Part three was a steak dinner. And from there on, the party continued into the night, me and the brothers. We shook the Pillars of Heaven and rattled the Gates of Hell. By the end of the night, I was good and drunk, and between all of us we finished that bottle of Jack. But I never puked. It was a rite of passage, and I had triumphed.

I spent the night at Sammy's house and drove home the following morning, even though Makala had asked me to come back that night or to call if I couldn't—which I didn't do. I was all attitude at that point. Add to that the fact that I still hadn't paid Makala back for the car, or the ring I lost... the whole situation was like a wire being twisted back and forth in opposite directions until sooner or later, it *will* break. My birthday had been the final bit of stress.

Makala kicked me out of the house.

And who could blame her? Well, I did of course. Although I think even then a part of me understood, whether I wanted to admit or not. Still, it wasn't easy. I had no place to stay. I was legally no longer a ward of the court so I couldn't turn to Social Services. And even if I could, I was still determined to make my own way.

CHAPTER THIRTEEN:
COMMENCEMENT

I started alternating sleeping at the brothers' houses when and where I could, but they all had families and situations that didn't always allow for someone crashing on their couch. Of course, if I had stayed at Makala's, I would be sleeping on a couch there too, so what did it really matter? It couldn't get much worse, right? (Don't ask me why I hadn't stopped asking myself that. By this point, I should have known better)

There were a few nights that I slept in my car, and used the showers at the gym. And there were times that I slept in my car and came to school without a shower. Come June, the counselor at school started looking at me as a hardship case.

Somehow, the girl I had been seeing through all of this, Carly, didn't leave me. I wondered what she saw in me. Sammy joked that she wanted me for my car. No, my house!

I went to Carly's senior prom after scrounging up enough money (I wasn't paying rent, after all) to get a tux and kick in for a limo with a few other couples. In the limo ride, all I could think about was how much living space there was.

We had dinner at a fancy restaurant. We drank in the limo. Later we danced, we laughed, and as the night wore on we decided to hit the beach.

Carly and I wandered the beach in our fancy, now frumpy clothes. We kissed and talked about the future. What would my future really be? What kind of a future could I offer someone like her?

I was in a melancholy mood when the limo dropped us off at Carly's place that night. I wanted to do more than just kiss, but Carly had been clear that she wasn't ready. I fell asleep with my head in her lap, her hand stroking my hair.

In the final weeks before graduation there were many parties, and I was doing my damnedest to make up for 18 years of sobriety.

At one huge senior party in Anaheim Hills, I pounded screwdrivers all night, then got into the Jacuzzi in my underwear. I would only learn later that sitting in hot water speeds up blood flow and therefore circulates alcohol in your body that much quicker. At some point I stumbled down the hill beyond the house's backyard and laid down in a hammock, wondering why the world wouldn't stop spinning.

When I woke up hours later, everyone had gone home. I climbed up the hill to find the house locked up and my clothes nowhere in sight. The girl who threw the party found me the next morning in a fetal position outside her glass doors, shivering in my skivvies.

Graduation was drawing near. I stopped by Makala's house to check in. We chatted for a while... she gave me a letter that had been forwarded by Dad's attorney to Social Services. Makala offered the use of her address for future letters, saying I could pick them up anytime. I thanked her. She asked me to get her tickets so she could attend my commencement, and I said I would.

Dad's letter was addressed to a clerk for the Orange County court house, wanting to know where I was (he had been told at this point that I no longer resided with Renee and Shawn), why my address hadn't been given to him, and of course, whether or not I was free from the court now that I was 18.

I felt bad that I hadn't written to him in so long, and I vowed to myself that after graduation, when I got my life back on track, I would send him a letter.

Before I knew it, the day finally arrived—graduation! I had dropped off tickets to Makala, and she attended along with Fred and the new foster kids. I had provided my social worker with a ticket as well, but she had another urgent matter and couldn't attend. My therapist Allison had already moved out of state.

I sat and listened to the valedictorian speech—about the future, of course—and wondered again what the future held for me. How, exactly was I going to take the world by storm? The answer wasn't clear yet, but I was unwaveringly optimistic.

They called my name, I got my diploma and sat. The names of my classmates were called. I had been so petrified, when Renee and Shawn moved to Burbank, that I wouldn't get to graduate with my class, and now here I was, getting my diploma along with so many of the kids that I shared such incredible experiences—both good and bad—with. It was an incredible feeling.

Final words were said, we threw our hats into the air, and that was it. I was done with High School. Time to make my mark!!

* * *

A little over a week later, when my social worker arrived at AMC for a final visit, I was still sleeping in my car. She had helped me through so much, and she wanted to know that I would be okay. I had talked to one of my friends about a construction job, and I hoped that by working that job during the day and working the theater at night, I would be able to get a room or apartment. She was still worried, but I told her it was fine; I chose to live this way. I wanted to be on my own, to follow my own rules.

Joyce informed me that the state would continue paying for my braces, through Medicare, until the time came for them to be removed. Beyond that, of course, the state no longer had any responsibility as far as my welfare was concerned. I thanked her for everything. We said our goodbyes, and Joyce exited my life.

I was, as I wished, truly on my own.

CHAPTER FOURTEEN:
FATE AND ROSES

And so the time had come for me to stake my claim! And it would all start with... roofing.

After a week of carrying tiles all day and working the theater at night, I got hammered at a party, didn't show up the next day, and got canned.

So much for roofing.

If I wanted to have any prayer of getting a real place to sleep (I was spending more and more nights in my car at this point, in a parking lot Sammy and others at the theater started calling "BelongtaMick"), and maybe someday being able to attend college, I needed another job. A search of the newspaper listings yielded an opportunity with a place called "Rush Time On Time"—it was an attorney service. Basically the job was for drivers to file court papers and serve summonses. I applied for the job and got it! Now, I thought, now... the world would be my oyster!

During this time, Carly and I remained on good terms, but things between us weren't progressing. Our relationship was cruising steadily in neutral. I thought if I got an apartment that might change things. I was behind on paying my gym fees (Makala had been getting angry letters that I looked at once and threw away), but I hadn't gone to class for a while anyway, and if I got an apartment, I wouldn't need the gym's shower...

I found something I could afford, a single room with a bathroom. No furniture, no bed, no TV, but I had a roof and a space of my own where I could drink, read, and do whatever else I wanted.

At this point the Demon was hurting. When I would park, the brake would depress, causing my brake lights to stay on and killing my battery, so I had a wooden block that I put under the brake every time I parked. On top of that, someone had stolen my gas cap. So, I did the most intelligent thing: stuffed a rag where the cap used to be. I thought everything was cool until a police officer stopped me and said I was basically a Molotov cocktail on wheels. I scrounged up money to replace the cap. With one that locked.

My job at the attorney service was interesting, especially the process serving part. I served papers to all kinds of folks in all kinds of shady areas. I made sure to carry a knife, just in case.

Much of the court filing required driving to the Los Angeles Courthouse. I quickly discovered that I was very good at getting lost, especially when forced to navigate one-way streets. I would end up taking six hours for a trip that should have taken four... If traffic was backed up both ways.

After a few weeks, the secretary sat me down said, "The name of our company is Rush Time On Time, and well... you're never on time." And so I got fired. By the secretary.

So much for my career as an attorney service driver.

Meanwhile, Carly and I continued drifting apart. We hung out sporadically, and when we did, the distance between us was palpable.

I wouldn't be able to afford the next month's rent unless I got another job, so I started looking. When I stopped to check in on Makala and she asked how I was doing, I lied and told her everything was fine. She passed along a membership cancellation notice from the gym, and another forwarded letter from Dad, still trying to figure out where I was and what was going on and reading the riot act to various personages within the legal system.

I told Makala I'd write to Dad. Which I would... eventually. When I wasn't ashamed.

Some time later I was still job hunting when a sophomore girl from Villa Park stopped by the theater and asked if she and some of her friends could get into a movie for free. She was hot. I said yes.

"Some of her friends" turned out to be like 20 freshmen. Everything might have gone okay if they'd been at all stealthy about the operation, but they weren't, and the theater manager caught them filing in with me holding the door open.

I was immediately fired. And, though Carly still spoke to me, our relationship was over.

Now I was out of two jobs, one girlfriend, and rent was coming due. I explained my situation to the landlord, who told me I'd need to pay what I could and vacate.

Throughout these messes I got myself into Sammy and the Bros never judged me, and only offered their support. Their living arrangements, however, didn't always allow for me to crash at their houses.

Going back to Makala was a possibility, but I was too proud. I didn't want her to be right.

Overall the AMC folks remained close friends and I still hung out at the theater. And so it was that I found myself sitting in my vehicle—the same vehicle I would be sleeping in once again—in the theater parking lot after everyone had gone home, and it all just hit me at once. I broke down.

I was 18. I was free. I was supposed to be taking the world by storm. Instead I felt like a miserable failure. A complete and total loser. In that moment it seemed like my life had been better when it was just me and Dad out in the desert.

The next day I tried to pull myself together and refocus on the job hunt.

At this point I was desperate, and willing to take just about anything I could get.

And that's how I ended up selling roses door to door.

Once I got the job, the routine went something like this: I met the other salespeople first thing in the morning. The managers gave a pep talk to get everyone excited ("behind every 'no' there's a 'yes'!"), then we'd be split into teams, assigned areas on the map, and from there we'd sign for our roses. Each salesman would get 12 boxes of roses, along with a water bottle so we could spray them throughout the day, and then we'd be off.

I tagged along with one of their top salesmen on my first day. We drove to a business park and then set out on foot, going from business to business. He covered a lot of ground, ignored signs that said "no soliciting," and much to my surprise he actually sold a fair amount.

That night I hung out at the top salesman's apartment. He had a *Playboy* displayed proudly on his coffee table, and informed me that if I played my cards right, I could be making enough to get a *Playboy* subscription of my own.

Okay, I thought. *I can do this.*

After a couple days of shadowing the top guy I was on my own, and determined to excel. I weathered "no" after "no," and by the end of the day ended up selling two boxes of roses. I told myself the next day would get better.

It didn't. I learned very quickly that most people really don't like salesmen, and most people really don't want roses. I was rejected, ignored, sometimes even threatened. And, I wasn't selling for crap.

After a few weeks something amazing happened. For each of us, there are pivotal moments in our lives; moments that change everything. I was having a lackluster day pounding the pavement, trying to find the "yes," when I walked right into one of those moments:

I stepped through the door of an Army Recruiter and asked if he wanted to buy a dozen roses.

He was silent for a brief second. He looked me up and down, grinned and said "come into the back room, I've got a video I want to show you."

The video he showed me was one of the coolest things ever: guys my age, dressed in camouflage, rappelling out of helicopters, shooting massive artillery, driving tanks... GI Joe in real life!

Then the recruiter fired a barrage of questions (interesting sidebar: you don't have to be a citizen to be in the US military!) all of which I answered to his satisfaction. Actually, it was probably more like elation than satisfaction (recruiters get additional money if they hit a quota). Looking back on it now, I think he must have been salivating, wondering how this gift from the heavens had just fallen into his lap.

He started telling me about the possibilities military life could offer: good pay, world travel, free room and board, meals, excitement, adventure. I was interested, to be certain, but I wasn't sold. There were other things to consider. For instance, though I didn't have an opportunity to watch the news all that much, I was aware of the fact that Saddam Hussein had invaded Kuwait, and that there were American troops in Saudi Arabia. War seemed unlikely to me, but a possibility nonetheless.

Then the recruiter told me about the GI Bill. The Army would pay for me to attend college. All I had to do was sign up for four years.

College! I could actually go to college. I could stop sleeping in my car. I could stop going from one crappy job to another. I'd have to have my braces removed, but they were scheduled for removal after another year anyway. And I'd need to get a haircut, but I could always grow it back later. And I'd have to get a medical exam and pass a physical—that would be a piece of cake—and an aptitude test, which I wasn't too worried about.

The recruiter could see the wheels turning. He was still smiling, a confident grin that said: *Hook, line, and sinker.*

He told me I could take the physical in one month.

I said okay.

134

I told Sammy and the brothers about my decision. Rider had already been in the Army, and Tone Dog was in the Navy, so they understood. It was going to suck not hanging with them for a while, but I knew they'd be there for me through thick and thin, no matter what.

While waiting to take the physical, I would need to eat, and it would be nice to have someplace to sleep, but selling roses just wasn't cutting it. I needed a job that would actually pay some money.

Back to the newspaper job postings.

I was able to land another job quickly... this time with a telemarketing company.

The "company" was housed inside one large office, with telephone stations lining the walls. There was a manager with a desk in the center of the room, with his own phone line. The manager would walk around, handing out stacks of paper squares with names and phone numbers on them. We would call the numbers and launch into a spiel about how the lucky listener had won a free television! All they had to do was go to a timeshare presentation, where they would have an opportunity to win a vacation (the TV was a tiny piece of crap, and the vacation was only on certain weekdays, and didn't include anything other than the hotel stay). I never attended the presentation, those took place elsewhere, but from what I was told it was a high-pressure sales environment. Once we had called all the numbers in our stack, we put the numbers back into circulation and got a new stack (it didn't matter if the people we called said they didn't want to receive any more calls or not. In fact, depending on how rude the people were, that often led to marking those papers for special treatment: repeated phone calls).

In addition to minimum wage we would get commission, but we only got the commission when someone we called not only showed up to the presentation, but actually sat through the whole thing. The king of the place was a guy who smoked like a burning tire and drank swimming-pool volumes of coffee. He had a way of talking to people that enabled him to sell just about anything.

It wasn't the greatest job in the world, but... it was only temporary. And, it happened to be just down the street from Makala.

I stopped in, told her about the job and about the Army. She was worried. Things in the Middle East were getting worse by the day. Saddam Hussein was bragging about chemical weapons and saying that if Americans invaded Iraq they would be sent home in body bags.

It was certainly enough to cause concern, but I told her I felt like this was something I had to do. I also told her that with my first paycheck I would give her some money toward what I owed her. She told me I could stay at the house when I needed to. I swallowed my pride and accepted. And, I even found time to write to Dad.

Knowing how he felt about the government, I wasn't sure how he'd take the news of my military plans, but I felt a lot better writing to tell him that, than writing to tell him that I was sleeping in my car. I asked him to forgive me for not writing sooner; told him about the Army and that I felt like I was following in his footsteps, and that I hoped he would understand.

Sammy and Rider got an apartment together during this time, and offered up their couch whenever I needed it. Now I had a few places to crash.

When I wasn't working, I would go to Mile Square Park and run. For the physical test I would need to run two miles, do 50 pushups and 50 sit-ups. The pushups and sit-ups I could do in my sleep, but my running needed work, and I trained a couple times a week.

At the job it was clear early on that BS-ing people wasn't my specialty. Mostly I got bored of sitting at the desk, repeating the same speech over and over, dealing with (justifiably) irate folks who really just wanted to be left the hell alone.

So… I decided to engage in a bit of mischief. When a phone number came to my desk with the name Jorge Salvez attached to it, I crossed out the number, wrote "new number," jotted down the digits for Sam and Rider's apartment and put the paper back into circulation.

As I've mentioned, Rider wasn't the most even-tempered fellow, and he always seemed to be the one who was home when calls came in. Of course the employee would ask if Jorge Salvez was home. After a few of these, Rider was fit to be tied. I would talk to Sammy later, who would tell me about hearing Rider screaming into the phone "there's no f#@&ing Jorge Salvez here!!"

My best gag though, took place on a particularly slow day. I crossed out the number on one of my paper slips, wrote "new number" and noted the call-in line for the manager's desk. I put the slip back into circulation and waited. Sure enough, a minute later the manager in the center of the office was answering his phone. He listened for a second to the employee reading him the spiel, then looked around angrily and yelled, "who the hell is this?" Some poor new employee a few stations down looked over, wide-eyed, probably sure that his ass was grass.

Fortunately, the employee didn't get into trouble, and they never found out who did it.

I took my medical exam, which I passed. On the day of the physical I nailed the pushups and sit-ups without difficulty, then ran the two miles in a decent time.

* * *

Next up was the aptitude test. I went to the Los Angeles MEPS (Military Entrance Processing Station), took the test, then sat before a computer screen to see what jobs or "MOS's" (Military Occupational Specialty) I would be eligible for.

Due to my "alien status" I was not eligible for any job that required a security clearance for classified information, but aside from that there were a fair amount of options. I knew that whatever specialty I chose, I'd like it to be something that would be applicable to a civilian job when I got out of the military. One MOS on the list especially piqued my curiosity: truck driver.

The recruiter told me I'd learn how to drive five ton trucks, semis, all kinds of cool vehicles. And that felt like a skill that could make me some money when I got out.

So… if that was what I truly wanted, the recruiter could make it happen. All I had to do was sign on the dotted line. If I changed my mind, he said, I could always get out of the contract. If I wanted the GI Bill, though, I'd need to sign up for four years.

Moment of truth.

I thought about my options, about my failures, about the possibilities for a better life. And I signed on the dotted line.

The recruiter started the paperwork and informed me that I would be heading off to basic training before the end of the year.

CHAPTER FIFTEEN:
PROPHECY

All of a sudden it all became very real. I got my braces off. I put in my notice at work. I got my hair cut (that was a crazy experience. The barber pulled it into a ponytail and chopped it. The result looked like something a giant cat might have puked up). Then I got a letter from Dad.

He reiterated that we were foreigners, enemies of the State, soon to be deported and therefore I could not join the US Army. He told me he was trying to get the Peruvian Consulate to get in touch with me. He said he understood that I did what I thought was right, but he hoped I didn't do it in haste, and I needed to get out as soon as possible, that we needed to stand and fight together.

Dad had certainly claimed that we would be deported many times before, but he had provided specific case numbers and contacts in his letter, and I needed to be sure, so I contacted the Peruvian Embassy—they were unaware of any deportation proceedings.

Three days later I received another letter from Dad, this time saying that he would reveal to me where

I was really born: an Incan Indian village near the border of Peru. He restated that the Mormons were our enemies and that they wanted to destroy us, and he said the Mormons would use the Army in a plot to separate us. Again he told me to immediately resign.

In the meantime, a series of sensational claims were being made about Saddam Hussein, about the chemical warfare he employed, and the agonizing, slow death those chemicals could cause. With every passing day, speculation in the media grew that the situation would escalate into all-out war, and that a much greater number of US troops would be sent to the Middle East.

Three days after Dad's last letter, I received another, this one far more plaintive, beseeching me to trust no one, to sign nothing except a resignation from the Army, to make no statements. He said the war that was coming was a war man had brought against himself. He implored me to run away to Arizona.

I knew I didn't want to run away (especially back to Arizona!), and I was sure that what Dad had said about where I was born was untrue. I wrote back telling him that I didn't really know what to say.

I was also worried about the possibility of going to war, and dying a slow and painful death. I stayed at Makala's house and thought long and hard about the decision I had made, and with all of my heart and soul and will I sought some kind of guidance, some kind of answer. What should I do?

That night I had a dream. I was standing in line at the movie theater concession stand. Behind the counter was a girl who I had been infatuated with, but who never responded to my advancements. When it was finally my turn to order, she slid a napkin across the counter. On it was a phone number. That phone number had an Orange County area code.

When I woke up, I remembered the dream vividly, and though I can't explain just how I knew this, I was certain that the number was the answer to my question.

Makala and the kids were gone. I went to the phone in the kitchen, and I dialed.

A female voice answered and said, "Sunny Acres, how may I help you?"

I immediately thought that Sunny Acres must be a cemetery, and my heart skipped a beat. Was this the answer, that if I persisted with my plans I was sure to die?

I asked what kind of business Sunny Acres was. The lady responded, "We're a retirement community."

I thanked her and hung up, and I knew, I absolutely believed without a doubt that the message was: "You're going to live. You're going to live to a ripe old age, so don't worry."

I wrote Dad back and told him that I loved him, but that I had to do what I thought was best.

* * *

I hung out with Sammy and the bros and we partied like there was no tomorrow (though, thanks to my dream I was sure that there would be—many tomorrows, in fact). The recruiter notified me that I would be taking basic training in Fort Sill, Oklahoma.

The time for my departure drew near. The folks at the telemarketing company threw me a party, and I drank myself into a stupor.

142

Makala and I decided to retire the Demon. It was still a beast, but now it was more like an aged beast that had seen many battles and was on its last legs. Sad to say, but I had driven it into the ground. I got a few hundred bucks for it at the junkyard, which I gave to Makala.

I worked my last day, received my final check, most of which I paid to Makala. I said my goodbyes to the bros and everyone at the theater, promising to see them all soon.

Dad wrote one final letter urging me to resign, stating that Neilson wasn't my real last name, that they would kick me out, and that without my help defending him he would rot in prison; that we had to go back to Peru and conquer in God's name.

I knew that me staying out of the Army wouldn't improve Dad's situation. My course had been set. I had made up my mind.

Then, in late October, I went back to the MEPS. Makala accompanied me, with Fred. She promised to write, and told me that I would have a place when I needed it. I thanked her and we said our goodbyes.

There was a lot of paperwork to fill out, a lot of signing on many dotted lines. More testing, physical examination, height check, weight check, etc. while the Army made sure I was someone who was really fit enough to serve. Some people at the station didn't make it. At one point a personnel member informed us that we still had time to back out, that it wasn't too late yet. One person took him up on the offer. I waited. And then it was time to take the oath of enlistment.

I raised my hand. I swore to defend the United States against all enemies, foreign and domestic.

And that was it. I was in. Soon I would be flying out to Oklahoma, and my time in the military would begin in earnest. I was nervous but determined, and excited to embark on yet another journey in my life.

As I waited for my departure, my mind and the minds of those who would be shipping off with me was on the worsening situation in Iraq.

CHAPTER SIXTEEN:
BASIC

Our plane landed in Oklahoma and before long we were on a bus. Everyone was anxious—we had heard rumors from other enlistees who had relatives or friends who had gone to boot camp. Stories ranged from soldiers being screamed at nonstop to trainees being physically beaten. I wasn't quite sure what to expect when the bus passed through the gates of Fort Sill.

Turns out, the rumors of yelling were right on the money. Drill instructors stormed onto the bus, poking the brims of their Smokey the Bear hats into people's foreheads, bellowing at them to get the hell off the bus. No matter how fast you moved, it wasn't fast enough. And if you moved too fast and dropped something, God help you. It seemed like we were doing pushups every five minutes.

En route to the barracks, one drill instructor ordered me to do push-ups, then got down next to me and wanted to know if I had a problem with that. I committed the cardinal sin of saying "no sir." I thought several veins were going to burst out of his head as he screamed "Sir? Do I look like an officer to you? I work for a living!"

I wondered, not for the first time, and certainly not for the last, just what the hell I had gotten myself into. I also wondered if Dad went through something similar. What had the military been like when he went through basic training? And, the thought that was always at the back of my mind was: had he really been in the military at all, or was that a lie too?

There was a steep learning curve right at the beginning. Even getting into a formation seemed like something nobody could do right. Once we managed, our head drill instructor introduced himself and told us that he and the other drill instructors were going to do everything they could to break us. There were a few more introductions, a few more speeches, and then we got a first look at our living quarters—an open barracks. One metal bed and one metal locker to a person, and basically zero privacy.

Next we were issued all sorts of gear: everything from our BDUs (battle dress uniform) to a rucksack, mess kit, shovel, flashlight, etc. Some items brought back memories (Dad owned a military fold-up shovel, flashlight with interchangeable lens covers and mess kit) and seemed to validate Dad's claims of military experience. On the other hand, these were all accessories that someone could purchase at any military surplus store.

The first few days were a pressure cooker of intense physical training, almost no sleep, and meals devoured with the intensity of contestants at a pie-eating contest. We would get up before the sun, do physical training with steam wafting off our beanie-covered heads, change, do push-ups, eat, fall in (get into formation), learn how to do things like stand at attention, parade rest, etc., do more push-ups, attend

146

classes (if you fell asleep, you'd stand with your back to the wall, thighs parallel to the floor and hold that position until the instructor said otherwise), eat again, do more push-ups, learn how to do things like march, attend more classes, do even more push-ups, eat again, fall in, get changed, collapse into an exhausted sleep, get up before the sun and do it all again.

There were a few soldiers who just couldn't take it and broke down early on. They were washed out... which is exactly what the system was designed to do: get rid of the ones who couldn't hack it, and further toughen the ones who could. After all, the stress we were enduring there was nothing compared to sleeping in a ditch with bullets flying over your head. The military needed all of us to be ready, physically and mentally, for the hardships to come.

Everyone got shots. Lots of shots. They were efficient though—you'd stand in line, step up, and get shots administered in both shoulders at once from needle guns. Recruits had a great time punching each other in the shoulders after that.

It was difficult that first week: I had left Makala's house because I didn't want to be told how to do things. In the Army, you were told how to do everything. And everyone did it exactly the same. You rolled your socks the exact same way the guy in the bunk next to you rolled his. You rolled your BDU sleeves the exact same way he rolled his. If your bunk wasn't made right, you paid with push-ups. If you didn't shave, you paid with push-ups. If your instructor couldn't see his reflection in your boots, you paid with push-ups. It was insane, but after what I had been through with Dad, I knew that I could handle just about anything. If I could get used to being ordered around every hour of every day, I would do just fine.

After that first week, the tension eased a bit. Then we started in on some of the juicier stuff, like becoming intimately familiar with the M16 rifle. Of course, we couldn't wait to shoot it, but first off we had to learn how to hold it, march with it, hit somebody with it (with bayonet attached), handle it in drill and ceremony and most of all, how to clean it. And cleaning it is something we did, and would continue to do, over, and over, and over again.

We were also issued gas masks, which we learned how to assemble, don and seal. Saddam Hussein's threats of chemical warfare were being taken very seriously. In the case of such an attack, we were told that if we couldn't get our gas masks on and sealed in six seconds we were as good as dead. We drilled repeatedly until we could accomplish just that.

Another dark rumor about basic that had circulated at MEPS and during the first week was the dreaded "gas chamber"—the scuttlebutt was that we would not only be exposed to tear gas with our masks on, but be forced to take them off, a notion that had many of the recruits freaked out. I remained convinced that the Army wouldn't thrust anything upon us that we couldn't physically handle.

The chamber as I remember it was a large, stand alone structure; one entrance, one exit. As we waited to enter the shelter, we watched recruits stumble out, waving their hands out at their sides, hacking and spitting up long streams of mucous into the grass. This didn't inspire much confidence, but we could tell that no one was dying.

We sealed our masks, went in and lined up against the wall. It was gloomy inside, clouded with a haze of tear gas that emanated from the center of the room. We filed to the exit one by one, and before we could step outside, we had to remove our mask and recite our name, rank and social security number.

The gas stung the eyes and played hell with one's sinuses, but all in all, it wasn't so bad. Experiencing the difference between having the mask on and off was a convincing argument in favor of the masks' effectiveness. After all, our lives might depend on those masks, and having complete faith in them was critical.

When we weren't drilling or training, we were cleaning. Everything was immaculate at all times, including the barracks floor, which was buffed daily. Running the buffer was an adventure in itself. The machine had a tall handle like a scooter, with a spinning pad on the bottom. It plugged into the wall and when you hit the switch, if you weren't ready, the contraption would take off across the floor and take you with it. Wrangling the beast at first was like trying to rein in a pissed-off mustang, but like everything else, it became easier with practice.

The interpersonal dynamics became very interesting a few weeks in. There were the people you got along with, and the people you didn't. Lines within the platoon and within the company were drawn. Friendships were forged. Enemies were made. But even with the friction that existed within our company, it felt like we were uniting toward a common purpose.

Pretty soon we were learning the various positions to fire our M16s from. Our drill instructor demonstrated dry-firing from a prone position with a dime balancing on the barrel. The trick was to pull the trigger without the dime falling. Many of us thought this was the coolest thing we'd ever seen and practiced religiously.

Excitement mounted, and then at last, the firing range was upon us!

Practicing without live ammunition was one thing, firing real bullets was quite another. M16s have a tendency to jam, and clearing the weapon quickly became a critical skill. We fired from all the positions we had practiced, and had a blast doing it. Human silhouettes at various distances would fall when you hit them with a satisfying "ding!" of the bullet striking metal. Over the next few days the firing range would become familiar territory as we practiced for our marksmanship qualification.

We had opportunities to fire other weapons as well—the M60 made famous by Sylvester Stallone in *First Blood* was a belt-fed monster. The first time I fired it, I was so spazzed out, I didn't lift the barrel and sprayed a full-auto burst into the ground just a few feet in front of me.

It's tough to beat the sheer thrill of holding down the trigger of a fully automatic weapon and feeling your teeth rattle in your head. Firing a grenade launcher after that didn't provide the same rush exactly, but there's something deeply satisfying about lobbing grenades downrange, even if they were just dispensing colored smoke.

We did get the chance to handle live grenades, however. Each recruit stood behind a reinforced concrete wall, pulled the pin, released the spoon and threw. There was a drill sergeant present wearing a flak jacket, whose job it was to throw himself on the grenade should a trainee get freaked out and drop it.

I tossed my grenade and was rewarded with a thundering BOOM! and a cloud of dirt beyond the wall.

It was somewhere around this time that we were introduced to Atropine. Needles were distributed for demonstration and instructions were given that if we were exposed to a nuclear, biological or chemical attack, injecting the Atropine into the thigh or buttocks would provide the only slim possibility of survival. Many of the recruits believed the Atropine was simply meant to provide a relatively painless death. Now of course it's easy enough just to look something like that up on the Internet to see exactly what it does, but back then the Internet didn't exist. So despite what we were told, the recruits still had their suspicions, and I suppose it goes without saying that we all hoped we would never have to field test the drug to find out the answer.

Soon it came time to qualify on the firing range. There were different levels based on how well you did—marksman, sharpshooter, expert… and there was a time limit. As I went about qualifying, moving through the various positions, I was hitting almost all of my targets, when my weapon jammed and I couldn't clear it before the target dropped. I hit the remaining targets, including the farthest one out, and ended up scoring sharpshooter, just one point below expert... not too shabby.

We had maintained our intense physical training throughout, and soon it came time for our final physical training test. I scored the highest overall in my platoon.

We were well into December and nearing the end of our training, when I received letters from Makala and Dad. Makala was doing well, and was hoping to see me for Christmas. Dad sent me some drawings, and asked me to draw as well so that I would "let your Dad know that it is MOKI, my SON—I am talking to or writing to." He told me that he was proud of me, and that my mother was proud of me. I wondered again if she was still out there somewhere, and if so, would she be thinking about me that Christmas? I felt the familiar anger of not being able to get at the truth, and refocused on my training.

As we entered the final stages of our training, which included several field exercises, I was getting sick. My tonsils had swollen and my throat was a mess. I spent a full day out of training and was told if I missed any more I'd be held back. I was determined not to let that happen and pushed through, letting the antibiotics do their work.

We set off into the field and learned how to build lean-to's, set up tents and... we had our first taste of MREs—"Meals Ready to Eat." The meals might have been ready, but we weren't. From what I had heard MREs had actually improved over the years. I'd hate to know what they tasted like before.

In the field we got to play war games, which was a lot like laser tag. Everyone's weapon was fitted with a laser and we all wore sensors.

At one point we did a night crawl underneath barbed wire, through the mud, with live rounds being shot high overhead, tracers lighting up the sky. It was meant to simulate an assault on an enemy position, and it was effective. We'd been told throughout basic that being sent to the war was a very real possibility for all of us, and during that exercise the reality of it felt closer than ever.

As if to punctuate that fact, we were soon told that our entire class would not be given the typical Christmas break. We would all be going straight from basic to our AIT—Advanced Individual Training.

The mood was somewhat somber as graduation drew near, but we all knew what we'd signed up for.

One of our final exercises was a 12-mile march, in full combat gear—rucksack, M16, Kevlar vest, helmet. It was grueling and brutal, the hardest thing we had done yet, but every single one of us finished.

Just before the end of basic, everyone got to visit the commissary to buy whatever we wanted. We could eat junk food for the first time in almost two months! After having every aspect of our lives monitored and regulated that small taste of freedom was refreshing.

And then it came time for me to go through yet another graduation—this time from the military. The plane fare was too much for Makala, so she was unable to attend. By the end of the ceremony we were recognized for the first time as true soldiers of the United States Army. Many of the recruits rushed into the arms of loved ones and spent what quality time they could before prepping to leave, while I celebrated quietly with some of the fellow recruits who had become my friends.

CHAPTER SEVENTEEN:
SHIELD AND STORM

Only a handful of the folks I went to basic with ended up joining me at Fort Dix, including a spunky young recruit from Alabama named Kurt. We arrived at night, and caught just a few hours of sleep.

In the pre-dawn hours, I heard a truly beautiful sound—a chorus of female voices. They were responding to cadence and after the many weeks of basic training surrounded by nothing but "swingin' jimmies," the sound of women's voices was undeniably music to my ears.

We were told in the very beginning that this phase of our training, which would normally take two months, was being shortened by half.

The first few days consisted of PT in the morning, followed by classroom instruction, then it was time to jump in and start learning how to drive... Makala's truck was a stick, so I had a bit of practice, which gave me an edge over some of the other students.

We learned how to drive five ton trucks... there was a new system in the vehicles at that time that would allow the driver to increase or decrease the amount of air in the tires with the press of a button. Less air would allow for better traction in the sand. And, if one of your tires was shot, you could continuously pump air into it until you were able to reach a safe location. We also got a taste of the older trucks, the two and a half ton trucks, or "deuce and a halfs."

In the backs of these trucks were the long, fold-down seats that I mentioned in the beginning of this book, the same kind of seats that were installed in the truck Dad drove out of Oklahoma when I was five. I hadn't remembered those seats until I saw them in the Army trucks.

We also had to become licensed on big rigs. Backing one of those things into an "alley" (which for training was just orange cones) is a lot trickier than you'd think—the trailer goes the opposite way the rear of the cab wants to go.

It was all new to me, but I was happy to be learning something that I could apply in civilian life later on. From what I understood, truckers could make pretty decent money. I was also meeting interesting new people, including some females who quickly became good friends, but not romantic partners.

Fort Sill had been cold, but Fort Dix was frigid in early January. We did field exercises where we took turns sitting in the cab to warm up. There were times when your feet felt like blocks of ice. By far the most fun was a driving course that consisted of shallow and steep hills, gullies, potholes, and a whole lot of mud. For the course we drove HEMTTs—Heavy Expanded Mobility Tactical Trucks. They were ten-ton eight-wheel drive monsters with a wedge-shaped cab, and they could take as much punishment as the course and the driver could dish out.

There is nothing like gunning the engine of one of those behemoths, barreling over a hill, and looking through the viewing window in the floor of the cab to see the ground rushing up to meet you. Driving big-ass trucks through a crapload of mud reminded me why I joined the Army in the first place.

Toward the end of our training we were called into one of the classrooms, and informed that the war against Iraq had begun. The Air Force had already started flying sorties to bomb key Iraqi targets. We would be receiving deployment orders, and we would be joining the fight in a very short time.

I walked outside and stood, letting the enormity of it sink in. Dad had said he served in Korea and Vietnam. If so, his advice and insight could be valuable, but of course there was that same question as to whether he had really served or not. Besides, whenever he spoke of his military past, whether real or imagined, his mood grew dark and even more intense than usual.

One of the female trainees came out and we talked for a while. "It doesn't seem real, does it?" she said. I agreed, it didn't seem real at the time.

Reality wouldn't take very long to sink in.

I informed Makala of what was going on, and I finished my training with the rest of the class. I soon received my license to operate light and heavy vehicles, and shortly thereafter we were issued our deployment orders.

A charter bus would take us all to Fort Jackson, South Carolina, our departure point.

When the bus arrived, alcohol was acquired for the 11-hour trip. There was a sense of finality as we set out. The alcohol, paired with the air of a communal date with destiny, provided an atmosphere unlike any other. The men and the women on the bus soon found comfort with each other, and at least one couple openly had sex during our travel.

I chatted with my friend Kurt for a while, then sat next to the female who had spoken to me outside the classroom not long before, and we shared each other's company for the remainder of the trip.

By the time the bus arrived at Fort Jackson, we were fatigued, inebriated and exhausted; spent, both emotionally and physically.

* * *

The clock ticked away, preparations were made. Some people tried to find a way out, without any luck. Soon we were all on a commercial flight to Saudi Arabia. It was one of the most bizarre, yet inspiring flights I've ever been on. The flight attendants played patriotic videos on a big screen and sang, and we all sang along. Lee Greenwood's "God Bless the USA" must have played 50 times during that flight.

Once we landed in Saudi Arabia, we were transported to an airfield where C-130s waited. We were separated and given our unit assignments. Kurt and I were disappointed to find that we were being sent to separate companies. We had gone through basic and AIT together, and we'd hoped to serve together in the war, but it wasn't meant to be.

We said our goodbyes, and I piled into the C-130,

sat against the netting, strapped in, and before long we were off.

We landed in the evening and caught another transport. En route to our destination, a Hispanic soldier kept saying, with a crooked smile, "we're riding into the eye of the storm." Soon we had arrived at a massive tent city. It felt like its own bustling little community. We were told we'd spend the night there, and proceed on to our assigned company the next day. We were also told that there had been warnings of possible SCUD missile launches—these were the missiles everyone believed would deliver chemical agents. Soon we bunked down for the night. Noise from air traffic overhead was constant. One of the soldiers next to me was so scared of a missile attack that he slept with his gas mask on. I didn't, but I slept with it in my hands, out of its case.

Most of the next day was spent waiting, until finally the time came to move on. That evening I was stuffed into the back of a five-ton truck, along with about 14 other soldiers. We had a long truck ride ahead of us through the night. After the first few hours, people basically made room wherever they could, even if that meant sleeping partially on top of someone else.

Hours later I arrived at my company, 84th Transportation, literally out in the middle of the desert. There was absolutely nothing to see on the horizon other than sand in every direction. I had no idea where we were, other than the fact that we were still in Saudi Arabia. Introductions were made, I was shown to my cot, and I started to get my bearings.

There was a small group of tents—larger bunk

158

tents, one for males, one for females, a separate tent for officers with slightly better accommodations, a mess tent, supply tents, fuel bladders, hastily constructed latrines. This would be my home for... well, I had no idea for how long.

What followed was a long period of inactivity. I mostly kept to myself, especially at first. Our platoon leader was a real hard-ass but he was pretty good at chess—one of the many diversions the soldiers engaged in to pass the time. There was also reading, cards, singing, and more physical exercises.

Every once in a while I had an opportunity to ride with someone on a supply run. On one particular trip into a nearby town, I rode shotgun as part of a convoy. The driver was a female named Donna. We stopped to drop off our supplies, and Donna removed her kevlar helmet, revealing red hair. The Saudis were amazed. They had never seen a redhead. Some of them were superstitious. One of the soldiers later told me that red hair was believed to be connected to witchcraft. I don't know if that's true or not.

On the way out we decided to eat some local food. Walking into the eatery, I saw something I'll never forget—a monkey, sitting outside the door, a rope tied around its neck. We ate chicken and rice that was a delicious departure from our normal meals of MREs and Dinty Moore stews.

After dinner I purchased an entire box of Snickers from a nearby shop. As we drove out of town, we tossed bags of M&Ms from our MREs to children who ran alongside the trucks shouting and waving their arms. It was a small gesture, but it left me with a good feeling.

Back out in the desert, we asked when we would get some orders, when we would see some kind of activity. The Master Sergeant believed that we would get some news in the next week or so. Time seemed to crawl. Soldiers traded magazines for MREs. *Hot Rod* magazines with girls in bikinis were a favorite.

Days passed, and I accompanied a group of soldiers to a small sand drift not far away where we were given a chance to fire a .50 caliber machine gun from a turret. The turret was mounted on the passenger side of a five-ton. You stood inside a ring and gripped both handles of the monstrous weapon. It made a sound like deep thunder. We were told that it was against the Geneva Convention to shoot a human being with a .50 cal because it would rip them in half.

More time elapsed. I accompanied Donna on a supply run to a nearby company. As I was backing the truck up, Donna was spotting me. She called out, "stop, Yaki!" A sergeant nearby asked what she called me. She said my name was Yakimoki. The soldier said "Yakky monkey?" and had a good laugh. I was stewing about it on the ride back but Donna put me in good spirits. She and I made a good team.

At night we rotated shifts for guard duty. Two of us were on duty at any given time. We were given night vision goggles which we used to watch the perimeter. We would walk through the camp and keep our eyes open for any signs of enemy activity. We were told that our weapons, however, were not to be loaded. We carried magazines in our cargo pockets.

One night as I walked with another E2 rank, I looked over and spotted several figures dressed in black emerging from behind a tent. My heart raced as I searched for my magazine, slammed it into my rifle and prepared to swing the weapon around when one of the onrushing figures called out in a voice I recognized that they were friendlies, playing a prank by raiding the female tent—a good way to get themselves shot. The rule of not keeping our weapons loaded probably saved their lives, but it also made me realize that if the enemy got that close, I wouldn't have time to lock and load. I kept a magazine in the weapon during guard duty after that.

Days later I was driving as part of a convoy on a supply run. We slept in our cabs overnight in the middle of the desert. Perimeter alarms were set up to detect missiles overhead. In the middle of the night, the alarm went off, even though I didn't hear it. I awoke to a Specialist (E4 rank) pounding on my door yelling for me to get my mask on. Less than ten seconds later I had donned it. My co-driver and I waited for several tense minutes before being told that it had been a false alarm.

Though we all understood how potentially lethal an engagement with the enemy might be, at times the waiting, the anticipation almost seemed worse. Everyone in the company wanted to know when we would get orders, and all the Master Sergeant could tell us was that we would know something when he did.

I was driving with Donna again, part of a convoy, when we took a small detour on the way back—"off roading" into a seemingly endless expanse of trackless sand. We sped across the desert, kicking up brown dust and weaving through the billowing clouds we left in our wake, a welcome distraction to the tedium of the past weeks.

Closer to our base camp we passed a shepherd ushering a massive flock of sheep. It looked like something straight out of the bible. I was struck by how ancient and enigmatic the land was, so close to the birth of many civilizations—Sumer, Assyria, Babylon. There was a dark undercurrent to the region as well, though; unsettling and vexing. I imagined some timeless god, dark, brooding and titanic, sleeping beneath the arid wastes like something out of a Robert E. Howard tale.

I'm sure of course that the circumstances of my stay; the constant threat of imminent danger, had more than a little to do with my unease.

At camp we always spoke of home, and all the things we would do upon our return. I received a letter from Makala, and I was grateful for it. I was grateful also for a letter I received from an elementary school class, offering me, some faceless and unknown soldier, best wishes. Though I had been in Saudi Arabia only a month, it already seemed like a lifetime. I tired of waking up to the same flat horizon day after day and I wondered how much longer we would have to sit and wait.

Then, in late February, a briefing was held. We gathered in one of the largest tents, and there we were told that we would be driving into Iraq.

The ground war had begun.

CHAPTER EIGHTEEN:
DEATH HIGHWAY

We would be going in a few days behind the First Brigade Task Force, providing a continuous supply line and logistical support. The Chaplain gathered us all together, and told us that we fought to preserve our country's freedom, that our cause and our mission were noble and just. He also said that not all of us would return home from this mission, and offered his time to anyone who wanted to make their peace. As we prepared to depart, we all knew that for any of us, the end of the road might come soon.

It was well into the night when we set out. We would drive in a convoy, relying on the moon and special headlights that would illuminate reflectors on the back bumper of the truck in front of us. The headlights were difficult for an enemy to spot. However they also didn't reveal a whole lot of what was in front of you.

As we set out, I was toward the back of the convoy, and when I crested a small rise I saw a long, long line of trucks, their headlights casting a glow on the reflectors before them: a softly luminescent daisy chain stretching for miles over the night sand.

We drove, and drove, and drove. Sometimes stopping for long periods. At one point I closed my eyes and awoke to a hand slapping the door of the truck, signaling me that it was time to move on.

It was a harrowing journey, but we continued on until sunrise the following day. I switched out driving duties with a fellow soldier, but slept only in minute snippets.

In a combat situation, while in a convoy, all of the drivers were trained what to do if a certain signal was given that an enemy might be present. Every truck would pull to the side, facing forward at an angle, opposite the side of the truck in front of it, and the co-driver would have their weapon ready.

At one point the following day, the signal was given. Each truck did as the driver was trained, and soon we were at the side of the road, sitting idle. I was on the passenger side, M16 across my body, barrel pointing out the open window. There was a drift flanking the road, and all eyes were on the crest, waiting for a sign of enemy forces to come over the hill.

Once again I was transported back to Arizona, back to that hill as I lay there with an unknown man in the sights of my rifle, not knowing if Dad would give the signal, not knowing whether or not I would be capable of pulling the trigger. The difference was, this time, there was no doubt. The first head that popped up on that rise would get a bullet through it.

We waited for what seemed like forever, though it was probably no more than ten or 15 minutes. Soon the order was given to continue on.

I don't remember which day it was when we

reached the blacktop, but at a certain point the convoy moved onto a ribbon of pavement that cut a straight path through the desert for several miles. I vividly remember the first body I saw. We passed a truck that was pulled off to the side, door open, and there was something lying beside the road. We drove slowly, and as we passed, I saw what looked like a person. But it couldn't be, it just didn't look right.

The driver said, "That's a body."

I said, "What? No…"

The closer we came, the more I could see: red pants, a greenish brown jacket. He had black hair and a mustache. His skin was ashen. He was lying with his arms spread to either side, one leg out, one knee up. The first dead boy I ever saw, and I'll never forget it.

There would be many, many more on that highway. I learned later that it had earned the name "Highway of Death" or "Death Highway."

I was on the passenger side as we drove on, passing more and more carnage: trucks that were nothing more than blackened remains, some with figures that were barely recognizable as human sitting slumped against the steering wheel; ruined bodies and ruined vehicles strewn to either side of the road and across the sand; a bus with a hole the size of a child's trampoline straight through the middle of it; the occasional light armored vehicle; something that I couldn't even recognize at first, but realized upon closer scrutiny was simply a lower torso and a pair of legs. Sometimes we had to steer around bodies in the road. We didn't stop; we didn't exit our vehicles. We kept moving steadily on.

As night fell it was my turn at the wheel. At one

point I drove over something, something not completely solid. I tried not to think about the possibility that I had just driven over a corpse. Soon the vehicles were fewer and farther between. We continued on. Death Highway was behind us.

That highway weighed heavily on my mind as the sun rose. How many soldiers died, but how many civilians as well? How many more would die? I wondered; if Dad really had served in the military and had seen the kinds of things I saw, maybe that was at least partially what made him the way he was. If he was even slightly mentally unstable to begin with, maybe the horrors of war had sent him over the edge.

Later that day we reached a point where we could finally stop and rest. We started to hear rumors that the Iraqis were giving up. We even heard a rumor that a group of them had surrendered to a camera crew.

That evening we came to a place where Iraqi POWs were being held. There were basically rings of concertina wire with people sitting or milling around inside, guarded by soldiers standing just outside. The wire didn't rise much past the knees of a standing POW, but it certainly didn't look like anyone might try to escape. Our job was to load up POWs and move them out to another facility. Of course, most of them didn't speak English, but as we loaded prisoners one of them spoke to me. He was an English teacher, and he told me how much he hated Saddam Hussein, that he was happy we were there; that we were doing the right thing. He gave me an Iraqi coin and thanked me as I helped him into the back of the truck. We drove to our destination, and when we dropped off the POWs, I wished the English Teacher luck.

Soon after, I was partnered with a new co-driver temporarily, and we ran supplies along a dirt road where oil had been poured to prevent the trucks from kicking up dust. It also made the roads slick and challenging to navigate, but I learned quickly.

We drove several supply runs, always conscious of the fact that we were in the heart of enemy territory, always on a state of high alert. The only injury our company had suffered at that point was a cut face from the side mirrors of two five tons colliding as one truck passed the other.

Then it was announced that the ground war was over. We would be staying in Iraq for a while, but our mission would be to run supplies out as various units departed the theater.

It was on one of these missions, hauling tents, that I was partnered again with Donna, the red-haired female whose company I enjoyed. We were toward the back of a convoy on one of the main routes, a two-lane highway with steep embankments on either side. It was nighttime and I was exhausted, so I lay down on the passenger side and went to sleep.

I learned later that Donna and a friend were pulling into the opposite lane and skipping forward, then pulling back in, working their way further up in the convoy.

Donna pulled into the other lane, saw a vehicle bearing down on her, and couldn't get back over. She pulled left, off of the road.

I awoke to see the lights on the dashboard spinning, vaguely aware of a tumbling sensation, like being in a dryer. The noise was deafening. We rolled several times, then came to a stop. The vehicle was upside-down, and my right hand was wedged between the crumpled roof and the top of the dash. The windshield was destroyed. My left hand was twisted behind me, and Donna's legs were draped over my shoulder. There was a small fire in the engine.

Then there were several voices. Donna was pulled free, but my arm was still trapped and the pain was incredible. I wasn't even aware that I was yelling until someone told me to stop. My mind raced: if the engine fire wasn't put out and I wasn't pulled free, the vehicle would explode and take me with it.

While one soldier frantically threw sand on the fire, another used a large wrench, trying to create space to get my hand free. Thankfully the sand was enough to smother the fire. Several more minutes passed as soldiers worked to free my hand. I heard a siren. Then, a release of pressure on my wrist. I pulled my arm back to see that my right hand was bleeding profusely. I worked my left hand out from behind my back to see that that it was folded over so my fingers were touching the underside of my forearm. The soldier helping me said, "Do you know your wrist is broken?" Brilliant. I said, "Just get me the f#$k out of here."

Soon I was out of the vehicle and on a stretcher, then I was carried to the tiniest ambulance I've ever seen, a Saudi ambulance. As the ambulance pulled away from the crash site, I wondered if Donna was okay.

CHAPTER NINETEEN:
THE LONG ROAD HOME

I was taken directly to a Saudi hospital. The medical staff was composed of doctors and nurses from all over the world—Korea, China, France. They cut my clothes off of me and continued working busily, and though I don't remember a lot of specifics, I do remember the doctor bending my left hand back into place, straightening my wrist. It hurt like hell, but the doctor informed that at least the wrist wasn't broken. My right hand, however, didn't fare so well: the back of the hand had been lacerated, and the extensor tendon to my middle finger had nearly been severed. The first thing I thought of was that I might never be able to draw again.

I wanted to know where Donna was, but no one could tell me. I hoped she was okay.

The doctors operated on my hand, but confided in me later that they weren't sure if I would ever be able to close my fist or not. Only time would tell. For the short term, however, both of my hands were out of commission. I'd had a mild concussion and my back was in a great deal of pain, but beyond that I came through the accident in pretty decent shape.

A few days later two Americans in suits walked into my room. They were from the Army's CID, the Criminal Investigation Division. It had taken a while for the Army to track down the hospital I'd been taken to. The CID was completing a report on the accident, and they informed me of some of the specifics that I hadn't been aware of. I asked how Donna was.

They told me she was dead.

I couldn't believe what I was hearing. She had been talking, they said, when she was pulled from the wreckage, but she lost consciousness shortly thereafter and never regained it.

They asked me for some details about the accident, what I remembered, and I told them what I could. Then they spoke briefly about Death Highway, asked me if I had nightmares, or flashbacks of what I had seen there. I told them I didn't. And it was true—though I'll never forget what I saw on that stretch of highway, I haven't been haunted by it, something for which I am very grateful.

Before leaving, the investigators told me that I would be transferred soon to an American field hospital.

* * *

I was taken by helicopter to the Army medical unit, the fanciest tent setup I had seen—temperature controlled and comfortable. The doctor checked my wounds to ensure that there was no infection. Then a contraption was fitted on the cast of my right wrist: a rubber band stretched through a pulley attached to my middle finger. I would do several exercises per day, which consisted of flexing my finger down, then allowing the band to pull it back. The cast on my right hand extended halfway up the forearm. I also had a cast on my left, which went nearly to the elbow. This made some of the basics of day to day life challenging, but I managed.

Beyond that, there was nothing for me to do but rest, and read. The Staff Sergeant and Platoon Leader from my unit stopped in briefly, to tell me that they were glad I was okay. We spoke of Donna, and it was clear that the entire company felt her absence deeply. Before leaving, they told me that the unit would be heading back to the States in a few weeks. Whether or not I would end up with them or be reassigned upon my own return, was unknown.

* * *

From the field hospital, I was flown to a large Army hospital in Frankfurt, Germany. They checked for infection and had me continue physical therapy. During the first week there, my wallet, which I kept in a bedside drawer, was stolen. In it I had kept not only my military ID, but also the coin given to me by the Iraqi POW several weeks earlier. It was an irreplaceable item, and to this day I am saddened by its loss.

My recovery was going slowly and though I was determined, there was still a question as to whether I'd ever be able to close my right fist again. I was told I'd be in the hospital for the next few weeks. Frustration mounted, and I needed to get out. I had of course never been to Germany, and was anxious to experience the city. On top of that, however, my birthday was rolling around again and I didn't want to spend it in bed or wandering the sterile halls. Thankfully, I soon got permission for a day pass, and one of the other soldiers staying at the hospital took it upon himself to be my guide.

The first thing we did was go to McDonalds, where I was absolutely astounded to see beer on the menu. Beer. At McDonalds. My guide told me that the drinking age in Germany was basically "when you're old enough to see over the counter." We were off to a good start.

As I drank my beer in "Micky D's," my guide told me about the Red Light District, a section of the city consisting of numerous brothels. Basically, prostitution is not only legal in Germany, it's regulated by the government, which performs mandatory testing for venereal disease on all the service providers.

And so I found myself in a very interesting situation; here I had almost died in a truck accident fighting a war half a world away from home, my arms were in casts, I had an injured right hand that might never again function at a hundred percent... but I was alive, and I was turning nineteen! I found myself evaluating my life and all the things I wanted to do and had never done. Not surprisingly, sex was at the top of that list. And now I had an opportunity to finally check that one off. With a prostitute, sure, but it wasn't illegal, and based on what I was hearing I didn't have to worry about walking away with some kind of creeping funk.

After all I had been through, it sounded pretty damn good to me. But I wanted to see the women before I made up my mind. I finished my beer, and we headed off to wait for a bus.

When the bus arrived, I got up to enter at the front, but my guide stopped me and said we should get on the back. He told me that the way buses worked in Frankfurt, if you wanted to pay you got on in the front, if you didn't you got on in the back. I still don't know if that's true or not, but I noticed other people entering the back and followed suit.

The Red Light District featured several rows of tenement buildings. My guide took me into one of these, and we basically went from floor to floor, walking the halls where women in lingerie stood in the doorways of small rooms plying their trade. I went through a couple of these buildings before a slightly chubby Hispanic woman caught my attention. She was gorgeous, she had curves upon curves, and she promised to find several ways to work around any limitations my casts might pose. I made my decision then and there. My guide assisted in the negotiation then waited outside. A short time later (not TOO short, ahem...) my virginity was a thing of the past.

I spent the rest of my time continuing physical therapy, and toward the end of my stay, I was able to close my fist about ninety percent of the way. The doctors believed that I would regain total function of my right hand soon.

Before long the cast on my left arm was removed, and the contraption and cast on my right was replaced with just a half cast. Then, it was time came for me to fly back to the States.

I stayed at a unit in Georgia just long enough to buy some new clothes (my favorite was a shirt with

Saddam Hussein's head in the crosshairs of a rifle scope and the words "We Aim to Please") and get the official paperwork for my convalescent leave, during which time I would actually be able to go back to California. I also filled out my "wish list" for where I wanted to be permanently stationed. At the top of the list was Hawaii. I'd never been, but of course it seemed like a dream assignment. I had no idea where I'd end up; for the time being I was just looking forward to some R&R.

In *Wizard of Oz* Dorothy said "there's no place like home." She couldn't have been more right. When I came back to those old familiar streets and neighborhoods there was an absolute feeling of being exactly where I belonged. One of my first stops was Makala's house. She welcomed me back, and I spent a few hours catching her up on the craziness that had been the last six months.

Makala and I went to pick up groceries, and at one point she took a corner going a bit too fast, and I had a sudden flash of the truck barreling off of the road, rolling into the side hill. My heart raced. I forced myself to put those thoughts and fears outside of my head. It wouldn't do to go through life being afraid of erratic driving.

Soon it was time to meet up with Sammy, Eric, and Rider. Tony was on active duty and wouldn't be able to take leave in time to get there before I left. Regardless, the decision was quickly made that we all had much to celebrate: I was alive, I was back, and I was nineteen. It was party time.

And so we threw the rager to end all ragers. The Brothers and my old friends from the movie theater showed up at Makala's house and we cut loose until the wee hours of the morning. There were people hooking up left and right. At one point, Eric camped out in front of Makala's doorway, waiting to put the moves on her. It was debauchery on a grand scale. Sammy fashioned a Samurai helmet from a beer case box and drank from a Viking-style horn he had gotten at Renn Fair. Epic amounts of alcohol were consumed, and billions of brain cells were obliterated. Amazingly, we all survived to drink another day.

I wrote a letter to Dad catching him up on what I had been through, and I spent much of the remainder of my time hanging out with Sammy. It was just like the old days, although the Army had changed me a bit—I was a little more hot-tempered and foul-mouthed, and Sammy noticed. I wasn't really aware of it until he said something.

At one point when I went to the park with Makala and Fred, Fred pointed a toy gun at me. I yelled at him and took the gun away, and later that night I took a hard look at my behavior. I also vowed to be more mindful of those types of outbursts.

The rest of my leave went by way too fast, and before I knew it, the time had come for me to say goodbye to everyone once again. Makala and I had gotten along well, and as before, she told me that there would always be a home for me with her. I exchanged handshakes and hugs with the Brothers, and I was off.

I soon found myself back in Fort Jackson, South Carolina, but this time I was there awaiting assignment to my permanent duty station.

In the meantime, I received my military paycheck, which reflected the hazard pay from the war. Suddenly I had money to spend; more money than I had ever made at the movie theater, and certainly more money than my Dad and I ever possessed. I bought a gold chain necklace, something I had always wanted but could never before afford. I was also a huge fan of *Top Gun*, and did my damnedest to look like Maverick (Tom Cruise, for anyone who doesn't know. Also for anyone who doesn't know, shame on you). I bought a leather flight jacket and Ray Ban sunglasses, then struck up a friendship with some of the other soldiers awaiting assignments. We bar-hopped nightly.

On one night in particular, we had been drinking heavily and one member of our party got into it with a member from another group of soldiers, and pretty soon they were fighting in the street.

The fight went to the ground, and when it did one of the other guy's buddies walked over and kicked my friend in the head. I shouted at him and he approached me, threatening to knock my teeth in. I rolled my eyes as if to say "you don't stand a chance, pal." Now... I'm going to dispense some self defense advice here that, while obvious, is still worth mentioning: don't ever take your eyes off your opponent. As I made silly facial gestures, he took the opportunity to crack me in the mouth. I fell back and hit the base of my skull on the bumper of a parked car and was out cold. My only contribution to the fight was that I drew the honorless scumbag off of my buddy, but at least that was something. Of course, the thought that I had no business getting into any kind of altercation, with my hands still on the mend, never crossed my mind.

I woke up a few minutes later with a sore mouth

and a throbbing head. One of my other buddies had laid down an ass-whooping and the fight had broken up.

A few days later, my orders came in. I got the top pick on my wish list: Hawaii! My buddies were all jealous. I was elated. When I got back to my locker (which I hadn't purchased a padlock for), my leather jacket was gone. Stolen. In the pocket had been my Ray Bans. Crash and burn, huh Mav? Oh well, at least I was headed to paradise!

CHAPTER TWENTY:
LOST IN PARADISE

Upon landing on Oahu I was sat down in an Army classroom with several other new arrivals where we were all given an orientation. The biggest takeaway was that we mainlanders would be known to the locals as "haoles" (pronounced "howl-e") and that the name had negative connotations. What it really boiled down to is that most Hawaiians wanted the islands to be autonomous, and there was a fair amount of resentment over being a sovereignty of the US.

Tourists were treated very well, of course, partially because they pump a lot of money into the economy. Military folks, however, weren't as well received and were oftentimes targeted for assaults and sometimes worse. To be fair, drunken military personnel were known for starting trouble as well, so it wasn't a one-way street. Whatever the case, my first impression of Hawaii was a warning by the military basically telling us: "you're not all that welcome here."

Next I went through processing at Schofield Barracks for the 25th Transportation Company. A PFC showed me around the barracks, which were different from what I was used to. It was a two-story building with a "lanai," basically a balcony that wrapped around the second story and overlooked the courtyard. The weather was, of course, perfect. At this point I was thinking to myself, *warnings be damned. This is gonna be awesome.*

I was assigned to a platoon and quickly fell into the routine of PT, motorpool (where we did basic maintenance on our vehicles) lunch, motorpool again, dinner and then usually hanging out in the barracks drinking.

There was a serviceable gym directly across the courtyard and I was happy to get back to weight training. I can be fairly quiet, especially in a new environment so people don't always warm up to me right away. It was the same here, where I didn't start making friends until I became comfortable enough to speak up and really start engaging with people.

I hit it off most with newcomers to the company, like Delarosa, for instance: an above average height, tattooed student of human behavior who enjoyed heavy metal and had half the company convinced he was a devil worshipper (he wasn't, but he found that allowing people to think that he was instilled an instinctual fear in them that he enjoyed).

There was an old-fashioned dojo that was close enough for me to attend classes a few nights a week. It was Okinawan Kenpo, and had quite a Japanese pedigree. The instructor had been training most of his life and, as you would expect, was amazing. The students were a mix of locals and military, and they made me feel like part of the family almost immediately.

I made a few additional friends and some connections with some of the females at the barracks. One character who started hanging around with us was Gibbs, an intelligent guy who was in his thirties and gave less than a crap about being in the military. He never missed an opportunity to flout authority. Case in point: there was the time he was walking back from the mess hall and he passed an officer, but didn't salute. The officer dropped him for pushups. When Gibbs stood up, as the officer was turning to leave, Gibbs pointed to the officer's hat and told him "excuse me sir, I just thought you should know your rank is on upside down." Now the officer was a first lieutenant. Their rank symbol is a single vertical bar, straight up, straight down. The officer removed his cap, looked at the rank, shook his head with a smirk, then turned and walked away. He'd been had, but he took it graciously.

Gibbs was dying to go back to civilian life. The daily grind of permanent duty was soul-leeching to him, and it wasn't too long before I understood where he was coming from.

I lived for the evenings I could go to class. One weekend at a beach party, one of the soldiers got a few drinks in him and decided he wanted to fight me. Every time he rushed in swinging I side kicked him. He tried the same tactic about five times before he gave up. The next day he could barely move. Gibbs had watched the display and decided to join my Kenpo class. It was a welcome diversion for him, and it was nice for me to have a training partner in the company.

We had an opportunity to drive the five-ton trucks in convoys around the island every week or so, but for the most part, the daily routine remained constant. And boring. I started to build up quite a movie collection, to the point where my room in the barracks became the local "Blockbuster" rental. I even had a sign-out sheet. The weather was amazing, but I've never been a huge fan of the ocean. I hate digging sand out of every crease in my body. I never tried surfing and had no interest in it. Waikiki was a fun city, but the club/bar scene got old pretty quick.

I wondered exactly what I was accomplishing. I was making a steady paycheck, but it felt like my life wasn't really going anywhere. Somewhere I read once that there are two very broad types of people in the world: competitors and achievers. Competitors feel fulfillment when they beat someone at something; achievers feel fulfillment when they accomplish something (personally I would add a third type—"loafers," who don't want to compete or achieve). After years of trial and a whole lot of error I came to realize that I'm an achiever. I need to feel like I'm making some kind of progress toward a goal. If I don't feel that forward momentum I get anxious. Anyway, I wrote Dad a letter telling him how confused I was; that I didn't know if the military had been the right choice.

He wrote back and told me that it had been natural for me to choose the military, that the military was in our blood. He told me to have faith, and to be the best at whatever I chose to do. He told me to be proud, to become an officer. He said that the life ahead of me was whatever I would make it to be. He said there were no limits.

I knew I didn't want to become an officer, but something about Dad's advice sunk in: to be the best at whatever I "chose" to do. That was the key, really.

There were plenty of folks in the Army who were attending college classes at night, working on degrees, thinking about life beyond the military. I needed to think that way; I needed a goal to work toward. One thing I had always wanted to do was write.

And so I bought a computer at Radio Shack, along with a typing tutorial program. I practiced my typing every night without fail. I had a bunch of stories inside my head and I wanted to get them out.

After about a month of typing practice I wrote my first masterpiece. It was set in the late 1700s, a short story about a Franciscan monk who asks to be assigned to a secluded monastery in the Pyrenees Mountains. Unbeknownst to the friar, this particular monastery had been taken over by vampires, who took advantage of its location: wedged in a deep canyon, the abbey never received direct sunlight.

Granted, the concept was a bit hokey, but there are still aspects of it that I like, and who knows, maybe I'll revisit it someday. At the time of course I thought it was brilliant. After completing it over the course of a week, I took copies to my Kenpo class, handed them out, and waited anxiously until the next training session where I was convinced praise would be heaped upon me. One of the students, a high school teacher, handed it back to me, saying it was "neat." He then proceeded to mock vampires. For everyone else who read it, they were polite, but I could tell the response was lukewarm at best.

I resolved to take it out on all of them in class, and to rededicate myself to the craft of writing back in my room.

Meanwhile, Delarosa proposed that he and I

should buy a car. With both of us splitting the payments we could afford it, and we could trade off driving. It sounded like a great idea. Even with the two of us chipping in, however, the best we could afford was a little piece of crap Justy.

After several months on the island, I was no longer one of the new guys. Of course those of us who had been there for a while decided to give the fresh meat as much grief as possible in the motorpool. We had green soldiers fetching left-handed wrenches, blinker fluid, filling tires with "winter air" (that one was awesome—we were in Hawaii for God's sake)... one thing I loved to do was call a soldier's name, then roll under the truck when he came running, call his name from the other side, roll under again when he went around, call out, etc. (and of course pretend to be angrier and angrier—"get over here, what are you waiting for?").

One of the new guys was a meek but lovable character named Birmingham. Delarosa, Gibbs, and I had started messing around with a Ouija board to pass the time, and Birmingham was fascinated by it. We used it several times in the barracks, but it wasn't working as well as I knew it could, so one night we decided to take the next logical step—play the Ouija board in a graveyard, on top of a grave.

The four of us drove out (Gibbs drove the Justy— he was the only one who hadn't been drinking). We arrived at the cemetery, found a grave not far from where we parked, sat down with the Ouija board in front of us, and asked if there were any spirits present. We got an immediate response. We asked several questions, and it soon became apparent that our spirit wasn't

183

necessarily the friendliest soul. Birmingham was skeptical of the whole thing, convinced that we were pushing around the oracle to mess with him. I elected to have a little fun, so of course I asked if the spirit wanted to kill any of us. It said yes. I asked it to move over the first letters of the first and last name of the person it wanted to kill. It went to G. Gibbs started freaking the hell out. "Oh my God, oh my God, oh my God…" I said no, I had asked it to go to the first letter of the *first* name, then the last. Sure enough, the oracle moved over the letter B next. GB… for Greg Birmingham.

Just for the sake of clarity, I asked if Birmingham was the person it wanted to kill, and it answered yes. Now it was Birmingham's turn to be nervous. He took his hands off of the oracle immediately and said that was it, he wanted to go. Everyone else removed their hands from the oracle as well, trying to convince Birmingham that even if there was such a thing as spirits, they couldn't really do anything to him. Then, I looked down at the board, where the oracle was sitting back in the middle. "Uh, guys?" I said, "Wasn't the oracle on 'yes' when we took our hands off it?" I heard Gibbs cry out as he bolted like a shot back toward the vehicle. Birmingham and Delarosa were off immediately behind him, which left me to pick up the board and beat feet after them.

Gibb's hands were shaking on the steering wheel as we drove back to the barracks, and we gave Birmingham crap for weeks, telling him that his days were numbered. He lived, of course, and to this day I still don't know if the oracle moved back to the center of the board on its own that night or if one of the others moved it. I know I didn't.

184

The incident at the graveyard inspired me to refocus on my short story. I spent several days on a revision, which I mailed off to a small horror magazine, along with a black and white illustration of a hooded, glowing-eyed monk. *They'd be crazy not to publish it*, I told myself.

That weekend I hung out with a female soldier, a free-spirited former ballet dancer named Hope. I drove us to a beach party being thrown by friends of hers in Military Intelligence. We all ended up skinny-dipping in the wee hours of the morning. I still vividly remember a heavyset Texan with a Coors in one hand standing buck naked in water up to his knees saying: "Can you believe we're Military Intelligence?" Yes, I could.

When I got back, I found a note from Delarosa on my door. He was pissed because I took the car without telling him or leaving a note, and he'd needed the car that weekend. I felt like crap, and I tried to mend the rift but he wanted out. He signed the car over to me and I kept it, at the cost of our friendship.

Not long after, I received a letter from the horror magazine: they weren't interested in printing my short story. The good news? They liked my drawing! I would receive a check for 10 bucks upon publication. So, my writing needed work, but maybe artwork could lead to something? Who knew.

As 1991 drew to a close, I still had that terrible sensation that my life was aimless. I had really taken to writing but any kind of success seemed so far out of reach. And the artwork... what could I do? How could I make any kind of decent money drawing pictures?

On New Year's Eve, I found myself tagging

along with a group from my unit, folks I didn't normally hang out with, hopping from one club I wasn't interested in to another. It was New Year's Eve and I was bored out of my skull. I wandered into another crappy bar and was hoping to drink enough that I wouldn't remember the night at all when I looked up to see... none other than Tony!

The last time I had spoken to him, before I left for Iraq, he'd told me he was stationed in Pearl Harbor but I had completely forgotten. Even Sammy didn't make the connection that Pearl Harbor and Schofield Barracks were right there on the same island. I couldn't believe it. What were the odds that, on that night of all nights, with thousands of people celebrating in downtown Waikiki I would run into Tony? An old pal from home... just what I needed. It was like a breath of fresh air.

* * *

I started off 1992 with renewed determination. Tony was a great motivator, and had a good head for story. He and I hung out every weekend and brainstormed ideas, but we needed a medium to express those ideas... it quickly became obvious that with my artistic ability and our combined storytelling, comic books would not only be the most logical fit, but would be a ton of fun as well. The problem was, drawing that much would take a heap of time. But what if we could recruit Sammy?

I called the Brother, who told me he had gotten a new job, but he was interested. Sammy had been working at this little video game company called

Silicon and Synapse since December of that last year, and he was having the time of his life, getting paid to draw every day. Most of the art he did was 2D computer art, but it was drawing nonetheless. I remember thinking: *Man I would love to be doing that!*

Of course, I still had almost three years left to serve, so I would have to be content with our comic book venture. Sammy was excited, and pretty soon we had a name (Empire comics, based on the Queensryche song) and a plan: I would pencil, send the pages to Sammy, and he would ink. Tony and I went out and picked up the large lined paper that comic artists use, and we got started with a hero called the Gauntlet. Our main guy was a scientist who had created an indestructible metal, but only enough of it to make one gauntlet for his right hand. We also created a story called Memwipe War, that took place in a post-apocalyptic future where brainwashed humans were controlled by an alien race, challenged only by a small band of freedom fighters.

When I wasn't in the motorpool or working on pencils for the comics, I was at class. Tony joined the class as well and soon became one of the family. He was also quickly becoming a fixture at our barracks, which, while never that exciting to me, was the Four Seasons compared to his ship. At one point one of my roommates took off on vacation, and Tony slept in the other guy's bed. We got a knock on the door early the next morning and I opened it to see a Staff Sergeant staring me in the face, asking if I'd seen one of the soldiers. If this guy found out I had let someone from outside the company sleep in our barracks, I was screwed. The Sergeant looked over to where Tony was

187

lying, in the top bunk with his back facing out, and asked, "Who's that?" I said as matter-of-factly as I could: "Oh, that's Tony." The Staff Sergeant stood there for a brief second with a confused look on his face, said "Mm," and then left.

I couldn't understand why I hadn't gotten busted. Then, it hit me: Almost none of our superiors knew any of us by our first names. Those who knew me pretty well in the military called me "Yaki," but I was "Private Neilson" to all the sergeants and above. The Staff Sergeant who visited didn't know whether "Tony" was a member of our company or not, and didn't want to look uninformed by asking. I had dodged a bullet.

* * *

I soon learned another valuable life lesson: cars like oil. I had driven the Justy without putting any in it, and the engine seized up. I eventually ended up with an Isuzu Pup. It was new, but it was straight out of the factory—no radio, no automatic anything… but it was all I could afford.

Most weekends Tony and I would sit in his vehicle at the end of the airport runway, getting drunk while watching planes depart and land, recording tapes for Sammy, just me and Tone talking about anything that sprang to mind. We endeavored to try every single kind of rum there was, and we were making a hell of a dent in that plan.

When we weren't recording drunken rants, our work on the comics continued. We were going at a decent pace, but we hadn't seen inked pages from

188

Sammy yet. Then we got the phone call: Sammy's Mom had passed away. Tone and I were both devastated. Sam's Mom had always treated us like family.

Tone and I both felt that Sammy needed a get-away. His art gig with Silicon and Synapse was paying off. The company had developed a game for the Super Nintendo called *Lost Vikings*. Brother Samwise was making good money, and he had built up some vacation time. Before you knew it, the plans were set. He would come out to see us in the next month.

I kept plowing away on the comics. Of course, staying up late drawing meant that I was getting less sleep than most soldiers get, which is minimal anyway. I started seeking out ways to catch a few minutes' shut eye at the motorpool without getting caught. Interesting fact about five-ton trucks: there's a tiny space in the undercarriage that you can crawl into if you're skinny enough, which I was. I would lay there for 15 minutes or so, sleep, and come out covered in grease and grime, looking like I was working hard doing basic vehicle maintenance. I pulled this off for weeks, right up to the day of my promotion to Private First Class.

I received my promotion in the morning, and celebrated in the afternoon with a long nap. Unfortunately my snooze was abruptly cut short by the sound of my platoon sergeant shouting, "Neilson! Get the hell out of there!" I'd been caught. This of course led to a half hour ass-chewing, and then a long wait to find out what my punishment would be. I was penalized with a month of steam-cleaning undercarriages. Could have been worse.

By the time Sammy came for his visit, I was

ready to cut loose. Tone and I took Sam to all our favorite spots, and we drank enough booze to fill an oil tanker. The whole time Sammy talked about how awesome his job was. My old foster dad Shawn had always said comic books would rot your brain, and here was Sammy, pulling from all of his favorite influences in pop culture—movies, comics, anime—to create characters and environments for video games. I seriously wondered if I could do that as well. I felt like there was an opportunity here, a huge one. But I also felt like the clock was ticking—that this window wouldn't be around forever.

Sammy left Hawaii with a couple thousand fewer brain cells than he'd arrived with, and I started to think about the fact that Tony would be leaving soon too. He was due to be discharged in July.

The company continued its periodic convoys. Every once in a blue moon, if we were lucky, we'd get a surprise job. I got called on one morning to take part in a convoy transporting special forces trainees from nearby parade grounds to field exercises. I dropped the soldiers off in the morning, then went to pick them up that evening. The process of getting the soldiers boarded in the back of the truck took a while. On one of the days, the truck ahead of me left by the time the soldiers piled in. Since I didn't know the route, I rushed to catch up, putting the pedal to the metal on the freeway. Apparently the troops in the back got jostled pretty good, cause when we arrived at the company, they were pissed. There also happened to be a Captain back there. He had me in the parade rest position, yelling for a good five minutes before going to seek out my Platoon Sergeant.

It turns out there was a final truck in the convoy, that had also fallen behind. This truck was driven by a young guy with glasses who was missing part of one finger. We all called him Nine and a Half. Out on the parade field, the Captain found my platoon sergeant just as Nine and a Half pulled up and offloaded the final few soldiers. At that point the Captain turned and pointed, but he was pointing at the wrong truck. He must have thought I was the last truck, because he was pointing now at the last truck in the queue, the one driven by Nine and a Half.

I waited to see what would happen next, but we were all told to head back to the motorpool. After we had parked our vehicles, I was heading to the office when Nine and a Half came out, head hanging low. As he neared he said, "Man, I just got my ass reamed." He went on to say that he had gotten yelled at for speeding. I thought about it for about half a second before responding, "Well, you were driving a little fast."

* * *

For longer convoys, I had found that when I sat in one position for extended periods of time, my back started to hurt like hell. Over time that situation didn't improve. I went in to see the doctor, who referred me to physical therapy.

Tone and I continued to pound away at the comics during the remainder of his time on the island, but all too soon it seemed, the time for his discharge came. He promised to get with Sammy and keep things moving on the comic front, and then he was gone.

Without Tone around to inspire me, my own progress on the comics slowed. I continued physical therapy for my back, but the next time we went on a long convoy, I had the same pain. Martial arts class didn't hurt my back at all, but driving for more than a half hour caused me problems.

Several weeks later Tone wrote me a letter saying that Sammy was swamped at work. The company had put out *Lost Vikings* and it was a big hit. They were already working on a sequel. I felt that needling sensation once again, that there was a window of opportunity that would draw to a close if I didn't act soon.

I called Sammy and asked him if he thought there was a chance I could get a job at Silicon and Synapse. He said I'd have to learn how to draw on a computer, which had its own set of challenges, but I had natural talent, so yes, there was a shot.

That was all I needed to hear. I bought a book about back pain, and found that it's really difficult to effectively diagnose and treat. That was it. That was my way out. I would have to make the pain out to be worse than it was, but if it resulted in a medical discharge and gave me a shot at the Silicon and Synapse job, it would be worth it.

* * *

The last half of 1992 was a blur of doctor's appointments, X-rays, and more physical therapy. At every turn, I told the doctors that nothing was working, and that the pain was preventing me from doing my job. The process dragged on for months.

In the unit, the overall opinion of the soldiers turned against me. There was a camaraderie among everyone, a pride in doing the job. In their eyes, what I was doing was an act of betrayal. Some of them knew that I still attended martial arts class, even though I had been issued a doctor's note saying I couldn't run or do push-ups, and that made matters worse.

I considered quitting the class, but the folks there were now my only friends. Gibbs was still on my side, but aside from him I had become persona non grata to pretty much everyone in the company. There were several times I tried to tell my fellow soldiers that I was proud to have served my country—I still am—but that I felt there was another life waiting for me, one that was slipping further and further from my grasp every day. Those sentiments fell on deaf ears.

I hung out with students from my class on weekends, and I kept my eye always on the goal: get out of the Army, get a shot at working for the video game company. That was my focus, my purpose, and I was determined not to let anything deter me.

As 1992 drew to a close, I was issued a paper saying that I didn't have to do PT, and that my driving was limited to 15 minutes.

By the end of the year I was taken off of motorpool duty altogether. The end was in sight.

* * *

Early 1993 saw me assigned to the BOM Squad—it sounded really impressive until I told people what it really meant: B.O.M. stood for "Barracks Office Maintenance." Basically it was a small team composed of other folks who were on their way out of the Army for one reason or another, tasked with the job of maintenance and upkeep around the company. We learned how to change out light switches, ceiling tiles, outlets, fluorescents, faucets, even toilets.

I kept in contact with Sammy. His company was putting the finishing touches on a game called *Rock and Roll Racing*, and he was loving life. I told him that I would be joining him soon. Word was that my medical discharge would go through, it was just a matter of time.

Tom Petty sang that the waiting was the hardest part, and boy was he right. It had already taken six months for me to get as far as I did, on the verge of being released, and time continued to drag on. The only things keeping me sane were martial arts, writing, and drawing.

And then finally, mercifully, I received the greatest news ever. My orders came through. I would be medically discharged from the Army on May 3rd… my birthday! What were the odds of that? It was the greatest present I could imagine.

CHAPTER TWENTY-ONE:
CHAOS

My transition processing took a little bit longer than expected, but by June of '93 I was back in Cali.

The first thing I did was go see Makala. She offered me a place to stay if I could pay rent each month. I agreed. My separation pay totaled a little more than $6,000. Within a few days I had reimbursed Makala the amount she had spent on the Demon years before.

With the home situation sorted, I turned to Sammy about the job. He advised me that I would need to spend time learning how to draw on the computer. It would take a while, but we could work on it at night and on weekends.

Later in the week, he took me to a building in Irvine. Inside was a cluster of offices, the walls plastered with posters of everything from games and movies to scantily clad babes. Sam led me to the office he shared with two other artists and said I could practice on his computer. That's when I looked over to see one of the potted plants outside the doorway rustling. Then suddenly, out popped a thin young guy in a kimono, doing an amazing imitation of a velociraptor from *Jurassic Park*. It was Roman Kenny, one of Sam's fellow artists. Roman not only worked late most nights, but quite often slept in the office in his kimono. Roman was a complete nut, so of course I liked him immediately.

Nowadays artists have tablets and special pens that they use for computer illustration. Back then, you drew with the mouse. The first few nights I went in to practice were spent just getting accustomed to using the mouse as a pencil, pen or brush. That, and learning all the ins and outs of the 2D paint program all the artists worked with.

Sammy was right, it was going to take a while for me to become proficient enough on the computer to have a real shot at landing the job.

In the meantime, whenever someone at Silicon and Synapse threw a party, Sammy invited me. As you would expect, these people knew how to have fun. I started getting to know the other folks Sammy worked with, including the president, Allen Adham, and the other founders, Mike Morhaime and Frank Pearce. Allen was mild mannered and highly intelligent. He had a magnetic presence. Mike could be a "difficult read" at times, but he came across as sincere; genuine. Frank was the most boisterous of the three. Where Allen was soft spoken, Frank was outspoken. He gave his unvarnished opinion, and he gave it loudly. Despite any personality differences, however, what these three young guys all shared was an unflagging passion for making video games.

Outside of the work parties, I reconnected with Rider, Tony, and Eric. Tone was anxious to get back to our comic project, but I had to prioritize; keep my eye on the ball.

Sammy showed me the Super Nintendo games the company had completed and gotten awards for, like *Lost Vikings* and *Rock and Roll Racing* (a racing game with rock music, which amazingly, no one had done yet). They were fun games to play, and of course there were a ton of other games there as well. It took a great deal of willpower for me to balance "play time" with actually learning the craft of computer art.

The trickiest thing I had to learn was called anti-aliasing. It's basically a method of positioning different colored pixels in close proximity to create a desired effect. Highlights, shadows, backlighting—all sorts of tricks were achieved with anti-aliasing, and it was taking a while for me to get the hang of it.

At home, Makala informed me that she was a month behind on her mortgage, and she wasn't going to be capable of making her payment. I saw an opportunity to make up for being such a shit to her before joining the Army, so I gave her the cash she needed. My separation money, however, was running dry. By this time my vehicle had been shipped over from Hawaii, along with all of my other personal goods (a bunch of my movies were missing, including all of my Jean Claude Van Damme flicks. Man, I was pissed. After all, some things are just sacred). I had decided to put my driving experience and my vehicle to use by getting a temporary job to pay the bills until I could interview for an artist position at Silicon and Synapse.

And so I got a job as a courier—mostly it consisted of picking up and dropping off blueprints from a lithographic company to the architects. Sometimes it involved transporting packages from pharmaceutical companies. It wasn't the most exciting vocation in the world, but it would pay the bills.

Shortly after starting, I was informed that they needed someone to drive to San Diego every day for the next few months. Not only would I be working late with Sammy, but I'd be waking up at 5:00 every morning to make the nearly two hour commute. I said I'd do it.

And that's exactly what I did. For almost a month, every weekday. It was an incredible pain in the ass, and there were days when I would slap myself repeatedly in the face so I wouldn't fall asleep on the freeway. But I had changed. I was actually being... responsible. No matter what, I woke up every day and I got the job done. It felt good. I had come a long way, but there was still the ultimate goal before me: get the job at Silicon and Synapse.

One night I drew a dragon head on the computer. Highly detailed, with the proper light and shadow, all brought to life through anti-aliasing, and that was it. Sammy told me I was ready to interview.

* * *

I sat down in an office with Allen Adham, who knew me pretty well at this point from the various times we had all hung out. He had taken a look at the sample I'd done and liked what he saw. He asked me some questions, the most important one being: do you love playing video games? I answered an emphatic yes and told him about the games I had been playing recently. He asked a few more questions, and then it was time for me to take the drawing test.

We went into an empty office with a single table, where I was given a stack of blank paper and my choice of pencils. I would be tasked with drawing a human, a creature-type of my choosing (zombie, alien, whatever), a spaceship, a building, and a landscape. I would have the rest of the afternoon if I needed it. Allen left the room, and I got to work.

Don't screw this up, I told myself. And I drew. And drew, and drew. Sometimes I would get halfway through a sketch, decide it was crap, and start all over. Hours later I was completely drained, and ready to show my work.

Allen looked at each sketch, his face inscrutable at first. Then he pointed out the ones he liked. Looking at the drawings I completed later in the afternoon, he said, "I can tell you started to get tired here." Overall, though, the prognosis was good. Allen told me he'd get back to me soon.

The next few days were murder. I did my courier tasks, but all I could think about was that interview and test. Were the drawings good enough? Did I give him the answers he needed in the interview? I had come so far, and now all I could do was wait.

And then it was time to get the verdict. I figured there were two possibilities: either I got the job or I didn't. Turns out there was a third option...

At that time the situation with Silicon and Synapse was that both Interplay and an educational software (or "edutainment") company called Davidson and Associates were looking at buying the company. Allen explained that he couldn't hire me until events surrounding the acquisition played out. Something else about the company's situation at that time that I wouldn't find out until later: Allen, Mike, and Frank were paying the employees by getting cash advances on their credit cards.

The future of the company was somewhat uncertain, so Allen's offer was this: bring me on board as an intern. This way I could continue to learn, but it was also an "extended interview" opportunity to assess the long-term potential of my employment while the company waited to see how things with Davidson or Interplay would pan out. The catch was, nobody knew how long that would be, and during my internship I wouldn't be making any money.

Despite the unknowns, I said yes immediately.

The courier company was sad to see me go. They even offered me a raise to stay: it seemed they didn't have a ton of employees who had displayed the kind of competence and dedication I had, and that made me feel proud. I kindly declined the raise and walked away.

Next I wrote to Dad, letting him know what was going on, then I spoke to Makala. At this point money was quickly going to be an issue. Up until then I had earned enough at the courier job to pay rent and keep up vehicle payments, insurance, etc. but during the internship I wouldn't have enough money to do both; I only had enough for a few months of truck payments. I asked Makala if she would give me a break on the rent at least until I officially got the job. Makala remembered very well how irresponsible I was in the past, and she argued that there was no guarantee I would even get the job. She could either take the chance, or use that bedroom for another foster kid or maybe even a roommate, where there would be monetary compensation involved. And so she told me to move out.

This put me in a tough spot but Sammy was there for me. His Dad's house had an enclosed back porch, carpeted and everything, and Sammy and his Dad agreed that I could stay there for free until the job came through.

I moved my stuff over to Sammy's house, and my internship began.

At that time there were few other artists at the company. There was Sammy, of course; there was Roman, who would quite often fly one hand around the office as if it were an X-Wing, being chased by the trailing hand, which was a TIE fighter, while vocalizing sound effects (which were pretty spot-on). There was Ron Miller, a tall Scot with a short fuse who would soon become a drinking buddy of mine; there was a Renn Fair chap by the name of Stu Rose, and a tall guy named Joeyray Hall. Joeyray also acted as a sometime receptionist, which was interesting because his favorite phrase was "f#@k you" and his favorite gesture was to flip the bird. Finally there was Dave Berggren, who started showing me 2D animation. Dave was an absolute stud when it came to animating, and the project he was working on at the time was *Death and Return of Superman*, a Sunsoft game for the Super Nintendo.

The company had also recently been asked to develop another superhero-themed game: *Justice League Task Force*. My first training project was learning how to animate the Flash. Sure, it wasn't Conan, but I was a comic book geek all the way through, and working on a legendary DC icon like that was truly a dream come true. I was ecstatic.

Frank Pearce and Mike Morhaime worked on

coding pretty much non-stop (interesting anecdote: Frank also ended up serving as receptionist whenever Joeyray wasn't doing the job. Why two of the angriest employees were chosen to deal with the public is beyond me—probably for entertainment value). Allen did a ton of coding also, in addition to the day-to-day tasks of running the company.

I quickly got to know the other programmers. There was the ladies' man James Anhalt; there was the proud mullet-wearing Pat Wyatt, who lived at the time with Dave and Ron, and then there was Bob Fitch, uber programmer. This guy was a machine and would help to shape the future of the company in a big way.

Rounding out the group was Glenn Stafford, the one-man Sound Team. He created the music for the games, as well as the sound effects. Not only that, he had a great low, deep voice which was used for many of the early characters.

While working on *Justice League* we all learned something very interesting: Superman doesn't kick. Yep, that's what we were told. I don't know if that came straight from DC comics or from Sunsoft, but the art team was advised that absolutely under no circumstances would Superman be allowed to kick. It necessitated some adjustments for Dave, but he adapted and the animations looked incredible.

Meanwhile, I had the opportunity to animate Green Arrow and even Batman (I've always been a huge Batman fan, so that was epic beyond description, even though my Batman didn't end up being used in the final game). Another interesting tidbit: back then, there was not only no Internet, but there was no network linking all of our computers. When an artist

202

or programmer handed work over to a fellow employee, they had to save the work on a three and a half inch disc and walk it over to the other person (Roman would of course fly these to the other person's desk, complete with sound effects).

Roman also started his own side project, "Bitchfighter." As you might guess, it was intended to run on the *Justice League Task Force* engine and would have been comprised of sexy young females wearing variations of almost nothing at all. Roman could draw women better than anyone, and yet, despite enthusiasm for the project from several folks, it never reached climax.

Along with *Justice League Task Force* and *Death and Return of Superman*, the company was finishing up another game: *Blackthorne*, an adventure/puzzle title with a longhaired tough guy toting a shotgun. I was given the task of writing some of the dialogue for the slaves that the hero would come across during his adventures. These lines included such gems as "Curse this terrible life!" and "Could it be? Are you the Chosen One?" We're not talking Aaron Sorkin here but the dialogue was good enough to demonstrate that my writing had potential.

The games everyone was playing at that time were *Xcom* and *Dune II*. *Dune*, based on the series of books by Frank Herbert, was a real time strategy game—a type of wargame where the player builds up forces and collects and manages resources. This particular style of gameplay was a huge inspiration for the team, and provided a major influence for the other big game the company was working on: *Warcraft*.

Warcraft was a departure from the console games

the company had developed up until then—this was a PC game, featuring two major races at war against each other: orcs and humans. Players would be able to choose either side, and build up armies using various resources.

Everybody was excited for *Warcraft*, but no one knew just how popular it would become.

* * *

During this time I still kept in contact with Dad; even spoke to him on the phone. He sounded... old. As usual, he ended every sentence with "praise God." He was proud of what I was doing, and said that he was doing okay, that he was eating right and exercising and stretching and he wanted to make sure I was doing the same. I assured him I was.

By the time October of '93 rolled around, I was getting anxious. *Death and Return of Superman* and *Blackthorne* were in the final stages. Several weeks had gone by with no pay, and my cash reserves were running low. Then, toward the tail end of the month, the verdict finally came in: Davidson and Associates wanted to buy us, and we had accepted. The best news of all though...

I was hired!

My determination had finally paid off, and I vowed to make the most of the situation. Allen and others within the company had clearly resolved to do the same.

First, the company moved offices. The extra space was needed for the new employees (a few more artists and programmers) that were being hired. In those days we didn't hire a moving company. No, we all spent a weekend hauling furniture from one location to another.

Along with the new building we took on... a new name! A lot of people simply didn't "get" the name Silicon and Synapse. So, as we settled into our new, more spacious offices, votes were cast and a list of names was checked for copyright conflict. Among the frontrunners was Ogre Studios, but that was vetoed by our new parent company. Davidson was run by a husband and wife team, Bob and Jan Davidson, and Jan felt that the name was too scary for the kids.

The next runner up was Chaos Studios, and so the choice was made: Chaos it was! We had a logo designed, business cards printed up, we even had a sign made to hang above the reception desk.

And, we hired a few new folks, including an artist who would also sub as a new receptionist! A female, you ask? Of course not! He was, however, a gregarious Portuguese fellow by the name of Brian Sousa.

The company's future, and my own future within it, was looking bright as Christmas arrived. Since I wasn't talking to Makala, I spent Christmas with Sammy's family at his grandmother's house. His grandma knew me very well, well enough in fact to understand that the perfect gift was a bottle of Jack Daniels.

As 1993 made way for 1994, I was the happiest I had been in a very long time.

Come January, we got another new hire: he was a skinny dark-haired kid who was an absolute D&D freak. He brought in an art portfolio filled with giant pencil illustrations of the various characters he and his friends played. There was a very unique style to the artwork, and a sense of detail that reminded me of Roman's intricate pencil work. That kid was Chris Metzen, and over the following years his imagination would prove to be one of the company's most valuable assets.

A new artist we'd hired (not Brian) was let go for being flaky (he would party all night and basically show up whenever he wanted), so Metzen took over his desk in the artist's bullpen with me, Dave Berggren, and Roman. He quickly jumped in on *Justice League* animations, and became one of the guys, quoting movies and "speaking geek" right along with the rest of us.

That same month the company traveled to CES (the Consumer Electronics Show) in Las Vegas. We stayed off the strip in a Motel 6, but... we were in Vegas! Not only that, a few of us learned there was another convention, part of the Adult Video Awards, taking place nearby. A few of us *might* have gotten lost and wandered over to the AVN convention during our stay. Maybe. Who knows? I was drunk most of the trip.

After returning from CES we hired a handful more employees, including, at long last... our first ever female! As you can imagine, she had to put up with a lot, including (several months later) a surprise visit by a stripper. It was a birthday present for one of the programmers, from his dad, to "make a man out of him." The performer arrived, pulled the guy out into the main bullpen, laid him on the floor, and did her routine. Talk about casual Friday!

206

Meanwhile, I had received another letter from my Dad, and this latest was even more inscrutable than others in years past: he said that our "lifelines" were "Atrociously severed by the Innumeral enemys," that our "ESP was WARTORN, WARDAMAGED, Greatly WARABUSED," and that we must "Regenerate Resuscitate Magnetisms Intrinsic Magnitudes" within our "Intrinsic CONCENTRICS."

I was starting to worry that maybe Dad's mental health was declining even further. Not knowing quite how to respond, I sent him a letter basically just giving him an update of how things were going.

And things were going well.

In February, at a Valentines/housewarming party Dave Berggren introduced me to a couple friends of his, two sisters, Sharon and Deborah. Deborah and I hit it off and were soon going out.

At work, well, there were a lot of times when it really didn't feel like work. We were making games, after all. And when we weren't making them, we were playing them.

At this point we were hooked up to a network (no more having to fly three and a half inch discs around the office!). The video game *Doom* came out just before the end of the year, and man we had a blast playing that. It was a first person shooter, which meant your screen showed the point of view of the soldier, running around a complex of tunnels and buildings, blasting the crap out of your fellow players with a variety of badass guns. We would play until the wee hours of the morning, then drift back into work by 10:00 a.m..

During lunch a bunch of employees would sit on

the floor in the main bullpen and play a trading card game called *Magic: The Gathering*. Whoever wasn't playing that was in the break room playing a fighter game called *Samurai Shodown*—one of the most well-made fighting games any of us had ever played, and to this day it's one of the most fun.

We had a blast outside of work too. Dave and I even got to be in a porno!

Allow me to elaborate...

Everyone listened to Howard Stern on the radio, and that's how Dave Berggren heard a casting call for a porno that was being filmed over the weekend. They needed folks to be extras. Both Dave and I felt this was just too good to pass up, so we woke up early on a Saturday, drove out to Van Nuys, and waited in line with a bunch of other guys outside a strip club. We were eventually ushered in, told to sit at the tables and line up at the catwalk as if we were patrons during a busy night.

The stars, Janine Lindemulder and Julia Ann, came out and did a sexy routine while the crew filmed and we all watched. This went on for half the day; then we got some signed posters and left.

The movie was called *Blondage*, and when Dave and I got our VHS copies later that year, we were happy to see that we were indeed visible in a few of the scenes. So... I can say that I've been in a porno! (Unfortunately, Dave has since told me that in the DVD version our parts were cut out. Damn that newfangled technology!)

* * *

208

We were just growing accustomed to the name Chaos when we were notified that there was a conflict with another company. Unless we wanted to pay a large sum of money, we would have to give the name up.

And so, we went through the voting process again. There were a lot of interesting choices, but one in particular stood out to almost everyone, a name that would become legendary in the gaming industry…

CHAPTER TWENTY-TWO:
BLIZZARD

New business cards were printed, a new sign was made: the company was now officially Blizzard Entertainment.

One of our first actions as Blizzard Entertainment was to go to war… a paint ball war against Interplay.

Before the date of the battle, they employed some psychological warfare when they drove by the offices and fired paintballs at the windows. A couple of us got them back by going to their offices in the middle of the night and using sponges to spell out BLIZZARD in water soluble paint across their glass doors. Allen even left his business card. I heard later that Interplay's security company called the president that night and told him the building had been vandalized, but they didn't know who did it. If only there had been clues!

Shortly after that, we had our battle, and we beat Interplay two to one.

By the time of my birthday, things had reached a point between me and Deborah where we knew the relationship wasn't going to progress any further. Over the course of our time together, though, I had come to know her sister better. Pretty soon Sharon and I were going out.

With *Blackthorne* basically done and some work continuing on *Justice League* and *Death and Return of Superman*, focus at work shifted mainly to *Lost Vikings 2* and *Warcraft*.

In July we got another new hire, a friend of Stu Rose's named Bill Roper. Bill, who had been working as a graphic designer and desktop publisher, quickly became instrumental in shaping the story for *Warcraft*. He wrote the manual for the game, drawing on lore and character groundwork laid down by other folks, including Ron Millar.

Everyone was incredibly excited about *Warcraft*. We knew that it was a big deal—it was the first game we had real ownership of. Not only in the sense that we were self publishing it, but the marketing, the packaging, the entire vision of what that game was, came from Blizzard alone. It was truly ours, and for the first time our company's name—instead of Sunsoft's or Interplay's—would be displayed prominently right there on the box. Not only that, but the more we played *Warcraft*, the more we realized that it was really, really *fun* to play.

Soon another artist came on board, a surfer named Nick Carpenter. Nick's art style was super technical, which really lent itself to "the big new thing" that all of us artists would soon be dipping our toes into—3D.

Joeyray had been messing around with different 3D drawing programs, and he found one that would work for all of us. It was called 3D Studio. *Warcraft* was being created in all 2D, but everyone knew that 3D was where the industry was going. Things were changing quickly; the handwriting was on the wall, and the old methods were fast becoming obsolete.

Although no one ever came out and said it, I worried that if I didn't learn 3D, I might be obsolete as well.

3D Studio was an intimidating program. When you first looked at it, the screen resembled the instrument panel of a DC10, and the tutorial book was bigger than Stephen King's *The Stand*. The unabridged version.

As you might expect, this learning phase could become monotonous, so in the meantime several of us chased the occasional diversion—one of these being the Jawa Wall.

The Jawa Wall was a series of yellow sticky notes with a play on the word "Jawa" and a simple drawing that illustrated the pun. For instance, I drew a Jawa with a Mexican sombrero and a donkey called "Jawan Valdez." Other Jawa entries included: "Indiana Jawones" "Jawan Holmes" "Jawoptimus Prime" "Jawassic Park" "Jawawa pedal" and my personal favorite, a drawing of a coffee cup with a Jawa chillin' inside, titled simply "Cup O Jawa."

Star Wars wasn't the only source of entertainment. Bob Fitch was a *Star Trek* nut, which everybody knew. At one point he ventured into the artist's bullpen, and Chris Metzen let loose a barrage of *Star Trek* quips under the banner "Porn Star Trek." The improv performed from his desk suggested that the entire crew from *Next Generation* was engaged in sexual escapades, and of course poor Wesley Crusher took the brunt of the jokes, leading to Metzen's spot-on imitation of Captain Jean-Luc Picard telling Wesley to "bend over and put your hands on the counter!" Poor Wesley's mom, Beverly, was not immune either, as evidenced by a bit where Captain Picard was informed that Beverly Crusher was taking a shower, to which the captain replied "on screen."

Bob was literally on the floor laughing, and yes, laughing out loud. And this was all before leet speak.

We had fun, but we kept working as well, and after about a month, I finally reached a point where I was building geometry in 3D Studio that looked like whatever I had set out to create. There was still a long way to go, but I had gotten over my initial dread of the program itself and its telephone-book size manual.

Before long we hired a specialist in 3D, a tall guy named Duane Stinnett who started working on *Warcraft*. He also took on the role of mentor for many of us. We had been making progress before, but Duane was the one who really raised everyone's expertise to the next level.

Soon I became semi-proficient in creating textures that I would then map onto the surface of the geometry I had built. I reached a point where I could actually create buildings. One of the first things I made was a simple watchtower with a brick texture map. It was very basic, but it was another big step.

It wasn't long before 3D was put on hold as the time came to playtest *Warcraft*. This would be the first of many "crunch modes" for our games—periods of time where basically everybody in the company would play a game until we were ready to send off the gold master for production. Quite often we would stay until the wee hours of the morning, playing, trying to find "bugs" (errors) in the game. The known bugs would be listed on a whiteboard in order of severity, and we'd work through that list until the number of bugs was reduced to only minor concerns that would not prevent us from shipping the game.

This was something that separated us from other

game developers early on: other developers would either ship games when they hadn't taken the time to fully playtest them, or test the games but ship them with outstanding issues anyway. With Davidson, we were in a position to take our time, and do it right.

Warcraft was the first major game that exemplified our "don't ship it till it's ready" philosophy—a doctrine that has made Blizzard one of the most respected game companies in the world, and still holds true to this day.

* * *

When *Warcraft* was finally released in time for Christmas 1994, it was a huge hit. We artists (Sammy and Metzen especially) had developed an exaggerated style for the orcs, humans, trolls, elves and all the other fantastic characters, a style that really resonated and popped off the screen. That slightly over-the-top visual aesthetic would influence every Blizzard game from then on.

The game was innovative in its design, as well. It employed something we called "The Fog of War," which allowed you to see the terrain of the map you were playing on but obscured other players' buildings and units. The game was carefully balanced, and when it was released the world discovered what we had already known for several months: that it was incredibly exciting to play. For every strategy, there was a counter strategy, yet another feature that would become synonymous with Bizzard games moving forward.

Warcraft won several awards, including game of

214

the year. It was a great feeling, knowing that we had all been a part of something that was such a massive success.

Still riding that high, I called Dad to see how he was doing. As usual, he was working on being deported to Peru and wanted me to go. I told him the same thing that I told him before: that I had a life, but now it was much more than that—I was finally succeeding at something. I had a girlfriend. And I was happier than I had ever been before.

I could tell that Dad was in low spirits, and I really didn't know what to do. I simply wasn't going to lie and tell him I'd love to relocate to Peru. I tried to placate him as best I could but I knew that the damage was done.

I received several letters from Dad that December. In the first, Dad reiterated that Mom had been assassinated by the government, and that their last names had been changed to Zeilzonahua Quipu so they could act as covert operatives.

The second stated that I didn't need to worry, that he would never interfere in my life.

The next came a few days later and was difficult to read. Dad said that I had no need of him, that he would be returning to Peru soon, and when he did, he would report a second assassination, that of his son Yakimoki.

I spent that Christmas Eve with Sammy's family again (and scored another bottle of Jack Daniels from Grandma) and had Christmas dinner with Sharon's family.

Shortly after Christmas, I received more letters from Dad. I had written a response to his last letter and attempted as best I could to explain to him that I did still need him, that he shouldn't feel abandoned. I also told him that I worried about him, but I was frustrated at not getting answers about the rest of my family. Finally I told him that since I was making pretty decent money, I was hoping to come and visit him.

Dad said in his first post-Christmas letter that basically people had been calling him crazy his whole life, and now I was calling him crazy too. He also said that the only thing keeping him going during all those years of being locked up was dreaming about "liberating" me upon his release, and about the two of us continuing our lives and our adventures together.

In the second letter Dad questioned whether or not I was really the same son he had known; he said I was enchanted, consumed and entranced by a world that was not mine... then the tone of the letter changed. I realized that he had received my reply letter as he had been writing. The rest of the letter was cordial, even effusive, though he told me never to visit and not to call because all visits and calls were monitored. He said if I visited my life would be in danger.

Then, just before the end of the year I received one final letter. Dad seemed to be in much better spirits at first. He was being transferred to a lower security unit. Then, as in the previous letter, the tone shifted. He said that he was to be deported to Peru and executed as a prisoner of war. He said if I denounced him, he and I would never be reunited again.

CHAPTER TWENTY-THREE:
TO HELL AND BACK

The second half of Dad's letter was written days later, after the first of the year. He said he tried to call me but couldn't get through (this time he didn't say anything about calls being monitored). He responded to my pleas regarding the truth about our family, saying my grandmother and grandfather were Incans living in Brazil, and that my brother was "Mijikuai Zeilzonahua Quipu" and that he was in a top security sanctuary in "Sidney, Australia." He ended by saying that he wanted me to answer his questions from previous letters, so he could ascertain if I was really his son.

I dismissed the family information as more ramblings, though I didn't say as much in my return letter. I asked him to try and call again.

In his response later that month, he said that because of his impending deportation, I would be rid of him forever, that I would have my own life and profession, that I would have "no more Dad to be ashamed of." He said that he didn't understand my attitude, my statements, my refusal to answer his questions. He said I was trying to outrun my heritage and find a peace and a truth that was never lost.

I really didn't understand how he could tell me the truth was never lost when I had never been able to get a straight answer from him about the things I considered so important. My heart ached and the more I thought about it, the more impossible the entire situation seemed. I decided to focus once again on my work, on the aspects of my life that were bringing me joy.

Even before *Warcraft* launched, we had begun work on the follow up game. *Warcraft* featured buildings and units that were entirely 2D, but for *Warcraft 2* we built the units, buildings and doodads (extra things that go on the map like trees, boulders, etc.) in 3D, then touched everything up in 2D.

One early idea for *Warcraft 2* was that someone opened a time portal and the game would feature jets fighting dragons. That idea was scrapped early on, however.

For *Warcraft 2,* Metzen really took the reins on storytelling (Bill Roper moved into a position as the public face of Blizzard, doing interviews and press tours, evangelizing our products). Chris expanded the overall scope of what was established in War 1, creating a much larger world. He added new races, each with their own unique history, and because War 2 would feature the ability for up to eight players to go up against each other on networks (War 1 supported network play for two players), he created nations and clans with themes that coincided with the different unit colors used to differentiate the players. For instance, the yellow human color resulted in the nation of Alterac, cowards who betrayed their allies. For the yellow orc version, since orcs simply cannot be cowards, Metzen created the Burning Blade clan.

There was a great deal of progress being made on War 2, but as usual, there were shenanigans as well. Particularly between Metzen and Duane. Duane had long, thick, curly hair, and like I said, he was tall. At some point this inspired Chris to draw a caricature of Duane, naked, in the classic "Bigfoot looking over his shoulder pose." That was just the beginning. Somehow this led to the creation of Duanetaur, an elusive half man, half horse, with a dark flowing mane. Duanetaur sightings occurred on a frequent basis as drawings appeared on walls throughout the building.

The mighty Duanetaur would have his revenge, however. I won't go into details, but suffice it to say that the payback involved a Photoshop-ed picture of Chris, and a horse.

* * *

Warcraft, as it turns out, hadn't just gotten the attention of the gaming community. Other studios were impressed by what we had done and came to us with pitches. One of these studios was called Condor, and their pitch was for a turn-based claymation game called *Diablo*.

Allen thought the game showed promise, and he knew the developers were solid (Condor was developing the Sega version of *Justice League Task Force,* a sister product to the Super Nintendo version we were doing). All the Blizzard execs were excited about the idea, but suggested Condor pursue 3D rather than claymation, and go away from the turn-based element. Based on the feedback, the Condor folks started making adjustments.

219

* * *

March saw yet another correspondence from Dad, and this one was the most disturbing and abusive yet. He started off by calling me "interloper." He said those who cohort with the enemy become the enemy. He called me an evil Mormon intruder with no skills, a make believe, phony hypocrite antithesis Yakimoki. He said I had a microchip device planted in my brain. He said he didn't know this fake Yakimoki, nor did he wish to. He said that I had no soul, and that if we should meet, we would engage in war, in a fury of revolutionary conflict.

At this point I was getting completely fed up. Fed up with the lies, the erratic behavior, the riddles. I had pretty much reached the point where I didn't want to see Dad again. As usual, I fell back on my writing, my friends, my relationship with my girlfriend (though we were experiencing rough patches), and my work.

* * *

Blizzard was making solid progress on War 2. While working we passed the time by listening to Jerky Boys (hilarious crank callers who recorded their interactions with clueless victims), Pink Floyd, Beastie Boys, etc. but the most entertainment came from a guy we'd hired to be our IT tech.

His name was Alan Dabiri. We had hired his brother Shane a while before, and whenever Shane entered the artists' bullpen, he was subjected to a merciless barrage of mom jokes. Of course Chris and Nick, the main instigators, were kind enough to tell

Alan "we're talking about Shane's mom, Alan, not your mom."

Nevertheless when it came time for Alan to work in the bullpen, the verbal taunting was handed down. Whenever he entered the room, Metzen and Nick would take the opportunity to let loose. Sometimes Alan would be there for quite a while, long enough for the merciless flogging to eventually trail off. I felt it was my civic duty to keep the status quo, so I'd throw out a small-targeted comment such as "did you hear what he just said?" then sit back and watch the sparks fly all over again.

Eventually the artists saw a picture of Shane and Alan's mom and couldn't bring themselves to bag on her anymore.

Part of what Alan was spending that time doing was hooking all of the company computers up to a glorious new advancement in technology, a real game-changer; the milestone after which no one's life would be the same... the miracle of mankind's evolution known as "the Internet."

How could this technological and societal breakthrough change the face of modern civilization? One word:

Boobies.

Gone were the days of buying seedy magazines, perusing the adult sections of video stores, or recording Saturday night Cinemax on worn-out VHS tapes. Now mankind had access to boobies at a whim. It was, to quote Connor MacLeod from *Highlander,* "a kind of magic."

* * *

During this time period Thursday night was karaoke night. Metzen, Sammy, and Roman especially had amazing voices. A couple of these folks would even go on to become a very unique brand of rock star, but we'll get to that a bit later.

The main thing is this: we all worked together, and we all partied together, and one informed the other. We forged lifetime bonds and friendships, and along with the execs, we were the core of the company. I would even go so far as to say that the foundation of what Blizzard is today was built on a bedrock of karaoke, *Samurai Shodown* and Jack and Coke.

* * *

The only real detours on this rollercoaster ride were the letters from Dad. April brought another, two pages of symbols and foreign language that appeared to be Incan. It looked like some kind of code, but I had no idea what to make of it.

Not long after my birthday, another letter arrived, wanting to know "who killed Yakimoki," and claiming that it would be an eye for eye, a tooth for a tooth, ashes to ashes, and dust to dust. I filed the letters away, out of sight, but not entirely out of my mind. I tried my best to ignore the ramblings, but there was a deep, growing concern that could not be denied.

* * *

At work I hit my stride creating buildings and doodads in 3D, then touching them up in 2D. I had a blast taking a bunch of the buildings we made and painting them to make it look like the lights inside flashed on when you would click on them. The company overall was blazing through the development of *Warcraft 2*.

Something else I was just starting to sink my teeth into right around this time: writing screenplays.

The '90s was a golden era for screenwriting. This was a time when studios were buying spec scripts (meaning scripts that people had written not on assignment, but under the speculation that they would get sold) for six figures. Some scripts even sold for a million dollars. Hollywood was taking chances on all kinds of new, innovative and experimental ideas. I wanted a piece of that pie.

I started brainstorming with Sammy. Our first script idea was a time travel story with a twist: the Japanese discovered the secret to time travel during World War II, and jumped forward to create a virus they could take back to the 1940s to use against the U.S. The script was called *Eternal Sun*.

Screenwriting really is a discipline all to itself, and it's one that takes a great deal of time to hone. The first script we wrote was terrible. We vowed to keep at it until we got it right, but it was clear that learning how to do it right was going to take a while.

As the end of summer approached it was once again a time of great change.

Sam's dad decided to sell the house, so I would need to find a new place to live. Also right around this time, Sharon and I came to the conclusion that the relationship wasn't working out, and that we should go our separate ways.

As luck would have it, a room opened up in a

condo where Joeyray, one of the programmers, and one of the sound guys lived in Irvine. So I rented a room.

Mike Morhaime had a small house just down the street, and he started hosting "*Highlander* Night," where a few of us would get together and watch the TV series on VHS. Sammy and I would buy 40 ouncers and get sloshed, heckling the entire time.

The moving bug hit work too. We were growing fast and needed more room, so it was time to pull up stakes. And yes, we moved everything ourselves yet again. The relocation landed us just down the street, in a business loop called Corporate Park.

August also brought another letter from Dad, written as if the previous threats never existed. Dad wanted to know why I hadn't written, whether or not I was still doing martial arts, writing, etc. Was he playing mind games? Or had he blocked out the tirades from before? Either way, I wasn't ready to talk to him yet.

* * *

Meanwhile, Condor had continued development of *Diablo*, taking into account the feedback we had given them. They had made so much progress and showed so much promise that Jan and Bob Davidson basically said, "Why don't we acquire the company?"

It wasn't too much later that Condor Studios became Blizzard North.

Soon, crunch time came around again. We had knocked out *Warcraft 2* in record time. From what I've been told, the entire development of War 2 took

11 months, a timeframe which, for Blizzard, is pretty much unheard of now. Everything really seemed to come together. The game played well, we put in the necessary crunch to iron out the bugs, and by the time Halloween arrived we were celebrating War 2's completion.

When the end of the year fell upon us the company, as always, was looking ahead. Aside from *Lost Vikings 2* (which was a joint development, so it wasn't really our baby), what was going to be next after *Warcraft 2* and *Diablo*? There was work already being done on an expansion for War 2, but there were other concepts floating around as well.

At one point, we had approached LucasArts about doing a *Star Wars* RTS. Despite genuine interest from both sides, the deal fell through. The idea of doing a sci-fi RTS, however, stuck.

CHAPTER TWENTY-FOUR:
REACHING FOR THE STARS

All the reviews of *Warcraft 2* agreed that the game was better than the first *Warcraft* in every way. With our combined talent and enthusiasm and the backing of Davidson, it seemed there was nothing we couldn't do.

Then we learned that Davidson was being acquired by a company called CUC. We immediately wondered what this would mean for us. Would some suits step in and tell us how to make games, what to do and what not to do?

Allen, Mike, and Frank all shared with the company how important it was for Blizzard to maintain its autonomy. This was something that they would fight for. As the acquisition played out, the rest of us could only continue working, waiting to see how we might be affected.

At this point work had begun on the *Warcraft 2* expansion, *Beyond the Dark Portal*. War 2X would expand the story line and add new maps and new campaigns. The majority of the game design would be outsourced, but developed under Blizzard's watchful eye.

With the *Warcraft* expansion well in hand, the team focused on our next big project. Everyone had been operating in the *Warcraft* universe for quite a while, and the employees were ready for a "change in scenery."

Around that same time, Duane Stinnett built a mech in 3D and generated a walk animation. Sammy went in and gave it the "Blizzard Treatment," blowing out the proportions, and the result was amazing. It showed just a glimpse of what was possible for a sci-fi RTS. The idea had been floating around for a while, but this proof of concept was really the shot in the arm the project needed. And with that, the game we called *StarCraft* was moving full speed ahead.

Chris Metzen and James Phinney were tackling the story for *StarCraft*, and they started working out major races and characters, including the conception of one of the most iconic villains in all of gamedom. There was a character in *Command and Conquer* (a game by one of our closest competitors) called Tanya. This made James think of Tonya Harding, and resulted in the creation of Sarah Kerrigan (for those who remember, Tonya Harding was a skater who was involved in a scandal over an attack on fellow skater Nancy Kerrigan). Together, Metzen and Phinney crafted a storyline that would start off with Kerrigan as a protagonist and end with her ruling a malevolent alien race as the infamous Queen of Blades.

At that time we were also still working on *Lost Vikings 2*, and once again I had an opportunity to write, generating the game's dialogue along with James Phinney.

On my off time, I wrote scripts with Sammy. We

had revised *Eternal Sun* several times and had begun work on another screenplay titled *The Hunt*, a supernatural western. We would craft various story points during lunch hours, heading off to the pool at Sammy's apartment complex, where we would sit, soak up the sun, drink beer and talk story.

When Sammy broke up with his girlfriend and moved out of the complex, we took our sunbathing lunches to a neighboring area. The first day we spotted a Jacuzzi. Sam and I both sat in it, legs straight out in front of us, wondering where the button was to turn on the bubbles. Turns out we were sitting in a kids' wading pool. Despite this early setback, we held many more "business lunches" poolside.

At the condo, Joeyray had moved an old fridge into the backyard, which inspired a party to end all parties: white trash night! We moved the couch and TV into the backyard, ran an extension cord, stuck beers in the fridge, and ate animal crackers, Webers sandwiches and some unidentifiable meat from a bucket while watching *Every Which Way But Loose* and *Deliverance*.

Meanwhile, development of the *Warcraft 2* expansion was moving rapidly. One of the elements of our games that was beginning to show a lot of promise at this time was the cinematics. Duane brought a lot to the table, and he outsourced some work with a friend of his, Matt Samia. Along with Joeyray Hall, Nick Carpenter and others, they were creating some really kickass 3D. That group of artists would go on to form a team dedicated solely to cinematics. Their first official project together would be the 3D "flicks" for *Diablo*.

Warcraft 2: Beyond the Dark Portal was released in April and was a resounding success. By this time our concerns regarding a heavy hand from our new owner CUC, were laid to rest. It seemed that CUC was more than content to let us keep doing what we were good at, and not to interfere with the way we did it.

* * *

In those days the UFC, the Ultimate Fighting Championship, was still fairly new. It was a mixed martial arts competition that many of us at work had been following since it premiered a few years earlier. I was fascinated by the different styles, and back then the guy to beat was Royce Gracie, an average-sized man who employed a fighting style many people had never seen, called Brazilian Ju Jitsu. Royce was winning just about every fight, against opponents twice his size. I thought this was amazing, so I sought out a Brazilian Ju Jitsu school nearby and started classes.

Sharon continued to visit me at the condo every once in a while, but beyond that I didn't have a romantic interest at the time. I continued to work feverishly on screenwriting. Sammy and I finished *The Hunt*, as well as a thriller about a psychic called *The Gift*. I scoured the internet looking for small production companies that would accept unsolicited scripts. We were very excited about the projects, but early on we couldn't find any takers. Despite this, we were already conceptualizing our next script. It was a comedy about a town overrun with vampires, called, aptly enough, *Vamptown*.

229

Not long after, we met Dan Sullivan, a writer from a canceled TV show. Dan was looking at getting into producing. He and his wife invited Sammy and me to dinner, to pitch them some of our ideas. I told Sam before we sat down at their table that we shouldn't mention *Vamptown*, because there was really no story, just some goofy ideas for scenes we thought were funny.

We sat through dinner, pitched the scripts we had written, and got shot down repeatedly. By the end of the evening it seemed like a total bust. As we were about to leave Sammy said: "We did have one more idea, it's about these kids in a town full of vampires..." I thought, *Oh man, here we go, the nail in the coffin* (as it were).

When Sammy was done they sat there for a minute with blank looks, then they turned to each other and smiled. They loved it, and wanted to know how soon we could start writing.

* * *

At work, progress continued on *StarCraft*. We had created three distinct races—humans (or terrans), protoss and zerg. The game's "engine" (the underlying programming) used the same engine as *Warcraft* and was getting close to a playable state.

In May, the company presented *StarCraft* at an electronics show called E3, confident that the response would be huge.

Unfortunately the feedback was not what everyone expected. The game was described as "orcs in space," because it was obvious to players that the game was using the *Warcraft* engine. Despite the differences in appearance and functionality, to many people the underlying game still felt like a retread of what had come before.

The mood in the aftermath of E3 was somber. It was at this point that Bob Fitch, the programmer extraordinaire I mentioned earlier, spoke up and said, "Gimme a month or so and I'll rebuild the entire engine." Conventional wisdom said it couldn't be done, but if I'd learned anything at this point, it was that conventional wisdom didn't always apply to Blizzard.

While Bob isolated himself in his office, the artists worked on the aesthetic of the game. As with *Warcraft 2*, *StarCraft* would feature buildings and doodads created in 3D from concept sketches, then touched up in 2D. Trevor Jacobs and an artist named Maxx Marshall knocked out almost all the zerg buildings, while I took on several of the terran and protoss structures. By this time my skills in 3D had improved a great deal. One area I was still really weak in, however, was animating. I did some simple animations for some of the buildings, but adeptness at complex animation still eluded me.

* * *

In June I got a bizarre letter from a fellow inmate at Dad's prison. He claimed to be a pilot who flew me and Dad into the country in 1978. As I described early on in this book, I did remember being in a plane at some point (and throwing up)... but then the letter went on to say that this guy flew us from Edwards Air Force Base to John Wayne Airport in January of 1983, which I knew was a lie—in '83 we were "hiding out" from the law, probably still in Albuquerque, but I knew we didn't do any flying during that time. The letter used similar language and terminology to that which my Dad often used. Later the "pilot" said that he was framed by Mormons. He said he was being released soon and had agreed to fly me and Dad back to Peru when Dad got out.

My thinking was that the letter was actually from Dad, just using a different style of handwriting. I wrote a cordial letter back, saying that I did not intend to fly to Peru, but thanks for the offer.

Years later while going through legal records I found out that the pilot was a real person, someone who Dad roped into lying to try and get them both deported.

* * *

After two months, Bob Fitch proved good on his word, delivering a completely new engine for *StarCraft*. Soon we were creating builds that were playable once again, and the results were outstanding. The game felt fresh and exciting. We had even changed the perspective from top down to isometric (basically looking down at an angle). It was suddenly light years away from "orcs in space." These changes were a huge leap forward, but as we would discover, the game still had a long road ahead of it to reach completion.

Meanwhile, Blizzard North had made significant strides with *Diablo*. The early levels we played were rough, but even then it was evident that the game would be incredibly fun.

In our off hours Sammy and I worked feverishly on the *Vamptown* script. We cooked up an entire backstory for the vampires, and after a few months we had something resembling a first draft. We showed it to Dan, got notes, and started rewrites.

As *Diablo* neared completion and *StarCraft* development continued apace, there was yet another game in the works: *Warcraft Adventures*.

Many of us had been playing games like *Monkey Island*, *The Dig*, and one of my all-time favorites, *Full Throttle*. They were a particular genre called adventure games, which basically put your character in a situation where he or she had several options, including things in the background you could click on, or combine in order to solve the puzzle and progress to the next level. Many of these games used an animated style so that it was very much like playing a cartoon.

Blizzard wanted to dive into this genre, and so the concept for *Warcraft Adventures* was born. The game would feature a character named Thrall, an orc enslaved by a human, who would escape and lead his fellow orcs to a better life.

Since Blizzard didn't have the resources or necessary bandwidth to do the cartoon-style animations, that work would have to be outsourced. The group we began with was an American company with a studio in Russia. The language barrier presented a challenge when it came to our artists giving their artists feedback on style. At one point, Sammy, Ron and Metzen even flew to Russia to provide specific direction (and apparently had an adventure of their own being whipped by burly men with saplings in a Russian bathhouse—probably best not to dwell too much on that). After that. the art improved, though it still had a ways to go before reaching Blizzard quality. Nonetheless, the project moved forward.

Halloween was another festive affair. There was a *Saturday Night Live* skit about Superman's funeral (I think I'd seen it first when we were developing *Death and Return of Superman*), where a B-list hero named Black Lightning shows up (played by Sinbad) and nobody knows who he is. When asked, Sinbad would say "Man, I'm Black Lightning! I taught Superman how to fly!"

I bought a Michael Jordan mask, made my own costume complete with yellow lightning bolts, then picked up a Bride of Frankenstein wig and spray painted over the white streaks.

The Michael Jordan mask went over my entire head, so when I showed up to the party nobody knew who I was. Whenever someone would ask I'd say, "Man I'm Black Lightning!" The highlight of the evening though happened when I went to AM/PM to buy beer, in full costume. Joeyray still has a picture of me standing in line with a case in each hand.

* * *

Around that time, I decided to go on a little road trip. I had been thinking a lot about my childhood, about my situation with Dad, and about writing a book. The whole thing seemed like such a crazy story that it absolutely had to be shared with the world. The biggest problem was: I had more questions than answers, and I didn't really know the best way to approach the story. For some inspiration, reflection, and maybe just a bit of investigation, I decided to drive to Arizona.

I hadn't seen Tombstone in years, but when I arrived it was just the same as I had remembered it—same wooden boardwalks, same old west facades, hitching posts... same statues of the gunfighters at the OK Corral. It brought back a lot of memories, some of them pleasant, some of them not.

After spending the night in Tombstone, I drove out to Gleeson. It was still a tiny little outpost in the middle of nowhere. From there, I struggled to remember where Dad had built his compound.

It wasn't too long before I found the big hill that I used to dread when riding my bike. I knew I was close. A bit later and I found what looked like the spot. I got out and walked off the road, into the desert, up a hill, and then I looked back down at the road and knew that I was standing on that same hill where I had pointed my rifle at the man Dad had yelled at, the man Dad told me to shoot if he gave the signal.

I spent a moment there, thinking about how far I had come, thinking mostly about how incredibly grateful I was to God or the universe or whatever's out there that Dad had never given that signal.

Then I walked farther out into the desert and found some old wooden posts, some rusty barbed wire, and a single, warped bicycle wheel. There was almost nothing left of the compound. Whatever wasn't taken had been reclaimed by the sand and scrub brush.

The next day I made a phone call to Dad's prison, asking about visitation. I was informed that the inmate would need to fill out a paper that would allow me visitation, and that no such paperwork had been filled out with my name. I remembered Dad telling me not to visit, that I would be putting myself in danger, and while I didn't believe that was the case, I also didn't want to upset him... but there was more to it as well: as much as I hated to admit it, part of me was afraid to come face to face with him after all those years, to see what had become of him.

Later that afternoon, after quite a bit more driving, I arrived at the road outside the Arizona State Prison. I pulled over and took a long, hard look at the facility, wondering what it must be like to live your life behind those walls. I thought about how different my own life could have been.

And then I drove away.

CHAPTER TWENTY-FIVE:
GROWING PAINS

Back at work there was a major push to get *Diablo* out the door before Christmas. We fell short, but were successful in launching the game just before the end of the year.

At that time the holy grail of multi-play was over the Internet. With *Diablo*, the company introduced multiplayer matchmaking through a service we created called Battle.net. It was fast, easy and efficient, and that service alone would change the way people played games from then on.

Diablo would become a monster hit (pun not intended, but I'll take it), earning Blizzard another Game of the Year award.

On the *Warcraft Adventures* front, Sammy and Metzen had worked tirelessly with the animators to achieve a Blizzard style, but it was taking a lot longer than expected. The game that we'd hoped to get out that year still had a difficult path ahead.

By January '97 Sammy and I had completed several revisions of *Vamptown*, and our producer friends said it was time to start shopping it around to production companies. We held our breath and kept our fingers crossed.

A month later I decided to give Dad a call.

He sounded strange on the phone. He had adopted some kind of accent that I'm guessing was meant to be Peruvian. It sounded like a cross between Native American and Arabic. I asked how he was, and he assured me that he was in "perfect health, Praise Almighty God." We didn't discuss the content of his previous letters, and he didn't accuse me of being an impostor. He did say that he would be released from prison soon, into INS custody, and God willing he would be deported.

We talked a bit more and by the time we hung up I found myself feeling bad about not contacting him earlier. I couldn't believe he was finally being released after all that time… he had served 12 years of an 18 year prison sentence. What must it have been like, spending that much time incarcerated, then being thrust back into the world once again? I had been and continued to be absorbed in my own life, my own aspirations and my own problems. Knowing what I know now, would I have done things differently?

Some things no, but a lot of things yes.

One of the most important lessons I've learned in recent years is that it's so important to try to see things from the other person's point of view. That's probably the biggest change I would make if I could: I would try to see more of the situation from his point of view—and I don't mean the paranoid schizophrenic point of view. I mean the point of view of a man who loved his son and honestly wanted the best for him, even if he went about it in the strangest of ways.

I vowed to call Dad more often, and to write.

* * *

Before long Dan Sullivan and his wife started hearing back from several Hollywood production companies. One by one, they passed, until all of the contacts had been exhausted.

Sammy and I were bitterly disappointed, but determined to keep our eye on the ball. We began work on our next script, a story about a medical research facility that unlocks the hidden potential of the human mind with disastrous results, titled *The God Project*.

For the time being, *Vamptown* moved to the back burner.

While one door closed, however, another opened: a fellow named Morris Frank applied for a job with the Cinematics Team. He didn't get the job, but Sam was impressed by his demo reel. Morris had graduated from film school, and was looking to be a director. Sam and I struck up a friendship with him, and pretty soon we were talking about how we might get some of our projects made. Wheels started turning.

In May, Sammy and I celebrated my birthday at our favorite karaoke bar. I noticed two women sitting at a table nearby, and struck up a conversation. The two (a mother and daughter) were avid karaoke enthusiasts and Sammy hit it off with the daughter, Christy, right away.

When I wasn't hanging out with Sammy or brother Rider (who I had moved into an apartment with at this point), I was heading out to bars with Ron Millar, drinking a lot of booze, and playing a lot of pool. Some mornings I would wake up and realize I couldn't remember hours of the previous night. It didn't bother me all that much, though. I figured it was just part and parcel of being a party animal.

Later that month, an announcement was made that our parent company CUC would be merging with another company, HFS. Again we wondered if the maneuvering at the corporate level would have any effect on our company. As before, all we could do was wait and see.

Meanwhile, though, Sam and I had an opportunity to partner with Morris Frank on a small film project.

Morris got a crew together (folks who had worked with him in film school) and headed out to some salt flats to film a trailer for our script *The Hunt*. Metzen came out with us, in full Old West costume, and we even snagged Rider, and put him in special makeup (the bad guy in *The Hunt* has a scar and milky white eye). We filmed throughout the afternoon and overnight, on 70 millimeter (which was more expensive, but Morris told us the quality couldn't be beat).

In the following several weeks we got the film processed, color balanced, etc., and Joeyray helped us cut together the footage. We added sound and after a few more weeks we had ourselves a trailer that looked good. In fact, it looked better than good, it looked outstanding. This opened up a few doors for Morris, who added the trailer to his demo reel (recut to be a cologne commercial). Pretty soon Morris was working on other projects, and I pitched in where I could, just trying to learn as much about the business as possible.

* * *

Over the course of the previous year, Sharon and I had been seeing each other off and on. By August of '97 we decided to have another go at a relationship. We talked about the issues that resulted in our breakup, and decided to work toward solutions. I moved out of the apartment with Rider (at this point he was in a serious relationship of his own and ready to pull up stakes anyway) and moved into another apartment with Sharon.

Sammy had really hit it off with Christy, and the two of them were dating each other exclusively. Erick and Tony were in relationships as well. It seemed like everyone was settling down.

At work, the new improved *StarCraft* was really taking shape. The races were all fleshed out, and we had a story in place. We were still adding maps, and sometimes we would need new buildings, but for the most part it looked like we were nearing the finish line.

Things for *Warcraft Adventures*, however, didn't look so good. Much of the content had been completed, but overall Blizzard folks weren't entirely happy. The prevailing opinion was that the game wasn't as fun as the adventure games we had all come to know and love. Beyond that, however, even the adventure games of that time were moving to 3D. It seemed we were falling behind the curve.

At this point, we'd had a CO by the name of Paul Sams for a while. He had come over from Davidson (he'd actually handled the contract for Davidson to purchase us). He and Metzen sat down with me and talked about the game, saying that they were looking at doing an overhaul and gauging my interest in doing some writing. I said yes, then didn't hear anything for a while. Later I was told that an adventure game designer was being brought in. It was clear they were doing everything they could to make *Warcraft Adventures* the coolest game possible. Whether or not it would be enough, we'd just have to wait to find out.

As the end of year approached, we undertook a massive effort to ship *StarCraft*. It was the most complex game we had done, with three very different races that needed to be completely balanced when played against each other. A producer and game designer named Rob Pardo had just started at this time; he jumped in on testing and tweaking game balance.

We went into crunch mode, with the goal of launching before Christmas. Once again a bug list went up on the white board, and we did nothing but play the game all day long and into the night, including weekends. Then we'd wake up and do it all again.

Time passed, Christmas loomed, and at the end of each week, Allen Adham would get us all together and say, "Okay guys, we're getting close. We're in the home stretch."

In December the merger of CUC and HFS became official, and the name of our parent company became Cendant. As with the prior acquisition, there was no recognizable effect on us employees.

Meanwhile, Christmas came and went, and it was obvious that *StarCraft* just wasn't ready. We were all suddenly faced with the harsh reality that *StarCraft* would not ship that year. And with *Warcraft*

Adventures still undergoing triage, there was another bitter pill to swallow: 1997 would be the first year that Blizzard would not ship a major title.

Enter 1998. As the first of the year passed, our routine at work changed very little: play the game, report bugs, repeat. At the end of each week, Allen would get us all together and say, "Okay guys, we're looking pretty good here. We're in the home stretch."

Eventually, in the years after StarCraft, the phrase "we're in the home stretch" came to mean, "we're really not close at all."

The crunch was wearing on everyone. Most people would think "what's the big deal, you're just playing a game"—true, but try doing it for 12–16 hours a day, seven days a week, for six to eight months. Sharon just about forgot what I looked like. When I would finally go to sleep at night, I was still playing *StarCraft* in my dreams. For some folks it was worse. Bob Fitch's son was born around this time. His wife would bring the baby into his office and lay him on Bob's desk while she slept on his couch.

January stretched into February, which stretched into March. Finally, mercifully, it was done. The game was ready and was launched at the end of the month.

A bunch of us took time off. Sharon and I went out to movies and dinner often, and I had gotten accustomed to drinking wine, to the point where I could go through a whole bottle by myself. At one point Sharon and I went to Santa Monica and stayed in a nice hotel. I had way too much to drink.

When I woke up the next day and swung my feet off of the bed and onto the floor, the floor was wet. I asked Sharon why and she replied in an irritated voice:

"because you peed on it!" Apparently I had sat at the side of the bed sometime in the night and relieved myself.

I was blacking out longer blocks of time, as well.

* * *

It had been a while since I had talked to Dad, and I decided to call.

I learned that he wouldn't be allowed to leave Arizona for some time yet. He would be under observation. He wasn't happy about it. He said they thought he was crazy, and he was still talking in that strange adopted accent of his, but for the most part he sounded okay.

What Dad didn't tell me at the time; what I learned when I went through legal records later, was that Dad had spent several months (from April to December of '97) in a mental health facility named the Superstition Mountain Mental Health Center. I just want to go on record as saying that is one of the coolest names for any place ever. Period.

The new place Dad was being sent to was called Mountainside Psychiatric Acute Care Facility. Something else I found while going through records about Dad's stay there: they stole his peanut butter and jelly sandwiches, and man was he pissed. Dad said in a complaint that the authorities raided his pod and stole peanut butter and jelly sandwiches that he had hidden away. Apparently they took his shampoo as well. Dad said in his (six page) letter this act would result in "all out war." The subject of his ire during that time was not limited to peanut butter and jelly, either: I found another letter in which he said that the coffee dispenser dispensed nothing but pain and misery.

* * *

Things in Southern California, however, started off rosy: in February Sammy had secretly married Christy. All of my friends at this point were hitched. So, also in February, Sharon and I decided to take the next logical step: we got engaged, with plans to be married in June of the following year.

Meanwhile, *StarCraft* was our biggest success yet. It sold over a million copies and would be the bestselling game of 1998.

Many of us who had gone through the crunch reveled in playing against folks in the general public and wiping the floor with them since we had been playing the game for about eight months longer than anyone else in the world. After a few weeks though, a funny thing happened: we all started getting our asses handed to us. People were playing the game a lot, and they were getting really, really good.

You know who ended up playing the game more than anyone? Koreans. Eventually it seemed like the entire country was playing *StarCraft*. They went nuts over the game, and still love it today. Professional gamers in Korea are celebrities and get sponsorships just like professional athletes in the States.

Once again, we were riding a wave of success. But the company in those early days was still finding its path. We were all still young, still learning, and in many ways we still had that small developer mentality, even though the company was growing into something huge.

In April, Sammy and Christy had their official wedding ceremony. They wore kimonos, which made me think of Roman Kenny.

Also in April, unbeknownst to any of us at work, our parent company, Cendant, was being investigated for fraud. In April "accounting improprieties" were uncovered and the company's stock plummeted. Many of us at the company had stock options that basically became worthless.

From what I've read, the company's earnings were misrepresented by about $500 million. It was the largest case of accounting fraud in US history.

In the aftermath of us being served this colossal crap sandwich, Blizzard was sold to a French communications and advertising company called Havas. Havas was then acquired by a company called Vivendi, and that company became Vivendi Universal. At that point, many of us didn't really care who the parent company was, as long as A) they left us alone, and B) they knew how to balance their books.

In May, Blizzard announced that *Warcraft Adventures* had been canceled. In the end, it was determined that the game was good, but it wasn't good enough. If we would have released it, *Warcraft Adventures* would have been a "B" title, and that was unacceptable.

For a game company to spend a year in development on a title and then not release it for the simple reason that it wasn't going to be the best product possible was unheard of. The words "Blizzard quality" already stood for something, but from that day on those words took on a whole new meaning. The cancellation sent a message to the fans of our games, that we wouldn't settle, and we wouldn't compromise. Similar to the famous Orson Welles Paul Masson wine commercial in which he said "We will sell no wine before it's time," Blizzard's motto became "We'll ship it when it's ready."

* * *

I called Dad again and found out that in August he would be released for real... no more being kept under observation. He sounded very happy. Though he would still need to report to INS frequently, he would be out in the world and on his own. He had been in the system for 13 years.

At this point I had no idea what to expect. I hadn't shared my home address with Dad; nevertheless I was concerned that he would track me down, interject himself in my life, bug me about going to Peru, or who knows... maybe even flip his lid and start calling me a clone and attack me. His behavior had become so unpredictable that I really didn't want him to become a permanent fixture. Not to mention the fact that I had just gotten engaged. What if he showed up at our doorstep and didn't have a place to stay? Sharon knew about my Dad, but knowing about him and living with him would be two very, very different things.

But the way Dad talked, it sounded like he was content to stay in Arizona. He talked about friends he had made, that he might be able to stay with.

As selfish as it sounds, I hoped that was the case.

* * *

Meanwhile, Sammy and I continued working on our screenplays. Our latest was an action thriller tentatively titled *The Fourteenth Floor*. It was about an assassin working his way through a high rise, killing mob members. In between floors flashbacks would occur to explain how he got there. We continued our creative partnership with Morris as well, and sometimes I would head up to LA and work on the set as he filmed more spots for his reel.

* * *

At that same time, progress on the expansion for *StarCraft* was ambitious to say the least. The epic storyline would continue, and not only would new maps and campaigns be added, but new music and units as well. We started off by entrusting development of the game to a third party, but ended up taking on the lion's share ourselves. Once we took back control of the game, development blazed along at a record pace.

Things seemed to be going smoothly, and as we all know, that's usually when a bomb gets dropped.

This was indeed the case, and this particular bomb took the form of a whole group of folks leaving the company. Roughly ten artists and programmers (mostly artists) departed.

A lot of factors contributed to the walkout: the long hours on *StarCraft*, the Cendant fiasco, and for some the cancellation of *Warcraft Adventures* was the final straw.

Mike and Frank called us all together to deliver the news (Allen had stepped down as president at this

248

point. He had led the company brilliantly for several years, and decided it was time for him to follow a different calling in his life). Back then the company was still small enough that everyone pretty much knew everyone. Not only that, everyone contributed in a major way to each game that we worked on. The walkout was a pretty big hit to the company, but there were no hard feelings. In fact, the door was left open for many of those who left, and years later, several of those folks would return to Blizzard.

The executives looked at ways to make improvements after the employees left. They looked at what we were doing right, what we were doing wrong, and how we could do things better. They were going to make some changes, and those changes would have a huge impact on our lives.

Mike and Frank went to great lengths to identify ways in which the company could improve employee recognition. One recurring theme (unsurprisingly) among us all was a desire for profit sharing.

The executives were able to push this initiative through our parent company, and so, for the first time ever, all of the employees received profit sharing checks.

And those checks were big.

StarCraft was a very successful game, the company was profitable, and the employees received a sizeable slice of the pie. There were a lot of brand-new cars in the parking lot come September.

Me, I had set my sights a little higher. I didn't want a new vehicle, I wanted a house.

Sharon and I did some hunting, and it wasn't long before our real estate agent took us to a little neighborhood in Mission Viejo and showed us a cottage-style abode that we fell in love with.

Granted, this house was tiny. We're talking 905 square feet, with a detached garage. But it was a house, and if we could agree on a price with the sellers, and fight our way through a mountain of paperwork, it would be ours.

We offered a hefty down payment. A little over a month later, we slew the escrow dragon and found ourselves moving into our new home. It was a dream come true, and there were several times when I would wake up and walk out into the living room or come from work and just be amazed that the place was mine; I was an actual homeowner. Me! After growing up in the desert and sleeping on the floor of Dad's dojo or having little more than a room to myself, I had finally been able to take the biggest step forward in my life. It was an amazing feeling, and to this day I still think it's strange and crazy and absolutely wonderful to walk into a room and know that you own it.

Another example of Blizzard's new policies regarding employee recognition was the issuing of service awards. The first award was for five years of service, and it was a sword! My sword wasn't anything fancy, but it was still pretty awesome. Over the years, the swords have gotten better and better.

Over the course of the year, the *StarCraft* expansion, *Brood War*, had practically developed itself. On November 30th the game was released, and was considered by many to be almost a sequel rather than an expansion.

Sharon and I spent Christmas in our new home, with our own little Christmas tree. It had been a good year, an amazing year... but many of the issues that existed in our relationship previously had surfaced once again, and the arguments had become more frequent. I began to ask myself if getting engaged had been the right decision.

Months had passed and I hadn't heard from Dad.

The main thing I'd wanted to do when I received my profit sharing money was buy a house: check. The very next thing I wanted to do was to execute on an idea I had harbored for many, many years: to finally hire a private investigator to look into my past, and maybe get me some answers as to who I really was, where I was born, and whether or not I still had family out there somewhere. Thanks to the profit sharing money, the time had come at last to do just that.

CHAPTER TWENTY-SIX:
THE SEARCH CONTINUES

Nineteen ninety-nine, the last year of the second millennium BC was upon us, and I had things to do.

I was still training in martial arts. I had moved on from Ju Jitsu to Aikido and then decided to try something new: it was a martial art that was very similar to Israeili Krav Maga, called Hisardut. The instructor was a consultant for special forces, law enforcement, anti-terrorism, etc. He gave me a phone number of a private investigator whom he trusted implicitly.

I called this number and gave the man on the other end of the phone the lowdown on my past. He said that there really wasn't a lot to go on, but he could look for any ties to the name Shihan Calvin Neilson in South America, specifically Peru and Panama. He would also look into any Oklahoma connections. The cost would be $3,000.

It seemed like a real shot in the dark, but this was something I had waited a long time for. It was worth the risk, and I could afford it. I gave the go ahead. It felt good to at least be doing something.

At work, we had switched from the *StarCraft*

universe back to *Warcraft*, as we began development of *Warcraft 3*.

In March of '99, a game came out called *Everquest*. It was an MMORPG, which meant massively multiplayer online roleplaying game—a real fancy way of saying that you could play a character along with a ton of other folks online.

Nearly everyone at work was playing it. I went through the tutorial and got bored pretty quick. It just didn't grab me. At this time there was a question of what our next big game would be. *StarCraft 2* seemed like a given, but there were other ideas in the works as well. One of those ideas was for us to do our own MMO.

I remember going to lunch with Matt Samia and Chris Metzen, and them telling me that there were thoughts of us doing a game in the same style as *Everquest*. I thought it was a bad idea, basing my opinion on my own experience with the genre.

What I didn't understand at the time was that the company was looking at *Everquest* as a starting off point. The vision they had, as the world would eventually find out, was much greater.

Another game we were developing had the working title of Nomad. It was basically a post apocalyptic world ruled by various magi. There was a lot of design work going on, early concept artwork, and a basic engine was being built. For several months the game would be in the roughest of stages.

My 27th birthday was a stressful time. For one thing, the private investigator had contacted me and said he spent the past few months looking into any Oklahoma connection and had come up with nothing.

He had started doing some digging in South America, but so far he was having no success.

The ultimate cause of concern, however, was my impending marriage. Our marital issues had only gotten worse, to the point where we both believed that in roughly one month we were about to make the biggest mistake of our lives.

I couldn't help but think of *Warcraft Adventures*, the game our company had canceled because we knew it wouldn't be an A title. Here we were facing a marriage that we both knew would end badly.

With less than a month to go, we canceled the wedding. Shortly after that, Sharon and I broke up for good. It was immensely painful for both us, but we knew that in the end it was the right decision. Sharon left the house, and we agreed to remove her name from the title.

After the breakup, I drank more heavily than before. One night I came home, completely sloshed, put on some Hamburger Helper in a frying pan and passed out on the couch. I awoke to a black cloud with the smoke detector blaring. The hamburger looked like dried lava. The fact that I could have died of smoke inhalation wasn't lost on me. So did this incident curb my drinking? No! But I did start microwaving my meals.

Soon a very promising opportunity emerged at work. The development of *Warcraft 3* was still in the early stages, but the company was already making plans regarding the game's marketing. One deal that was made was to provide a demo, a small campaign that people could play for free, to generate interest. I was approached by Metzen and Pardo (who had moved up to lead designer at this point) and asked if I wanted to write the demo, to which I immediately said yes.

Come July it was time for the company to move once again. New business parks were being built near UCI, and Blizzard would have the entire top floor in one of these buildings. At this point, it really felt like we'd hit the "big time." Why? Because we had movers! That's right, all we had to do was pack up our desk and transfer our own valuables (which for me pretty much consisted of a Conan statue and an Elvira cardboard standup) and the movers would take care of the rest. It felt like the dawn of a new era...

For a while I even had my own office! And Sammy's was right next to mine. On the first day we moved in, Sammy and I were talking in my office when we heard a THUMP! one office over. We went to Sammy's office where we saw a kind of dusty bird imprint on the window, wings spread, head sideways like something out of a Looney Tunes cartoon. Just then THUMP! the same sound, from my office this time... we ran over and sure enough, there was another imprint on the window. We theorized that the birds were mates, and when the one saw that it's partner had died and/or committed suicide, it followed suit.

Mainly we just hoped it wasn't an omen.

I've discovered by now that I'm a storyteller first and foremost, not a game designer. That being said, working on the *Warcraft 3* demo in tandem with Pardo and Metzen resulted in a pretty damn cool little product. Metzen and I had cooked up the story (which continued the tale of Thrall, the main character from the canceled *Warcraft Adventures* game), and I knew how I wanted that story to unfold. Sometimes there were design limitations—"We can't flood that room in real time!" But we found ways to work around them: "What if we leave the room, and when we come back the room is flooded?"

Seems pretty simple, but you'd be surprised how many game development companies struggle with that basic concept. And I get it, sometimes the story does not drive the gameplay, sometimes it's the other way around... but the story should never feel shoehorned into a game.

Sammy and I had been talking to Morris for a while about doing a short film project, based on what we had originally called *The Fourteenth Floor* (the story about the assassin in the high rise) and was now called *Descent*. Morris had struck up a relationship with a small production company in New York, and he had access to their facilities. The company's main office was in an old firehouse, and Morris was convinced we could construct all of the sets needed to put together a 15 minute film that would tell the story we wanted to tell.

And that's how Sammy and I found ourselves in New York, auditioning actors and actresses in an old firehouse in the Summer of '99.

Morris was living in New York by this time, and working at the firehouse daily. At night, he was living in what used to be a convent. It was a sprawling, medieval-looking structure made entirely of stone... more like a castle than a nunnery. At night we sat under a statue of Jesus in a cemetery filled with graves marked by small white crosses and we talked story.

Sammy and I wondered why none of the crosses had names engraved on them. Morris suspected that it had to do with humility in the eyes of the Lord.

I thought about those women, dedicating their lives to their faith, with nothing left to show their passing but a simple white cross. I thought about my own name, about not knowing whether the name I went by was my real name or not... and I was determined that one way or another, my name would mean something. Maybe those nuns had moved on to a place where notoriety in the physical world meant nothing, but I wanted my name to be remembered.

We spent a week in New York, and by the time we were done, Sammy and I were satisfied that we could make our little film project work. It would take a fair amount of money; Sammy and I would split the cost, but when we were done, we would have a short film that we could submit to festivals.

As we returned to California, the plan was for Morris to do prep work in New York, and for us to return in a few months, at which point we would begin filming.

Meanwhile, I was ready to hit the dating scene. I'd never had much luck with women I met in bars, and it seemed like all the female friends of employees at work were taken, or simply not interested, so I went the "dating service" route. There was a place in Irvine called Great Expectations. Basically the way it worked was you would go in, give them a bunch of info, take a professional portrait style photo, then record a video talking about yourself. You could look through books and books of photos, then request the info on that person and ask to see their video. If you liked them, you could request a date through the service, and if the other person thought there was potential, they would accept and contact information would be shared.

I went in and made my video, then went back a week or so later and flipped through books, then watched a video from a girl named Tiffany, a cute blonde with big, bright blue eyes. She was from Washington State, and she talked about how she thought driving on California's four lane freeways was just the neatest thing in the world because the biggest freeways in Washington were two lanes. I thought she sounded interesting, and I was certainly physically attracted to her, so I decided to give it a shot. I asked the service to contact her, and then I waited... impatiently.

In August I received word that Tiffany had agreed to share her information. I called her and we set up a date.

When I saw her for the first time, what struck me immediately was that she was even prettier than her picture and video. There was no time to waste though as I had a full day of activities planned.

I remembered her saying that she liked the water, and where I lived there was an association... one of the perks of the association was access to Irvine Lake. The lake had kayaks, paddleboats, swimming, all kinds of fun activities. Tiff and I took out a kayak which I was convinced was going to capsize at any second. We made it through the day and had dinner at my favorite restaurant. Tiffany was a vegetarian, but I didn't hold it against her. We talked non-stop, and she asked me if I had read Anne Rice's *Interview With a Vampire*. I told her I hadn't.

That night we said our goodbyes, but agreed to see each other again. The date was a success.

The following Monday I went back to work, and when I came home that night I found a copy of *Interview With a Vampire* sitting on my doorstep.

* * *

I heard back once again from my private investigator, only to find out that he had come up with zilch. I knew it had been a long shot to begin with, and of course the thought crossed my mind that he simply took my money, but I trusted the person who referred him to me and I understood that there really hadn't been a lot to go on. I was disappointed, but unfortunately not very surprised.

While my investigative efforts into my past had hit a dead end, Blizzard was continuing to flourish, and pretty soon it was necessary for Sammy and I to give up our offices.

I moved into a large room with Trevor Jacobs, a fellow practical jokester, which was of course a recipe for trouble. We immediately named our domain the "Players' Club 54," and it quickly became party central. Soon we were joined by a Korean artist named Ted Park, whose quiet equanimity was a perfect counterbalance to mine and Trevor's antics.

And in those days, no one was safe. When Frank Pearce started bragging about killing a gopher in his yard with a shovel, we posted pictures of "the Shoveler" from the movie *Mystery Men* all over the office. We even stenciled the name "The Shoveler" onto Frank's favorite parking spot.

Some of our shenanigans were completely random. At one point we took an inline skate wheel (a bunch of Blizz employees skated for an inline hockey team) and we put it right in the middle of the floor in our office. The joke was, all three of us wouldn't speak a word to whoever picked it up or touched it. Sure enough, in walks a programmer, Colin Murray, who makes a beeline for the wheel, picks it up, then attempts to strike up a conversation, only to be met with an awkward silence. Colin kept asking why no one would talk to him, until he got worked up and finally turned off Trevor's monitor. At that point we broke silence, let Colin in on the joke, and by the end everyone hugged it out.

Sometimes for a good practical joke, sacrifices must be made. One of the new artists, Allen Dilling, was a good ally. He donated a pair of shoes, and I donated a pair of jeans to the cause. The joke was this: Allen snuck into one of the men's room stalls. We put cardboard toilet paper rolls in the shoes, ends up, and rolled the pair of jeans over them. The plan was to do it so that it looked like someone was sitting on the pot throughout the entire day. Allen set the fake feet up backwards though, and there was someone coming so he had to leave it that way and crawl out from under the locked stall door... which of course meant that it looked like someone was standing facing the toilet. All day long, with their pants around their ankles.

It's always a happy accident when a joke turns out even funnier than you intended, completely by mistake.

Several hours later, a tech wiz named Rob Bridenbecker (who would go on to become Vice

President of Online Technologies) went into the bathroom and called out "Hey, who's in there?" A moment after that the gig was up.

Allen never got his shoes back.

* * *

In October I received a brief note from Dad telling me that he was living with a couple in Arizona (or on their property, to be more specific) and that he was engaged in all sorts of activities, including teaching martial arts and anger management to seniors. Anger management? Yeah. Anyway I wrote back to him, telling him all the latest, but especially talking about Tiff...

Things with Tiff had gone well. At one point I was sick, and Tiff took the day off of work to nurse me back to health. That selfless and considerate act was really the point at which I started to love her.

My budding relationship with Tiff would need to be put on hold, however, as I traveled back to New York in November to shoot our short film. Sammy was set to accompany me, but due to a last minute emergency he had to bow out.

New York was quite the adventure. Morris had made some connections while he was there, including a producer named John Nemec who had recently worked on an independent film. We were introduced when I arrived at the firehouse, which was in a surprisingly unprepared state. The plan had been for at least the first set to be constructed and ready for shooting when we arrived. Morris was basically trying to build the sets himself, and he hadn't gotten to it, which meant we were scrambling on our first day to get our shots. The set we ended up with (which was supposed to be a baseball stadium bathroom) didn't look right at all. On top of that, the actor we had chosen for the part of the protagonist's father had other commitments, so we went with a number two choice, and he was having difficulties with the character.

Needless to say, we were off to a bad start.

Things pretty much went from bad to worse after that.

Every night we were feverishly building sets for the next day's shoot, but quite often the sets would be left unfinished, to be completed the next morning. It wasn't all Morris' fault; we partied a few nights, hanging out with John and others, getting drunk, and crawling our asses into the studio the next day. Even on the sober nights though the fates seemed to be against us.

Morris was still living in the converted convent, and I was sleeping in his apartment. In the middle of the week, after a full day of shooting, we went to crash at his place. As we were climbing the stone steps to the third floor, the lights went out. Morris had a dog, who immediately freaked out and disappeared. Morris went after the dog, and I was left in that crumbling nunnery in the most absolute darkness I've ever experienced. I made my way step by step to the next floor, and against one of the windows I could just barely make out a silhouette. I imagined the lights coming back on to reveal a nun, judging me and finding me wanting before dissipating before my eyes. My heart was hammering against my chest.

"Morris?" I called out.

For a brief second, there was no answer. I was ready to run as fast as my feet would carry me, though I would surely smack right into a wall or pitch headlong down the stairs. Then, mercifully, I got a response:

"Yeah, hey."

We made our way to his apartment, created a makeshift torch, and spent the next several minutes tracking down Morris' dog.

Roughly an hour later the lights came back on.

Over the course of the production, I grew more and more dissatisfied, and my partnership with Morris suffered. By the end, I had mixed feelings. I knew that we had gotten all our shots, but I also knew that the sets, lighting, acting, and cinematography were lacking. I wouldn't know how lacking until we got into post-production. Beyond all that, though, there was a disagreement as to who would ultimately own the film. We had signed contracts beforehand, so in my mind the matter was settled, and at that point I felt that Sammy and I would need to oversee post-production ourselves if there was any chance of salvaging the movie. When the film was processed I picked up the master tapes and flew back to California.

Morris was outraged, claiming that the project was his and that we stole it from him. We moved into the editing stage, and Sammy got his first look at the footage. He was disappointed, and kicking himself for not making the trip. Seeing the shots we ended up with, I was frustrated as well. Sammy and I had both spent thousands of dollars on the movie, and what he had to show for it was not at all what we had hoped for.

We were determined, however, to see it through to the finish, and so the editing process continued.

While I was in New York, I had received a letter from Dad. He wanted to know all about Tiff, what she was like, whether or not she was an artist, etc. He said "Strange as it seems Yakimoki, 'A Female is a Man's TODAY ~ The Male is a Woman's future';... and together they build their ToMorrows..."

I had sent him some printouts of my 3D artwork that he thought was amazing.

The other thing he was talking a lot about was Y2K. There was a lot of hype around that time about a massive crash of all the world's computers, as rumors circulated that due to programming concerns, the rollover from 1999 to 2000 (abbreviated as 99 to 00 for the computers) would cause global crashes, panic, an economical meltdown, etc. Dad felt that there may in fact be a global crisis, but he was basically of the mind that it would wake people up to his way of thinking.

Ironically, Dad was fiddling around with the Internet himself, and making his own website! He said he was even working with a local magazine (from what I could tell later on, he had submitted material to a local Native American publication, but I don't know if any of his articles were ever published). All in all it seemed that things were going well. Dad said he was in no hurry, that he had all the time in the world.

* * *

Our postproduction work on *Descent* continued. Our main actor was a star in more ways than one: he helped coordinate our efforts, and put us in touch with all the necessary people to get the project done. The movie was rough, and it really wasn't what we had envisioned, but it was nearing completion.

Meanwhile, my relationship with Tiffany progressed to the next level. On December 3rd, she moved into the house.

That Christmas the Players' Club threw the office party of the century... Hell, of the millennium! We had all been saving money in a Monkey Fund. As the name implies, the purpose of the fund was to rent a live monkey (we were hoping for a baboon).

We didn't get monkeys that December. However, thanks to an extra donation by the team's producer Chris Sigaty, we were able to throw a Mexican-themed party, complete with piñatas and, the piece de resistance... mariachis! It was an office fiesta that would go down as one of the best in Blizzard history.

And then, the end of the year was upon us. Would Y2K reshape the world as we knew it? We would just have to wait and see.

CHAPTER TWENTY-SEVEN:
GREENLIGHT, RED LIGHT

I don't think of myself as paranoid, but I do like to be prepared.

When the year 2000 hit, I was sitting with Tiff on the couch, shotgun within reach, ready for the power to go out and for the world to go to hell soon after.

Neither event happened.

Computers survived, the world's infrastructure and economy survived, and civilization continued on as if the paranoia never existed.

We had completed our work on *Descent*. It was, overall, a disappointment. Sammy and I resolved to premiere the movie in New York for all the folks who had contributed so much and worked so hard, but ultimately we felt it unworthy to promote through indie film festivals.

The premiere happened in January, at a small club. The stars and crew all celebrated. When we returned home the master tapes were put on a shelf, the copies were put into boxes, and the movie was largely forgotten.

Also in January I received a letter from Dad. The tone was different... he was confused by the Internet, and he lamented the state of affairs in Arizona, commenting on the cold weather, of how the people he associated with were senior citizens but it was the teenagers who were the real old people— "DISEASED, SICK and DYING." He spoke of how everyone was "sex crazy," that there were "babies having babies." He said no one exercised, that they all just sat around talking about the good old times as if they were born to die. Dad said the Immigration Department wouldn't give him a photo ID, so he couldn't secure a driver's license. He said he was living on $81.00 a month. As always, part of me wanted to reach out to him. I knew that if I sent him money, he either wouldn't accept it, or he would take it as an invitation to become a more permanent fixture in my life. I felt secure with the way things were: him in Arizona, me in California, with intermittent communication between the two of us.

Work on *Warcraft 3* continued, as well as the slow development of *Nomad. Diablo 2* was nearing completion, and would soon demand a large chunk of our time as we went into playtesting.

My relationship with Tiffany continued to evolve. We had certainly gone through some rough patches. Sometimes we fought like mad but no matter how bad it got, I felt that there was a reason we were together. She was headstrong and opinionated and I was determined and stubborn, which led to the inevitable locking of horns. We always managed to pull through, however, to the point that in the spring of 2000 I found myself back at the same lake where I had taken Tiff on our first date, sitting in a boat with her parents, asking her father for Tiff's hand in marriage.

He said yes, and I proposed to Tiffany shortly after. The wedding was set for May of the following year.

At work, we playtested *Diablo 2* feverishly, until yet another crunch phase was over, and yet another game was out the door. Once again, a Blizzard game became the fastest selling computer game of all time. *Diablo 2* was a huge hit.

June saw three letters from Dad. Positive overall—he was helping local senior citizens with legal matters. He talked about sharing an Internet connection with someone, then in the very next paragraph he talked about my mother, and her supposed assassination. He was calling her "Tah," a name he had used once or twice before. He said that he and Tah were married in Manous, Brazil, and that I was born there. He said my grandparents were alive in Brazil. He spoke of the US Army and Douglas MacArthur, and said that his fellow freedom fighters were "enconcentrationed" and that the reason he could not share detailed information with me about my past was for their safety.

To me it was just lies on top of more lies. Not knowing the truth, and having to contend with what I viewed as blatant misinformation was a constant source of frustration—something I believed would simply never change; I might never learn the truth. As usual, I took my frustration out on Dad by writing to him sporadically, calling him infrequently, and making no effort to visit him in Arizona. I would see him eventually, I told myself. There was plenty of time.

* * *

While Blizzard North focused on the expansion, I returned my attention to *Warcraft 3*. Before long though another writing opportunity presented itself. Metzen asked me if I'd like to try my hand at a literary format that we were told would soon be all the rage: ebooks! Specifically, I would be given the opportunity to write a short story set in the *StarCraft* universe. I jumped at the chance. Creating 3D buildings and doodads was all well and good, but where was my career really going? What was next? I was ready for a challenge.

Sam and I also hadn't given up on our screenwriting. Far from it; in September we entered Project Greenlight, a screenwriting competition run by Matt Damon and Ben Affleck, on the heels of their successful indie film *Good Will Hunting*. The way this first competition worked was, for the first round everyone would submit their script and agree to read and grade several other scripts. The highest scores for that first round of cuts would make it into the top 250. The point of the contest was not just to find a script, but also a director, so after that first cut, semifinalists would send in a short biography video of themselves.

The Hunt (the supernatural western) was our best work, so we turned that in, graded the scripts we read (a couple of which were pretty good) and waited.

Time seemed to crawl. The anticipation was driving us both nuts. Then, at last, it happened. The list was sent out.

And we were on it!

After all the writing we had done, all the hard work and dead ends, it was such an amazing validation to have our script chosen out of more than 7,000 to make that next round.

269

We immediately filmed our biography video, into which we injected our own brand of humor (one early version that Joeyray Hall cut together for us had a Mike Morhaime "endorsement" where he basically called us idiots, but we would have bleeped out the negative comments and dubbed another voice with positive ones. We had to jettison this idea when we learned that the video could only feature the writers) and sent the video off.

Just before Christmas, the top 30 would be announced. Once again, Sammy and I waited. This could be it... the big time!

Meanwhile I finished my ebook, *Uprising*, which was published by Simon and Schuster. The initial sales were nothing to write home about. I would soon learn that "Ebook's time" had not yet come as predicted. The world wouldn't really start to embrace ebooks until ereader technology improved and handheld devices became prevalent.

Then, in late December, the list was sent out for the top 30 finalists in Project Greenlight.

And we weren't on it.

I was crushed. Sammy was crushed. We had made it so far... what had we done wrong? What could we have done differently?

Sam and I started off 2001 with renewed determination. We would double our focus, double our efforts. At work I was expanding my horizons, going to VO recordings for the *Diablo* expansion. I sat in the studio and listened to the voice direction, observed how the process worked. Before long I was able to direct a few sessions of my own. I quickly found that I possessed an aptitude for communicating to the actors, and I had a decent ear for dialogue. Sometimes we would modify lines once we heard the actors read them. I tackled several writing tasks for the game as well.

Meanwhile, the indie producer Sam and I had met in New York started introducing us via email and phone to people he knew, trying to generate some interest in *The Hunt*. We spoke to other writers, producers, directors, and at one point we had an actor from *Law and Order* attached. Everyone had their own ideas for the script, and for everyone who might be able to get the movie made, Sam and I executed rewrites. It was a rollercoaster of optimism and rejection. But it was a kiddie coaster compared to what lay ahead.

The *Diablo 2* Expansion was nearly out the door as my wedding arrived in May. I've never been so scared in my life. Iraq comes close, but even the threat of death on foreign soil takes a back seat to getting hitched. Don't get me wrong, it was a wonderful feeling as well, but I was stepping into a whole new, scary world, and I'm the type of person who's resistant to major change.

The ceremony took place on a cruise ship. We invited all the guests to buy tickets for the cruise if they wanted to, but most of the attendees boarded while the ship was docked, stayed for the ceremony, then disembarked afterword.

It was a fairly small affair—less than 50 people, but it ended up being everything we had hoped for. Tiffany and I said our vows (it was non-denominational since neither of us are religious), we placed the rings on each other's fingers, we kissed, and it was done. It all seemed to happen in a heartbeat. The rest of the day would take on a dream-like quality, surreal, as if I were observing events from outside my body. Through it all I felt the weight of the ring on my finger, new and foreign.

The ring was heavy, but it was a perfect fit.

Having a wedding on a cruise ship is the height of convenience. You finish the ceremony and BAM! you're on your honeymoon. The strangest thing about the first few weeks after marriage is getting used to saying the words "my wife." The cruise was seven days, to Mexico, and we had a blast.

A short while later the *Diablo 2* expansion was out the door, and would become another huge hit.

In the meantime, Blizzard was approached by another small studio, Nihilistic. They had developed a game called *Vampire: The Masquerade —Redemption*, that was well-liked by most everyone at the company. Nihilistic wanted to develop a console game for us based in the *StarCraft* universe, and so the idea for *StarCraft: Ghost* was born.

The story would follow an elite operative (or "ghost") named Nova Terra as she regained memories of her past and uncovered a maniacal plot to overthrow the galactic Dominion. It was an exciting concept. Nihilistic went to work on building a demo.

Work on *Warcraft 3* continued as well, but it was slow going, as several members of our team shuffled over to help out with Nomad... but Nomad at this point was basically dead. The idea that replaced it, but would use an MMO engine, was simple: take the *Warcraft* setting, and the *Warcraft* characters and history, and allow players to run around in that world.

We could call it... the *World of Warcraft*. It seemed like a pretty cool little idea.

None of us had the slightest notion of what a behemoth that game would become.

* * *

At home, my relationship with Tiff was having its ups and downs, but the one thing we agreed on was our desire for a child. The time had come for us to begin planning. And to begin trying.

* * *

On September 11th, I was awoken by a phone call from Tiff. She left for work earlier than I did, and she had just heard on the radio that one of the towers in New York had collapsed. I asked if it was related to the wars in Serbia and Yugoslovia, but Tiff said there was no other information available. I went to the living room and turned on the news.

I took the day off of work, and I watched the events unfold, minute by minute, hour by hour. I was shocked, horrified, appalled and like so many others, deeply saddened by the events of 9/11.

For a short time afterword, work seemed much less important. After all, what was I doing? Working on video games. How important could that really be in the grand scheme of things? What was my contribution? My legacy? What *really* mattered?

Once again Tiff and I came to the same conclusion. A child was what mattered most. Children are the future (yeah it's hard to say that without hearing Whitney Houston in my head). Children are hope. Children are the best of us and yes, they can be the worst of us as well, but without them the world is a huge dead end, a one way trip to a final destination.

We had been trying for a while without any luck, but we resolved to keep at it.

CHAPTER TWENTY-EIGHT:
THE CIRCLE OF LIFE

Early 2002 was a busy time at Blizzard. *World of Warcraft, StarCraft: Ghost* and *Warcraft 3* were all in various stages of development.

The *StarCraft: Ghost* demo was promising enough to convince Blizzard that we should move forward, and the game was announced. I had an opportunity to work on the story, which allowed me to put some of my screenwriting chops to the test.

During that time I was also able to jump in with the Sound Team and really get involved in both writing and voice directing for *Warcraft 3*. One of the hallmarks of Blizzard games is something called "pissed lines." Pissed lines are basically just lines that the game character says after you click on them several times. It's a fun little extra that we had started in the first *Warcraft* when the orc would stay "Stop poking me!" after repeated clicks, as if he were "pissed." Over time pissed lines turned into an opportunity to have characters say all kinds of funny things and to break the fourth wall with pop culture references and running gags.

For *Warcraft 3*, we got together a group of

quirky, humorous employees and basically ran it like a writer's room, with everyone throwing out ideas and building on certain concepts, then refining until we ended up with lines that we thought were absolutely hilarious. They ran the gamut from snarky —the sorceress saying "I don't remember casting "slow" on you!" to the obscure —the dreadlord saying "This is not a dress, it's the standard dreadlord uniform!" (which was inspired by the line about wrestlers wearing tights in *Breakfast Club*), to painful puns — the deer-like dryad saying "I'm game!"

Once the lines were recorded, Chris Metzen would approve or disapprove them, and quite often we'd record lines that we knew had no chance of making it just in the hopes that others which were on the fence would squeak by. And sometimes that strategy actually worked.

* * *

At home Tiff and I were still trying, with no success. It had been several months and we both decided to consult doctors. After some investigation, one doctor had a theory—I had been going to a mixed martial arts class for a while, and would wear a cup a few nights a week when sparring and grappling. The doctor suggested that the cup was basically heating up my testicles and rendering my sperm ineffective. I decided to train without a cup for a while and see if that made a difference. It did. The most immediate difference was me getting hit in the nuts more often.

For my 30th birthday, Tiff and I stayed on the Queen Mary. We explored the ship, ate a fantastic dinner, drank bucket loads of wine and made love in our room. The Queen Mary is reputedly haunted, so later that evening I snuck out and went on my own little ghost hunt around the ship, with no success. Sometime in the wee hours of the morning, however, Tiff and I both distinctly heard scratching at the door. I've since found out that raccoons tend to scamper around the ship. Was it a mischievous spirit in need of a manicure making its presence known that night, or just some pesky critter looking to raid our Cheez-its? We'll never know.

One thing that did become clear shortly after that night, was that Tiff was pregnant. Apparently going cup-less at martial arts did the trick.

When our suspicions were confirmed, my mind raced. I was going to be a dad! Me, the bonehead who put fake penises in store mannequins and crashed his car into ice plant. A father! And I knew, somehow I absolutely knew, beyond a shadow of a doubt, that I was going to have a boy. And I knew something else right then and there, without question: that boy's childhood would be nothing like mine. I would make damn sure that child had everything he needed, but most of all I would move heaven and earth to give him the one thing I wanted most of all but never had: a normal life.

Tiff informed her parents, who were living in Washington. That very same day they put their house up for sale and decided to move down to California. Tiff and I made plans of our own. We got our finances in order. We both read about parenthood. We turned our second bedroom into a nursery, but Tiff didn't want to decorate until we knew for sure what the gender was going to be. I agreed to wait, but I knew we didn't need to. I knew I was right.

One major question did loom, however: should I tell Dad? Tiff and I talked about it. Obviously she knew about my past. She wasn't entirely comfortable with the idea, but it was ultimately my decision. I thought long and hard about it. The crux of the issue for me was this: we still didn't know what had happened to me when I was a baby. Had my mom died, or did Dad take me from her? And if he did take me and run, and I told him that I was now having a baby, would he somehow get it into his mind that if I wouldn't accompany him to Peru or the Cave of the Seven Winds or wherever, then his grandchild should?

We would already be worried enough about the baby, I didn't want us stressing about the possibility of Dad coming and grabbing the child as well. I made my decision. I wouldn't tell him.

* * *

Another crunch phase came and went, and in July, *Warcraft 3* was out the door. It was clear right away that we had another award-winning hit on our hands... although, when we developed our titles we didn't set out to win awards, we just set out to make great games. The awards followed.

The WoW team was still hard at work, and Nihilistic was making strides on Ghost. Our team, however, Team 1, was at a crossroads: we could launch right into the *Warcraft 3* expansion, or we could potentially work on an entirely new title. There was a debate wherein both sides were argued, but in the end it was put to a vote, and the majority opted to complete the *Warcraft* expansion.

* * *

Come September it was time to learn the baby's sex. In other words, time to confirm what I already knew.

The ultrasound was performed, but the baby was on its side. The doctor pushed around a bit and got the baby to move, and voila! The doctor smiled and said...

"Tiffany, you have a daughter."

I sat, mouth open, in stunned silence. The doctor confirmed one more time, saying there was almost a zero chance of error. It was a girl.

We left the doctor's office and decided to head to Baby's R Us. I finally started using my words again.

"Dresses," I said in a distant voice, still completely in a state of shock. "We're gonna have to buy dresses."

As we shopped, I told Tiff that I didn't know how to raise a girl. She reminded me that all the Brothers except for Rider had girls and they were all doing just fine.

But I had been so sure... I had never even entertained the thought that it wouldn't be a boy. I wondered what kind of dad I would be. Would I be good enough? And what would my daughter be like?

Like I said, I don't like change. And this was the mother of all changes. Not only were we having a child, but she was a different gender from what I convinced myself she would be...

And I didn't know the first thing about buying dresses.

Tiff took maternity leave in December. The baby was due mid-January. By Christmas, Tiff was sick of being pregnant and not looking forward to another month of discomfort.

She wouldn't have to wait that long.

At 6:00 on the morning of December 31st, Tiff's water broke. She went out and waited on the couch to let me sleep a bit longer, going through mild contractions. When I woke up, I couldn't believe that Tiff had let me sleep, but she wasn't in a hurry.

We went to the bank, had lunch, then finally around noon we arrived at the hospital. We walked the halls while waiting for a room, as Tiff's labor started getting worse.

A short while later we were in a room. The nurses checked in on us frequently, keeping up on contractions and dilation. Tiff's Mom and Dad arrived that evening. We spent New Year's eve in the hospital, waiting. When midnight hit, we all toasted with apple cider. I stayed awake into the wee hours of the morning until, around 5:30 a.m., Tiff started pushing.

This was it! Tiff had decided early on that she wanted to give birth without an epidural, but it wasn't too long before she was ready for drugs. She pushed for three hours, and at 8:27 a.m., out came Tatiana Alexis Neilson, 5 lbs., 13 ounces.

After the cord was cut, Tiff's Dad and I helped wash the baby off. Now, anyone who's seen a newborn knows that they aren't the most beautiful creatures in the world; they're covered in goo, their heads are misshapen, and they're roughly the color of a bruised apple. Tatiana was no exception. On top of all that, she had long, spindly fingers like Max Schreck in *Nosferatu*...

Which I thought was *really* cool.

The hospital had a button that you would press when a baby was born. It played a lullaby throughout the building. I got to press the button.

Tati was the first baby of the New Year at that hospital, which earned us a nice fruit basket. Since she was a preemie, Tati and Tiff both stayed in the hospital for three days. Tati was jaundiced, so when we brought her home we had to use a "bili blanket," which has a pad that emits blue light from the baby's back. It was like sleeping with a neon sign, if a neon sign could wail like a banshee. Tiff called her "glowworm."

After a few weeks Tati was off the bili light and sleeping in her own crib, and then began the routine of Tiff and I taking turns to get up with Tati through the night. Those first weeks can be rough, and there are times when all you want more than anything in the world is for the crying to stop. Nevertheless, I found myself in a constant state of bewilderment, amazement and fascination with this little human being that Tiff and I had created. Throughout those early weeks and months one thought repeated in my brain over and over: *I can't wait to get to know her*.

* * *

A few weeks more and I returned to work, where the *Warcraft 3* expansion was making huge strides. I was back on buildings and doodads, as well as character voice over. I was also reworking the script for *StarCraft: Ghost*, which had already gone through several iterations.

281

I hadn't spoken with Dad in a while, and I was putting off a phone call, because it would be hard to talk to him and not tell him about my new baby.

Tati was a joy. Tiff and I could take her to a restaurant and she would just sleep in her stroller, quiet and content. All in all, things were great, but at home we wanted more room. The house was okay for the short term, but we wanted Tati to have a yard to play in. At the time, houses in California were ridiculously high. The market "bubble" was still expanding. So, we put money down on a house that was being built 50 miles east, in Corona. The biggest upside? Corona was where Tiff's parents had moved to from Washington. We'd have babysitters not more than five minutes away!

Some of the folks who were working on the *Warcraft* expansion thought it would be fun to put a band together and have a song in the end credits. Sammy, Mike Morhaime, Dave Berggren, Alan Dabiri and Chris Sigaty became 10th Level Tauren Chieftain (named after a Warcraft 3 hero) and an in-game cinematic had characters playing their song at the end of War 3X.

Come July, the expansion was out the door and Blizzard enjoyed yet another massive success. Most of Team 1 then went "on loan" to the *World of Warcraft* team to help them finalize their game.

The situation with Blizzard North at this time was not rosy. After the release of the *Diablo 2* expansion, we were all wondering when we would see the next installment in the franchise. Development had been slow, and we heard rumblings of discontent at the higher levels in Blizzard North. In September, the rumors proved to be valid, as the president of Blizzard North and several top employees announced that they were leaving to start their own company. The remaining employees stayed in San Mateo to continue work on Diablo 3.

* * *

By October, Tiff and I had moved into our new house. It was over 2,000 square feet and had a huge backyard. The biggest downside early on was the commute, but when you drive a long route to and from work, day after day, your brain goes into "autopilot" mode and it's almost like being under hypnosis. I spent time going over stories in my head, solving problems. If I was having trouble with a particular story issue during the day, I would often find that by the time I arrived home I had found an answer.

* * *

In December I was called into Frank's office. I entered and saw Sammy sitting at a table, along with the HR rep at the time. The mood was somber. I wondered: had I done something to get fired? I couldn't think of anything that would get me axed. I sat down and Frank broke the news that they had received a phone call from someone in Arizona, who left a message for me that my Dad had passed away.

Nothing really prepares you for that kind of news. To say I was taken by surprise is a titanic understatement. I broke down almost immediately. My entire world was turned upside down. Frank, Lisa and

Sammy were very comforting and gave me all the support I needed but what I really needed in that instant was just to get away, and be alone with my thoughts for a while.

As before, the long drive home gave me ample time to reflect. I hadn't called Dad in quite a while. Frank had said he was told that Dad died of natural causes, but there were very little details. Had he died peacefully? How soon would the funeral be? How soon could I get out there? What kind of arrangements would need to be made?

When I was just a few blocks from home, I passed Tiff, who had just left the house with her mom and Tati. They circled back around, and once home I told them what had happened. Tiff was on the phone immediately, gathering as much info as she could. One thing she thought to do, which I have to say was a stroke of genius (because in my state of mind I certainly wouldn't have considered it) was to have the Coroner's office take blood samples.

The body was sent to a funeral home but there were no plans for a service—besides Tiff and myself and the man Dad was living with when he died, there really wasn't anyone to attend. The Coroner had already performed an autopsy, and the cause of death was determined to be atherosclerotic cardiovascular disease.

Tiff and I drove out to Arizona, leaving Tati with Tiff's Mom. Once in Arizona, we drove straight to the funeral home. We walked in and talked to the director, who said the body was available for viewing, if I wanted to say my goodbyes. I answered yes and the director led Tiff and I to a set of double doors. He opened them, and there was Dad, lying under a white sheet in the middle of a large room. The sheet was pulled down to his shoulders. He had a peaceful, almost blissful expression on his face. Tiff would later say that she half expected him to sit up and start talking to her, he seemed so alive.

The director asked if we would like to be alone, and Tiff said she would leave also. They exited the room and closed the doors and there I was, faced with this man who—let's face it—I had been avoiding for so many years. I was faced also with the inescapable reality that I would never hear his voice again, never receive another letter, never have a chance to tell him again that I loved him, or that he had a beautiful granddaughter who was the most precious thing in all the world; my dad, my partner, my compadre, my adversary, my ally, my opponent, my confidante, my stranger, my teacher and my enigma... was dead and gone forever.

I told him I loved him. I told him I was sorry that certain things hadn't been different between us. I told him that despite everything, I knew that he always loved me as much as one human being can love another, and I wished him peace.

Dad had always said he wanted to be cremated, so we looked at urns, picked one out and made the arrangements.

Tiff and I took Dad's blood samples to a lab. At one point, a friend who knew my story had wondered: what if Shihan wasn't my dad, but my grandfather (we had ruled out the possibility that he and I weren't related at all because there was a strong resemblance). Even though we didn't know how old Dad was, it was

285

clear that he was pretty old, and that he must have been in his forties when I was a baby, so the idea that maybe he was my grandfather, and that he had taken me from my parents wasn't an impossibility. It didn't seem likely, but we wanted to be sure.

The lab said they could do the test but it would take a few weeks. They would mail us the results.

Our next stop was the house that Dad had been sharing with another older gentleman at the time of his death. The other man was in his 80s, and none too happy to see us. He was very judgmental of my choice to not maintain a closer relationship with Dad, despite my reasoning. We were able to convince him, however, that he had no right to hold on to all of Dad's possessions, and we took several boxes and packed them in our vehicle.

One final thing we were able to do: we took Dad's death certificate to the courthouse and put in an official request for Dad's legal records.

Between the blood test, Dad's possessions and the legal records I hoped that maybe, if any good could come of Dad's death, it would be to shed some light on the mysteries of my past.

CHAPTER TWENTY-NINE:
RETURN TO OKLAHOMA

A few weeks into 2004 we received the lab results from Dad's blood test. It was 99.99 % positive that he was my father and not my grandfather. So at least that was one theory we could put to rest. Advancements in DNA research allowed other possibilities that hadn't previously existed, and now, being in direct contact with a company dedicated to the field, we decided to make the most of it. I had the company send me a "kit" which basically meant that we filled out some paperwork, and I used a cotton swab inside my cheek to provide my DNA. I requested a full workup of my geographical lineage, and I agreed to have my results submitted to a database where I could find "matches," and hopefully have a chance at connecting to relatives.

Meanwhile, we had come away with four or five boxes of Dad's possessions. He kept all kinds of things—business cards, trinkets, books. He had started numerous projects, including working with someone who apparently planned to build a casino with an Incan theme. He had written stacks of letters, and he had kept all of my letters to him. I gained a window into the last years of his life going through his effects, but by the end of the process I had very few leads that I could follow up on: some scribbled names, phone numbers, receipts. I separated these items and began methodically eliminating each and every one.

Concurrently, of course, there was my work life. *StarCraft: Ghost* was having problems. The gameplay just wasn't where it needed to be at that stage, and the story was in a continual state of flux. *World of Warcraft*, on the other hand, had evolved into something truly amazing. It had a vibrancy, a sense of its own being. Running around in that fictional world, inhabiting any number of online avatars and undergoing perilous quests was escapism at its finest. There was still a great deal of polish to be done, and many bugs to be fixed. The development team had been in "crunch mode" for nearly two years—an absolute marathon... but we all knew that *World of Warcraft* was shaping up to be exceptional. We all believed that it would be well worth the wait.

* * *

A few weeks after swabbing my cheek, we received DNA results. The workup they performed showed that my lineage could be traced almost exclusively to Europe: Scotland, England, Spain was even in there... but there were no South American "markers" in my DNA. None! I couldn't believe it. That whole quest I had sent the private investigator on not so long before was one big wild goose chase. It was frustrating, but it was also comforting to have some kind of hint as to my "identity." For so long I couldn't even tell people what my ancestry was with any kind of real conviction. Now, thanks to modern technology, I knew something at least of where my ancestors were from, even if I had no idea who they were.

In the early part of the year we received Dad's legal records, a box with stacks of papers. I spent several days studying the material, scanning each and every page for useful information. Some material had been redacted, which spurred me to enquire further. I was told that the information not included most likely contained personal data on someone other than my father, whether it be a fellow inmate, a prison official, etc. Overall I didn't find anything revelatory, but I did gain insight into what my dad was going through at various stages of his incarceration, and I acquired details about things like my dad's arrest, that I had either forgotten or never been told, which are now included in this book.

All in all, between Dad's personal items, the DNA results and the legal records, I had gained more knowledge, but the biggest questions still remained: who was Dad, really? Who was I, really? Did I have a family somewhere that might be searching for me? Was my mom really dead? What worried me most was the fact that Dad was now gone. I had never been able to get the answers I wanted from him, but I always held on to the hope that someday he would reveal the truth. Now, that was no longer a possibility. How many secrets had died with him?

At that point I was pinning most of my hopes on the DNA/genealogy website. Maybe a relative of mine, distant or otherwise, had submitted their DNA to the same database. All I could do was wait and see.

* * *

Meanwhile, Sam and I went back and started "revamping" our *Vamptown* script. Then one of the folks we had met in New York, John Nemec, introduced us via email to a producer named Paul Aaron. Paul was looking for good scripts, so we sent *The Hunt*. Paul's Vice President of Development, James Waugh, read the script, liked it, and set up a meeting.

Sam and I drove up to LA and sat down with Paul and James. Paul told us right away that *The Hunt* was a good script, but Westerns weren't selling. He was excited to see what else we had. We pitched *Vamptown* and they both loved it. We threw several their way: *The God Project, Eternal Sun,* even *Descent*, but the response was tepid. *Vamptown* was the script they felt had the most potential.

A few weeks later we sent our revisions to *Vamptown* and got notes. Paul made it clear that he was invested in the project, and that he would take as much time to develop it as was needed. We began a routine of taking meetings, taking notes, and making revisions.

At work, *StarCraft: Ghost* was still struggling. Development of the game was moved from Nihilistic to a game studio called Swingin' Ape. *World of Warcraft*, on the other hand, was nearing completion and the excitement around the office was palpable. As for Diablo 3, progress was being made, but it was still slow. The remaining employees at Blizzard North were invited to Orange County to continue their work. Many of them accepted the offer.

All the while, Tati was growing into a fascinating little person. She walked a little later than most kids, but more out of a determination to do it on her own terms than an inability early on. She babbled a nonsense language that amused me unceasingly. And, she was gorgeous. Any parent is going to tell you their child is beautiful, but Tati was truly the cutest kid you've ever seen: blonde curly hair, big blue eyes, fat little cheeks—the whole package.

Sam and I were getting close to a *Vamptown* script that Paul and James could shop around to Hollywood. Meanwhile, throughout the year, I visited the DNA website and followed possible leads. I found a couple people with markers indicating that somewhere in the past (usually several generations), we shared a common ancestor. I sent emails to all of these people, telling them the broad strokes of my story in a couple paragraphs. The ones who answered all said the same thing: they didn't know of my mom or dad or any immediate relatives, but they wished me the best of luck.

As time passed, I worried that the DNA database was going to be yet another dead end. I was at a loss.

Then, in early November, almost a year after Dad's death, I received a letter from the funeral home, passing on a message from a martial arts instructor named Scott in Oklahoma, basically saying that there was a group of individuals who had trained with Dad there, who had spent the last 30 years searching for him... and for me. The letter contained contact information for the instructor, Scott Wilson.

I was excited. This could be just the breakthrough I had been waiting for! I had done some digging but

291

never found anyone who knew Dad when I was an infant in Oklahoma. These folks might have clues as to where Dad had come from or what really happened to Mom. I called Scott immediately, my heart racing.

Scott was very polite, very well spoken and genuine. He had been a loyal student of a sensei named Bill Thurston for many years, and Bill Thurston had trained with Dad when I was a toddler. Scott himself never knew my Dad, but had heard amazing stories and experienced first-hand through Sensei Bill's training the style that Dad taught. The other thing Scott had learned from Bill was that Dad basically disappeared one day and no one ever heard from him again. There were others who trained with Dad as well who were still teaching, and they all shared a deep desire to answer the question of what had happened to Dad, and whatever had become of his son. Scott in particular took it upon himself to solve the mystery.

I asked Scott how he found me. As part of his Internet searching, Scott had come upon Dad's name listed in an online Arizona obituary. He knew the funeral home wouldn't share information about relatives, but he pleaded with them to pass on his contact information.

Scott shared Sensei Bill's contact information with me, and said I should feel free to communicate with him directly.

When the call was over, an incredible sense of fulfillment came over me. After so many years of nothing but dead ends, here at last was a group of people who knew Dad when I was still in diapers. The weight of the years lifted slightly. There was still a great deal of the unknown to sort through, but this was by the far the biggest forward step yet.

Shortly after that phone call, *World of Warcraft* was released. We all felt like we would have another big hit on our hands, but minus a crystal ball, nothing could have truly prepared us for the WoW phenomenon. The immediate response was overwhelming. Queues of people were lined up on servers for hours. The company had prepared for 400,000 subscribers in North America, long term, and this was considered a safe overestimation. The game exceeded that capacity within the first month. And this was a trend that would continue at a breakneck pace. Multiple times within the first year of WoW's release, Blizzard had to stop sending new boxes to retailers because the company just didn't have the support for the amount of players who were lining up to buy the game.

It was a crazy time. The entire company was riding high come Christmas 2004, an elation that would carry over into the following year, as critics praised the game and players flooded the virtual world we had created.

For me personally, there was the massive success that the company was enjoying, and there was the personal success of making contact with someone who had actually trained with my Father. Sensei Bill and I traded emails well into 2005. I had a ton of questions, all of which he answered to the best of his ability. I was tiny when he started training with Dad, but I soon learned that the Oklahoma network of martial artists who were digging for clues had made contact with a couple who owned a local church, and that Dad had brought me to this church when I was just a baby. I took time to process this while the Oklahoma folks continued tracking down other former students. I started making plans with Tiff and Sensei Bill for a trip to Oklahoma... I would need to see these people in person, visit the locations where they had spent time with Dad and me. We set the wheels in motion.

In the meantime, I couldn't stop thinking about the church. Dad had brought me to a church as a baby... basically seeking sanctuary. People who did that were usually on the run from something. The more I talked to Sensei Bill and the more I learned of that early time in our lives, the more I believed that Dad had in fact taken me from my mother. If that was true, then it was very possible, actually probable, that Dad had lied about Mom being dead. It seemed too much to hope for that she may still be alive, but I held onto that tiny glimmer and I didn't let go.

After reviewing our finances and coordinating with the Oklahoma folks, the plans were set for me to fly out in September.

On the screenwriting front, *Vamptown* was ready to shop around! Both Sammy and I had high expectations—we had rewritten or revised the script over a dozen times, just during our partnership with Paul. We all believed in the story and Sam and I allowed ourselves to entertain the notion that yes, we could actually sell a screenplay. Paul's Vice President of Development, James, took the script to all the major studios...

And they all passed.

We were again surprised, and again deeply saddened. Paul and James didn't lose faith, however. If the big studios didn't want to make the movie, fine, we'd go to the independents. James took meetings, sent the script out again, and we waited. And waited. At one point we gained some traction when Paramount Studios' former president, Michelle Manning, took interest in the project but ultimately that momentum was lost.

Sam and I were learning the hard way that sometimes selling a script to someone in Hollywood is very much like beating your head against a wall... except a wall would be more likely to return your phone calls.

Finally the indie studios responded. All in the negative.

So that was it. *Vamptown* had been sent pretty much everywhere. James said there were a few more places that he could try, but it was clear that whatever head of steam we had built was in the wind. Sam and I were crushed once again, but determined to keep writing.

Blizzard, in the meantime, was still basking in the afterglow of WoW. In 2005 we hit four million subscribers... an insane number. The company was getting bigger and bigger, hiring more people to keep *World of Warcraft* going. We leased buildings down the street and filled them with employees. And, the executives decided to buy the studio that was working on *StarCraft: Ghost*—Swingin' Ape—outright.

Despite the purchase of Swingin' Ape, work on *StarCraft: Ghost*, was still an uphill climb. Technology on the console side was moving faster than the development of the game could keep up with. Plans for a Gamecube version of the title were soon canceled. The gameplay still wasn't where we wanted it to be, and even as we recorded lines, the story remained in flux. *StarCraft II* was still in its infancy, and I found myself drawing concepts for buildings, doodads, etc., again. It was good work, but I had been doing it for over ten years, and I wanted a change of pace.

The commute to work from Corona was wearing on me, as was the constant barking of our neighbors' dogs. The neighbors below us and next to us both had loud dogs that didn't like each other, and the neighbors both thought it was perfectly okay to let their dogs out at 5:00 a.m. at which point they would rush to the fence the two properties shared and bark their lungs out as they apparently attempted to tear each other's heads off.

My relationship with Tiff was suffering as well. I had started questioning everything: my life, my work, the decisions I had made, where I lived, what kind of future lay ahead... through it all there was a single beacon, a guiding light that emanated from a tiny, precious source: a little two-year-old girl who lit up my soul with her smile, her laugh and her unconditional love. My daughter made everything worthwhile, everything okay. No matter how difficult things became or how much I questioned the path I was taking, she was always there to hold my hand and show me the way.

Come September it was time to go to Oklahoma. I was excited, nervous, anxious... undergoing a full spectrum of emotions as I flew in to meet Bill and Scott. They greeted me at the airport, Bill a gray haired-older man with a mustache and an infectious smile, and Scott a tall, athletic and well-spoken gentleman. We talked there for a while, then they drove me to my hotel. Scott and Bill had both offered up their homes, but I wanted privacy at the end of the days to process everything that was going on, which was exactly what I did after the three of us had dinner.

I lay awake in my hotel room that night wondering what the trip would bring, what my expectations were and whether they would be met. Would I find some clue, some nugget of information that I would be able to seize on that might lead me to living relatives? Was that too much to hope for? My thoughts raced late into the night.

The next morning Bill took me to his dojo, where I met many of his students and received a demonstration of some of the techniques Sensei Bill taught. I was amazed to see certain movements and executions that I recognized, but had forgotten, hallmarks that I learned were particular to Dad's style of teaching.

Later that day Scott and Sensei Bill hosted a get together for more of Dad's old students and other folks who knew of me and Dad and had shown an interest in our story. It was quite a turnout, held at a Chinese buffet, and it was the most enlightening activity of the whole trip. I heard several incredible stories about Dad; how he could do a thousand push-ups, how he could leap clear over a tall man, how he could move a ping pong ball on the end of a string without touching it… one of the most bizarre stories was of my Dad predicting the exact day and time it would rain three weeks before the fact.

I learned that Dad's teeth were partially missing

297

even back then. He told the students that he was in a bar in Panama (or Japan, depending on who you spoke to) and that someone came up from behind him and smashed his head down into a bowl of soup. He used this as a cautionary tale to never sit with your back to a door.

Some of the stories were a bit disturbing. One student recounted that Dad always ranted about how bars were breeding grounds of every type of sin, physical affronts against God. Not long after a new bar opened in the neighborhood of one of Dad's dojos, he asked a couple students to give him a ride late at night, and drop him off at a location that was a block away from the bar. Several minutes later Dad returned to the vehicle and told the driver to get moving.

The next day the students learned that the bar had burned down.

That aside, the most revelatory information came in the form of disclosures made by Dad early on to the students: he had said that he was divorced from his wife, that she had lived in California; that she had done something terrible to him, and… that I had a brother.

Like everything else divulged by Dad, this data was subject to a great deal of question. But, Dad had mentioned a brother before, in his letters. Why mention a brother if he didn't exist? Most of all, Dad's statements reinforced my thoughts that perhaps he had taken me as a baby and ran out on my mom. Of course he would tell the students that he was divorced, not that he had kidnapped his son.

Among all the accounts of Dad's life and actions in Oklahoma, there was one constant: all the former students said unanimously that he had loved me more than anything.

At the end of the luncheon, one of the old students presented me with a "gi" (martial arts uniform) top that Dad had worn, as well as a shirt from Scott's dojo, a plaque, and a black belt. It was all very poignant, and very humbling.

Afterward, Scott and Bill drove me around to the long-ago locations of Dad's dojos. One of the sites still existed with little in the way of modification, and Bill pointed out where the students would train, drink tea, where Dad would sit, etc. They hoped that this tour would spark some memories. There was a vague familiarity to it all, but it was cloudy at best, and any recollections connected to these physical locations remained largely out of reach.

Later that night I was taken to a new dojo where Dad's oldest former student currently held classes. The training area was basically in a garage, where mats had been laid out on the floor, and training equipment like Olympic-style rings hung from the rafters. Of all the locations I had visited, this one seemed the most familiar; not because I had been there before, but because the entire layout was so similar to the way Dad had set up his old dojos. This former student, named Larry, even had practice knives carved out of wood, just like Dad used to use—something I had forgotten about until I saw them that night.

I spoke with Larry, along with Myles Martin, another former student who was instrumental in bringing everyone together, for quite a long time. I could tell that Larry had known my Dad well. He was amazed at the difference in personality between me and my Dad, and even more taken aback by the fact that I had made such a success of my life. It was, in his words, "a miracle."

The next day Scott drove me to the church where Dad had sought shelter when he first arrived in Oklahoma. The pastor and his wife met us there and talked about seeing me as a baby, certainly less than a year old, still in diapers. Dad had been very quiet and secretive about his past, but he did tell them at one point that he had left my mother, who lived in California.

This just seemed to add credence to the scenario that had been taking shape in my mind and solidifying since the day before; Dad's marriage to some woman in California falling apart, and him taking me from my home and running to Oklahoma, hiding out, starting over.

In exchange for being allowed to live there, Dad had painted most of a mural (which another man later finished) on a wall facing the entryway of church. The mural took up the entire wall space. It was a reproduction of a famous painting of Christ and two apostles on the road to Emmaus. The dirt path led up and to the left if you were facing the painting, but the pastor and his wife told me to stand far to one side and look at the painting, then stand far to the other side— which required walking halfway up a shallow ramp— and look again. There was a bend in the road, and depending on which side you stood on, the road toward the end seemed to change direction. It was an interesting optical illusion. Whether or not Dad had intended this trick of the eye was unknown.

We had lunch with the pastor and his wife, and

they asked me if I was a Christian. I told them that I was not, but that I tried to be a good person. We said our goodbyes and soon I was back on a plane to California, head swimming with thoughts and hopes that perhaps I was one step closer to finding my family.

CHAPTER THIRTY:
DEVELOPMENTS

In October of 2005, Blizzard held its first "Blizzcon," which was, as it sounds, an entire convention dedicated solely to the company and its games. Again, insane. About 8,000 people attended, and at the show, employees were treated like royalty, signing boxes, talking on panels, and generally just interacting with the fans. What an amazing experience.

As 2005 drew to a close, I was asked to write "boss lines" for an event in *World of Warcraft* called Gates of Ahn Qiraj. It was for a "patch," which is basically an online update of a game that introduces new elements and institutes balance changes and bug fixes. During that time I also wrote a short story for the event called *War of the Shifting Sands*.

* * *

Through the end of 2005 and well into 2006 I spent mornings, lunches and any other free time I could find looking at an online database of missing kids. I looked at photos for babies who were abducted between the years of 1970 and 1973, searching specifically for kids taken from San Diego. Most of what I found were older kids, or girls, or boys of the wrong ethnicity. I spent months exhaustively searching the database, and it was getting me nowhere.

In Hollywood, Paul and James continued fighting the good fight for *Vamptown*, but the momentum had died. Sammy and I were hard at work on our next project, a script about two goofball ushers at a small movie theater in the '80s. Sound familiar? Yes, we drew from many of our own experiences, including "door posing" and "aisle dancing," and the script was a blast to write.

John Nemec, the producer we had met in New York, was doing some hustling on one of our old projects, the supernatural western *The Hunt*. At one point, as I was driving to my tae kwon do class I received a call from John saying that the script was at Mandalay Films, where a reader had liked it so much she forwarded it to the president of the company! I was ecstatic... if the president liked it, we were off and running.

A few weeks later I got the call from a dispirited John that the president had passed. Once again, the rollercoaster of Hollywood was plummeting downhill.

At work I staved off the doldrums by continuing to write. Our Hollywood projects were stalled out but at least there was fulfillment to be had from the games... sort of. After a prolonged struggle to whip *StarCraft: Ghost* into proper shape, the decision had been made to put the game on "indefinite hold." I had been hoping that a writing credit on *Ghost* would bolster Sam's and my efforts in the film industry, but unfortunately that was not to be.

I focused my writing efforts in another direction,

tackling a short story called *Unbroken* that would be released on the Web around the same time that the expansion for WoW, called *The Burning Crusade*, would be launched. I continued writing boss lines for the game, and I had moved into a position where I worked with the Sound Team to cast the actors; then I would go to LA and do voice direction. It's amazing how much you can learn about writing dialogue when you not only write it, but see the process all the way through to the recording phase. The cross-pollination of writing screenplays and dialogue for the game was creating fantastic results.

Later that year Sammy and I finished the *Ushers* script. As before, we would go through multiple rounds of revisions, taking notes, making changes, and doing everything within our power to create the best possible story.

In January of 2007, the next expansion for *World of Warcraft* came out, and it was huge. World of Warcraft subscribers hit the eight million mark. Every once in a while Mike Morhaime would send out an email comparing WoW subscribership to the populations of small countries, and how we were topping those numbers. We were getting bigger and bigger and the company needed more physical space as well. Plans were in motion to move everyone to a large campus.

Months later it was time to submit *Ushers* to some select studios. The response was good... but there were two major notes from almost everyone: they wanted to push the adult-rated content and they were all hung up on the fact that it took place in the '80s. They didn't think it would be relatable to a contemporary audience. We went to work on pushing the R-rated envelope, but we stuck to our guns on the time period of the film.

Several revisions later, the script went out again, this time to all the major studios. As before, Sammy and I waited anxiously as the rejections came in, one by one. Then James sent the script out to independent studios... with the same result.

As much as I hate to say it, at this point Sam and I had learned not to get our hopes up too much, so yes we were crushed, but not as devastated as we had been in the past. It was back to the proverbial drawing board.

* * *

At work the winds of change stirred once again. Chris Metzen had asked me if I wanted to join a new department he was experimenting with, called Creative Development... a place that would basically be an idea generator, a wellspring of imagination with opportunities to write and tell stories in abundance, which was really where my heart lay. The trick was, it was a gamble. The whole department was an idea that Chris was playing with, but there was no guarantee that the fledgling group would take flight. When you work in 3D art, the tools and knowledge that you rely on can become obsolete quickly, because technology is always changing. What if I took the leap, and the whole Creative Dev idea failed after a year? Then I'm in a tough spot because the company might not want to pay me to play catch up, learning the new tools, programs, etc. that evolved in my absence.

Ultimately I decided to hedge my bets. I told Chris I would do work for Creative Dev and the *StarCraft* team, Team 1, dividing my time and tasks between the two for six months to see if the new department had legs. I was very relieved when Chris and Sammy agreed.

The team was tiny, consisting of me, a producer, a historian and one other creative developer. It was the wild frontier, but it was exciting. One of the first major projects I worked on was story development for the *World of Warcraft* comic, written by a legend in the industry, Walt Simonson. Walt's wife, Louise was very active in the process as well, and though we had our differences of opinion, we soon found a rhythm that worked well in producing the monthly title. Issue One was a big hit, going into reprints soon after its publication. Once again, I applied my screenwriting/story structure knowledge in planning out the comics' arcs, working with Metzen to convey the overall vision. And, Sammy worked on several covers!

The six months I allotted myself seemed to go by in a flash. Come December, it was time for me to make a choice. I felt that there was a future to the team, although there were of course no guarantees. Ultimately I decided what the hell… and I took the plunge.

While our team was small, Blizzard was bigger than ever, and in December it was time also to move to our new campus… which basically looked and felt like a movie studio lot, complete with its own cafeteria, gym, a twelve-foot tall bronze statue of an orc riding a wolf, and a huge front gate with a big metal sign that read "Blizzard Entertainment." We had never used a sign on any of our previous buildings, partially to maintain a low profile, as well as for security reasons. The glass around our old reception area was actually bulletproof. Some players who broke the rules or hacked our games would get pretty irate when their accounts got canceled.

Within a month or so of moving onto the new campus, parking became nearly impossible and it was soon clear that we didn't have enough parking spots for all the employees. It got so bad that valets were hired to pack the cars in any way they could.

As 2008 arrived, Sam and I continued developing script ideas (this time for an animated show), and I was excelling within Creative Development at Blizzard. My title was Story Developer as I was once again writing, casting and recording all boss lines for WoW's next expansion, *Wrath of the Lich King*. The comic's success led to several manga titles published through Tokyopop, which I developed the story lines for as well, working directly with the editor, and through him, with the authors. On top of all that, I was writing my own four issue comic series, set in the WoW universe, called *Ashbringer*.

Things at home were generally good. The neighborhood was still driving us nuts, but Tiff and I were getting along well, and Tati, now five years old, was the coolest kid around. She was always surprising me. Several houses in our neighborhood shared one large mailbox, and when I went to get the mail I would take Tati with me. Folks would often post "missing pet" flyers on the side of the box. At one point someone posted a flyer trying to sell a television, with a picture of the TV printed at the top. Tati had asked about the other flyers, so when she saw this one she said, "Aw, look, somebody lost their TV!"

Once while driving past a farm, Tati looked at the identification tags on the cows' ears and, thinking they were price tags, wondered how much they were being sold for. I can't easily convey how much joy Tati brought—and continues to bring—into my world. I never really knew what was missing in my life until she became part of it.

And just as I had no idea what was missing, I also had no idea whether or not I would be a good father until I became one. After being a dad for five years, I could honestly look at myself in the mirror and be secure in the fact that yes, I really was a good dad. Not that I haven't made mistakes, mind you, but I've always tried to learn from those mistakes and apply that knowledge to improve.

Gaining confidence as a father soon influenced other areas of my life as well: at work I had always avoided being in any kind of management position, because I really didn't want to be anyone's boss. After having shouldered the responsibilities of parenthood, however, my outlook changed.

Later in 2008, as the Creative Development department was expanding, I decided that it was time for me to take on additional responsibility in a management role. We needed a Story Developer, and I knew just who to call.

I got James, our contact in Hollywood, on the phone. I knew that I wanted someone from the industry because I believed then (and still do) that some of the best storytellers in the world work in the film and television industry. When I called James, I didn't intend to try and lure him away from Paul, I simply wanted to see if he knew of anyone who might be interested in applying for the job. James surprised me by answering that he himself might want to throw his hat in the ring.

James aced the writing test and subsequent interviews, and in October I was a Senior Story Developer and James was my employee. It was an interesting kind of role reversal: as the guy giving Sammy and I notes on our scripts, James was telling us what to do. Now I was telling him what to do. But the dynamic worked: James excelled.

In November *Wrath of the Lich King* was released, and WoW continued to dominate the PC market.

2008 was a good year, and I was determined to keep the momentum going into '09. Creative Development was still expanding, and we were working with some of the most amazing writers in novels, comics and manga. The only downside was that I really didn't have time to write the boss lines or voice direct for WoW any more.

I soon realized that the itch I was trying to scratch by writing screenplays—the storytelling itch—was being appeased by my role as a story developer. Sam and I continued to work on projects, but not nearly at the same pace as before.

Then in the middle of the year, I got incredible news: the hardcover graphic novel of *Ashbringer*, my four-part comic series, had hit number two on the *New York Times* Bestseller List! When I got the email I believe my reply was "Oh my God I think I just s#*t myself!" Suddenly I felt as if I was part of an exclusive club... a NY Times bestselling author! I had them print that on my business cards. Our department director at the time joked during a company show and tell that I insisted on being referred to from then on as "*New York Times* Bestselling Author Micky Neilson." I embraced that joke. With all the things I had lost or never possessed early on in life, with all the questions of who I really was, that title was and is something no can ever take away from me; something with no ambiguity. It is simply fact.

Meanwhile, the housing market had taken a complete dive. This was good news for the family, because it meant we had a shot at moving back to Mission Viejo. We did some house hunting, found a place we could afford, and in August we relocated.

Life was good. Life was really good. I was living my dream. But there was one missing piece, still, one black hole in my increasingly perfect world... the unanswered questions of my past. The specter of the unknown still loomed large over all I had accomplished.

I had been wanting to write a book about my life for a long time. The success I had now enjoyed as a writer for Blizzard gave me the confidence to believe I could, but execution wasn't the problem. I looked at the project from a storytelling perspective: I didn't have an ending. I knew that everything I had gone through was pretty crazy, but how would I wrap up the book—"I still didn't know who I really am, when I was born, or if there's any family left alive out there... but everything's cool?" It seemed underwhelming to say the least, but when 2010 came around, I decided that I wasn't getting any younger, and if I was going to write an autobiography, I needed to get it done. I told Tiff that this was the year: I was going to write the book, happy ending or not.

CHAPTER THIRTY-ONE:
BREAKTHROUGH

By October of 2010 I still hadn't started the book, but I had been noodling it for quite a while, figuring out in my head how I wanted to structure it, what I wanted to include, etc. The ending, or lack thereof, still bugged me.

Then I received a message that changed everything.

I had signed up on Facebook that year, and was only moderately active on the site, posting photos from vacations every once in a while. Some Blizzard fans knew my name from the stories I had written and would send me friend requests, which I usually accepted after chatting with the person a bit via messaging. In late October I received a friend request from a fellow named Mijikai Mason. It read: "Little Worry, this is short timer. I need a safe way to speak with you."

What struck me immediately was the name of this person... the combination of a Japanese and Western-sounding name reminded me of me and Dad. It was rare. Could it be just another Blizzard fan? Maybe, but I had a feeling there was more to it than that. Maybe a lot more. I was a bit worried about this person needing "a safe way to speak" with me. Was Mijikai connected to one of Dad's old friends or students, maybe some fellow conspiracy theorist?

I sent a message back that basically said: "I received a friend request. Do I know you?" Then, a few weeks later, came this response: "Mick, my apologies for the lateness in responding. I was on a military retreat. My nickname is Mitch. My real name is Mijikai Mason. The first name is Japanese. I am a U.S. Army Chaplain serving in Germany. My Mother and I 'Betty' knew you when you were little."

Someone who knew me when I was little? Someone with a Japanese name? I was putting two and two together pretty quickly, but I didn't want to get my hopes up. Years of rejection in Hollywood had taught me to manage my expectations. I told Mitch I was excited to talk more with him, that I would be writing an autobiography soon and still had things to figure out about my childhood.

Mitch wrote back that he had "a good bit of information" about my "parents, sibling, and early life." He was concerned that Facebook wasn't the best place to divulge this information.

At that point I decided it was time to give Mitch my email address and try to learn more. I had never spoken to anyone who knew Dad before Oklahoma. Mitch mentioned a sibling... could this be the moment I had been waiting so long for? Could this be the resolution to 38 years of drifting in a fog of unawareness?

A few days later I received an email from Mitch. It was like a bomb being dropped in the middle of my life... but in a good way. A very good way.

The email told me that Mitch was, in fact, my brother... that my mother was indeed alive; that she was a nurse living in Texas. He told me when I was born (May 3rd 1972, which was the same date Dad had celebrated with me throughout my life); where I was born (Colorado City, Colorado); what my real name was (Yakimoki Mason), and what Dad's name was—or what he told Mom his name was (Todd Mason). He told me that Dad had kidnapped me when I was nine months old and that they had been looking for me ever since. Also, that I had a half brother and a half sister. What really clenched it though were the photos Mitch sent. Mitch and I looked (and still look) very much alike. It was crazy, staring at this image of someone who was another version of me. But Mitch had also done a great deal of digging and found a photo of Dad when he must have been in his twenties or thirties. The man in that photo looked like both of us as well.

I remember sitting at my computer, staring dumbly at the screen. James walked in and asked if I was okay. I told him what I had just learned, and he was nearly as blown away as I was. There it was, at last; the truth revealed; the lighthouse in the fog, guiding me home.

Mitch and I continued trading emails. I told Mitch that Dad had passed away. The reason for the secrecy on Mitch's side in his earlier communication with me was out of concern that Dad might do something drastic in response to me being contacted by family. Despite this, I could tell that Mitch was heavily affected by the news of Dad's death.

At one point Mitch and I talked on the phone. He

was in Germany, so it took some coordinating, but I was amazed at the fact that even Mitch's voice sounded similar to mine. We talked for at least two hours on that first phone call, and weeks later I learned more of the circumstances surrounding my kidnapping...

Dad and Mom had fought, Dad had actually taken both Mitch and I and drove away, but at some point he dropped me off, then agreed to meet Mom at a bus station. Mitch was retrieved, but somehow Dad was able to talk his way out of the situation and was allowed to leave. It is logically assumed that Dad then picked me up from wherever he had left me. After that, Mom received one more phone call in which Dad said, "You'll never hear from me again." And she didn't.

Mitch told me that he had informed Mom that he'd found me, and that she was waiting for me to call her. It hit me all over again: Mom was alive. After all this time of not knowing, she was alive. Mitch had sent me a picture of her. I stared at that picture for a long, long time, thinking about everything that she had been through; thinking about the many years that she must have wondered if I was safe, if I was okay, if she would ever see me again.

Calling Mom was the most emotional moment yet. I was a complete wreck. Mitch had set a time where he would try a conference call. I sat on the bed, shaking. Mitch called, but he had been unable to make the conference call work. He gave me her number and said I should just call her directly. I hung up with him, but couldn't bring myself to dial the phone yet. Tiff was in the next room, and she knew what I was going through. She asked if she should dial the phone for me, and I said yes. I heard her dial, heard her talking to someone for a minute... then she brought the phone into the bedroom and handed it to me. I said, "Hi Mom," and on the other end I heard my mother's voice for the first time in 38 years.

She said, "Hi Moki," and asked if it was okay for her to call me Moki, because that was the name she remembered me by. I told her she could call me anything she wanted.

We talked late into the day. Mom told me about how she met Dad: she took martial arts lessons from him at a dojo he ran in Pensacola, Florida. He was very secretive about his past, but he did claim to have a military background, saying he served in several conflicts including the Bay of Pigs. To this day, whether or not Dad really served in the military remains a mystery. Mom told me further about how Dad basically admitted to using an alias, and how at one point she discovered that he never divorced a previous wife who lived in San Diego. Dad and Mom argued... at the time they were doing search and rescue in Colorado. They were called out to rescue someone but en route Dad tried to drive them both off of a mountain. The car got caught up in barbed wire that wrapped around the axle and prevented their deaths, although Mom suffered a broken jaw and dislocated hip. Dad had told me a similar version of this same story, years before. Of course, he left out the fact that he had intentionally driven off the road. The incident where Dad took Mitch and me happened not long after, while Mom was visiting her Mother in Florida.

I related to Mom the various stories Dad told me about how she had either died or was killed, including the story about her having a cyst on her ovary that ruptured on a flight from Mexico. Mom told me that she did have a cyst on her ovary when she was with Dad, and that it did rupture... but not on a flight, and it caused no ill effects.

The more I learned, the more I realized that so much of what Dad told me had a kernel of truth to it, buried in all the lies and misdirection. In fact, while going through Dad's letters in preparation to write this book, I found the letter I refer to earlier which stated that I had a brother, and that his name was "Mijikuai." It hit me like a freight train: somewhere, on some level, a part of Dad was trying to share the truth, but I had no way to know it.

After the call with Mom I took some time to let it all soak in. I maintained contact with Mitch, learning about various similarities we shared (we both have a dry skin condition, we were both practical jokesters) as well as differences (I'm not religious; Mitch doesn't play video games). Mitch told me about a tiny pair of leather baby shoes of mine that were left behind when Dad kidnapped us, and about how he had kept those shoes throughout the years. They were packed away, but Mitch said he would find them and give them to me when we were reunited.

He also told me that our grandmother was still alive; that she would be notified soon that I had been found. Interestingly, Granny had at one point experienced a dream in which I came to her house and knocked on her door.

I was determined to make that dream come true.

316

Mitch was still in Germany, but we made a vow to visit Granny together as soon as Mitch could get back to the States. In the meantime, I had a mother I needed to spend Christmas with.

* * *

And so I flew into Texas, a complete emotional train wreck throughout the flight. We landed, I got the call from my half brother Marshall, we proceeded to baggage claim, and there was Mom and the news cameras and Marshall, my half sister Gynene and Mom's husband all waiting patiently.

The person went through the doors ahead of me, I went in and stopped, waiting for the automatic doors to move. I stood there and I thought about what an incredible journey my life had been.

I don't know exactly how long I stood there, but I remember hearing Tiff shout "Keep moving!" I took another step, the doors moved, I got out and Mom and I embraced. We held each other for a very long time, and we talked about how much of a miracle it all was. The moment was perfect. There's a still image taken from the camera footage that was used when the story was posted on the Web; it shows me with my arm around Mom's shoulder, my eyes closed with a look of utter serenity on my face.

Mom and I were interviewed by the reporter, various footage was taken of us there at the airport, and later that night the segment aired on the local news. It was truly amazing to see.

During the time that I was visiting, Mom held my hand everywhere we went, as if, now that she had found me, she would never let go. And that was fine by me. We all talked for hours on end. There was a lot of catching up to do, a lot of pictures to see, a lot of memories to share. I asked Mom what she thought about all those years, how she felt.

She said that a part of her knew I was alive. What was most heartbreaking was not knowing where I was, but also knowing that she had missed out on the formative years of my life. She talked about how she became overprotective of Mitch, Gynene and Marshall while they were growing up. Mostly she kept herself busy, distracted (which made me think about how I always turned back to my work or other personal pursuits when all of the unanswered questions would weigh on me). She wanted to help others, and contemplated social work or nursing. She opted for nursing, became a licensed vocational nurse and received a Bachelor of Science in Nursing. Part of what drove her was a desire to be someone I would be proud of when we were reunited.

And I couldn't be more proud. It's still hard for me to imagine what Mom went through emotionally, and I'm awed by her strength. She told me that the prevailing opinion in the 70s was that it was perfectly acceptable for a man to raise a child alone, and that Dad was just as entitled to me as Mom was. No female police officers discussed the situation with Mom after I was taken and there were times when it seemed her pleas for help fell on deaf ears.

As she grew older, she didn't want to leave the world without seeing me or knowing I was okay. And so I was able to tell her the one thing that was most important to me that she know: that I was okay. I was really okay. Despite the weird childhood and the hard times, and the foster homes and everything else, my life had turned out amazing. And now, things were better than I ever could have imagined.

Mom's husband Gary took me aside at one point and told me that through the years, during the holidays, Mom would become somber, wondering what kind of Christmas I was having; wondering where I was and if I was safe. He told me that this Christmas was the happiest he had ever seen her. Mom herself told me that finally after all these years, she felt complete.

When the time came to leave, I didn't want to go, but I knew that nothing would separate us ever again.

* * *

Mitch and I stayed in contact as we waited out his final months in Germany. Granny had already been notified that I had been found; all that was left now was for Mitch and I to walk up to her door. Unfortunately, that was not meant to be; Granny passed away before we could make that visit. The family was devastated. I flew to Florida for the funeral, to be with Mom. Marshall set up Skype and a monitor was positioned so that Mitch could read a eulogy from Germany. I was infinitely saddened by the fact that I didn't make Granny's dream come true. But before I had left, Tiff said to me "She knew you had been found. And that was enough for her to be at peace." I believe that what Tiff said is true, that Granny passed with contentment in her heart that all was well.

Roughly six months later I found myself in Texas

once again, this time to be reunited with Mitch. I was nervous and emotional, as before, but this was slightly different. With Mom it was the moment I had waited my entire life for; with Mitch it was a moment I had waited my entire life for without knowing I had been waiting. I reunited with my brother, and spent time with his amazing family (a wife and four daughters!). Mitch was writing about his own life at that time. I was still working on my story, but we were already planning a follow-up: a book about Dad that might answer some of the questions that surrounded his life.

Oh, and yes, I have my baby shoes now. They have a special place in our home, and a special place in my heart.

* * *

In September of 2011, I had a sharp pain in my abdomen. I went to the doctor and had some tests done, including an ultrasound. No, I wasn't pregnant, but I was diagnosed with a fatty liver due to alcohol. I was told that if I wanted to prevent cirrhosis and the need for a transplant, I'd have to lay off the booze.

I was irritable for a while, mostly just angry that I couldn't have alcohol if I wanted it. Despite my early frustration, I learned that I really didn't need alcohol. I haven't had a drink since the diagnosis, and today I feel great.

EPILOGUE

Starting sometime in 2015, I fell into a kind of funk at work, at home... I was getting restless again. Angry. Why?

Secrets had been revealed, questions (though many, about Dad's background, still remained) had been answered. But what was next? Even with all that I had been through and with the recent revelations, my life had fallen out of balance. I needed a change of pace, a change of scenery... I needed radical change.

In March of 2016, after 22 years at the company, I left Blizzard Entertainment. I moved my wife and daughter to a small farming town in Washington State, back where my wife Tiff had grown up. Not long after, her parents moved back as well. And now... now I spend my days writing. Writing my own original material, doing freelance projects, consultations. I still write screenplays, and *Vamptown, Ushers* and *The Hunt* are all still alive and kicking. Sammy and I are working on a book project. I still talk to Tony, Eric, Rider. Mom is no longer a nurse, and she had health issues for a while, but she's been making a strong comeback. Mitch and his family live in Washington as well and we're looking forward to catching up on so much lost time. The extended family is doing well. And day by day I'm regaining that balance that I lost.

When I left California I thought about Dad... about when he had decided to basically check out from humanity altogether and move to Arizona. Was I becoming like him? Then I thought about life in general, how it's like that revolving door I got caught up in. We get stuck. And we don't know if we can make it through but we cling to hope. And eventually we do make it through, and we learn.

Looking back, I've learned a lot. For so many years, there was so much that was missing in my life. But what I didn't understand, what's only become apparent with the passage of time is that in our lives there are the things that we know are missing; the things that we don't know are missing until we find them, and then... there are the things that we only think are missing but were really there all along.

So now what? What's next for me? What else is missing in my life?

I don't know...

But I can't wait to find out.

ABOUT THE AUTHOR

Micky Neilson is a two-time *New York Times* best-selling author whose graphic novels, *Ashbringer* (#2 on the list) and *Pearl of Pandaria* (#3) have both been published in six languages, selling especially well in the German, Korean and Brazilian markets. As one of the founding writers of Blizzard Entertainment, he has more than two decades experience in the cutting edge of the gaming industry. He is currently working on a graphic novel, *Rook*, as well as a horror novel, *The Turning*, and a number of film projects.

If You Enjoyed This Book, You Might Also Like

Norman Reedus: True Tales of The Walking Dead's Zombie Hunter, An Unauthorized Biography
By Marc Shapiro

Trump This! The Life and Times of Donald Trump, An Unauthorized Biography
By Marc Shapiro

Welcome to Shondaland: An Unauthorized Biography of Shonda Rhimes
By Marc Shapiro

A Star Shattered: The Rise and Fall And Rise of Wrestling Diva
By Tamara "Sunny" Stych

Bronx Bummers: An Unofficial History of The New York Yankees Bad Boys, Blunders and Brawls
By Robert Dominguez and David Hinkley